Battlefields of Gold

BATTLEFIELDS OF GOLD

How Gold Fields Fought for Survival and Won

Rex Gibson

JONATHAN BALL PUBLISHERS
JOHANNESBURG & CAPE TOWN

The author would like to thank the following:

Bill Jamieson, author of *GOLDSTRIKE! – the Oppenheimer Empire in Crisis* [Hutchinson Business Books, an imprint of Random Century Ltd, 1990] which he consulted in the process of writing this book.

mineweb.com for its account of the provenance of the Cockerill e-mail and its content which appears on page 276 of this book.

All rights reserved.
No part of this publication may be reproduced or transmitted, in any form or by any means, without prior permission from the publisher or copyright holder.

© Gold Fields Limited, 2012

First South African Edition published in trade paperback in 2012 by
JONATHAN BALL PUBLISHERS (PTY) LTD
PO Box 33977
Jeppestown
2043

Paperbook ISBN 978-1-86842-514-3
eBook ISBN 978-1-86842-515-0

Twitter: www.twitter.com/JonathanBallPub
Facebook: www.facebook.com/pages/Jonathan-Ball-Publishers/298034457992
Blog: http://jonathanball.bookslive.co.za/

Cover design by Michiel Botha
Typeset by Triple M Design, Johannesburg
Printed and bound by CTP Book Printers, Cape Town
Typeset in 11/15 pt Sabon MT Pro

Contents

PREFACE vii
ACRONYMS AND ABBREVIATIONS xiv

Chapter 1   A Death in the Family 1
Chapter 2   The End of an Affair 10
Chapter 3   Battle Stations Alert 19
Chapter 4   A Tiff in the Family 32
Chapter 5   Gloves Off 41
Chapter 6   Cloak and Dagger 53
Chapter 7   'Friends' Fall Out 62
Chapter 8   What Rhodes Started 72
Chapter 9   Enter the Heavy Hands 85
Chapter 10 When Euphoria Fades … 95
Chapter 11 Baptism of Fire … 107
Chapter 12 A Little Gold Mine 119
Chapter 13 Trapped – Three Kilometres Down 128
Chapter 14 Something Going Wrong 137
Chapter 15 Nightmare Start 148
Chapter 16 Strike to the Death 159
Chapter 17 Future Shock – Now 169
Chapter 18 Into a New World 181
Chapter 19 Shock Treatment 191
Chapter 20 An Imposter? 201
Chapter 21 Going International 210
Chapter 22 Life and Death 219
Chapter 23 One Ill-chosen Word 228

Chapter 24   A Bombshell Leak 239
Chapter 25   From Russia, with Anger 246
Chapter 26   Predator on the Prowl 255
Chapter 27   Deadlines, Damn Deadlines 265
Chapter 28   A Victory at Last 277
Chapter 29   Palace Revolution 283
Chapter 30   Brutal Ping-Pong 293
Chapter 31   Changing the Guard 301
Chapter 32   Looking Ahead 312
Chapter 33   A Woman's Touch 321

INDEX 331

Preface

THIS IS THE story of 25 years in the life of a gold mining company – a mere blink in history's eye. Yet it is a period so rich in drama and incident that it is almost as if a lifetime and more has been compressed into it.

It is not, however, a conventional company history. Company histories tend to sanitise the past, glossing over blips and modifying the bumps. Thanks to the decision of the people who commissioned this book, it is licensed to be a 'warts and all' account. I can't guarantee that I have succeeded in that, but I can guarantee that I have tried. And I can confirm that not one word of it has been changed simply to protect the company's image. For better or worse, the attempt at a balanced account is my own.

It's no secret that official company announcements often conceal as much as they reveal. In writing the story of a major company, therefore, there is one rule of thumb for a writer: the more bland the official announcement, the more likely it is that it is hiding something. Some human drama, perhaps, or boardroom battle, or clash of personalities.

This is not cynicism but simple realism. Nobody expects a great enterprise to wash its dirty linen in public. The object of official statements is to inform people, not titillate them. It is not necessary to record that some new development was pushed through the board over the dead bodies of several directors. Nor is it necessary to add the words 'good riddance' to a warm valedictory message for some departing employee.

Not necessary at all – but that is to eliminate half the excitement and much of the truth of what really happens in the necessarily ruthless world of Big Business.

The exercise has been made more intriguing by three things: the fact that many company records predating the year 2000 have disappeared; that human memories are fallible; and that people's perceptions of themselves nearly always differ from the perceptions of others. Sometimes the chasm is a mile wide.

I have made no attempt to reconcile contradictory views. Readers can draw their own conclusions. Perceptions become reality even when they are not correct. They colour decisions and have a profound influence on the direction of a business enterprise. Every step away from a previous path represents, by definition, a rejection of an old idea. It cannot help but be controversial.

There is a final reason why this is not a conventional company history. Time will provide an ultimate judgment on whether Gold Fields has secured its future for another hundred years. Too much is too recent for sweeping conclusions at the moment.

But some facts are clear, even now. The company is determined to succeed. Its leadership believes it is on the right track. There is a discernible vigour in its actions and its recent annual reports present an optimistic face. As ever, it gets its vitality and sense of purpose – its weaknesses and strengths too – from the interplay between strong characters in leadership positions. Strong leaders clash; it has always been thus.

Paradoxically, progress requires harmony and team spirit on the one hand; conflict and contestation on the other. Both ingredients are crucial. The jury of history will decide whether the formula has worked. But it looks promising.

BETWEEN February 1987, when Gold Fields celebrated its centenary, and February 2012, when a considerably different company with much the same name celebrated its 125th birthday, the face of the world changed. The Berlin Wall came tumbling down, international boundaries disappeared, political philosophies died, the Cold War ended. A new (and somewhat shaky) United States of Europe emerged to challenge, tentatively, the hegemony of the United States of America. The rise of the Asian Tigers tilted the balance of global economic power. The sleeping giant of China began to stir. The continent of Africa took its first halting steps towards democracy and participation in an emerging global village. International economies lunged from recession to prosperity to global meltdown. And the rising gold price signalled dramatic economic changes.

It was as if the world abandoned its past with a single shrug to begin anew. Old threats disappeared and old loyalties died, only to be replaced by undreamt-of new terrors, alliances and opportunities.

The face of South Africa changed. Apartheid disappeared overnight though its legacy clung stubbornly. International audiences watched engrossed as the country attempted what many saw as the impossible: a nearly bloodless revolution. History could find scant record of a country where a ruling minority had relinquished power voluntarily. It brought its own triumphs and torments. Democracy turned out to be both deeply satisfying and deeply unsettling. There was reconciliation and tension; relief and frustration. Yesterday's politicians disappeared with yesterday's policies, to be replaced by politicians of a different hue and contrary agendas. Amid the inevitable turmoil of change, only one thing was crystal clear to all.

The old South Africa had gone forever.

The face of business and industry changed. Closed doors opened. Phrases and buzzwords hardly known to a previous generation crept into the official lexicon: affirmative action, black economic empowerment, equal opportunity, racism. Labour flexed new-found muscles. Men abandoned ties and suits and ultra-formality. The glass ceiling that kept women out began to lift, though not nearly fast enough.

The face of mining changed. The mining empires that clustered on the Witwatersrand had seemed impregnable for more than a century; fortresses against ill-fortune. When GFSA celebrated its centenary with unconcealed optimism, seven great gold mining companies dominated not just South Africa's economy but that of much of the globe; household names like Anglo American, Anglo-Vaal, Rand Mines, Union Corporation, General Mining, Gold Fields. Their designated meeting ground was the Gold Producers Committee of the Chamber of Mines. Here they sat in conclave to settle the direction of the industry and the prosperity of a nation, displaying a collegiality that was not always apparent in their business encounters.

By 2012, a scant quarter-century later, the scene was unrecognisable. South Africa was no longer the world's largest gold producer. New finds in other places were shifting the balance. Of the seven great gold mining houses, the most powerful of them all – Anglo American – had abandoned gold. Other big names had been swallowed up by mergers, takeovers and attrition. Only one mining house remained in something like its old form. Even then, critics said it was no longer Gold Fields but an imposter in Gold Fields livery. Was the accusation justified? We shall see.

In any event, the working environment had changed so much that it hardly mattered. Competition at home and abroad had become more intense; acquiring mining rights more problematic; keeping labour satisfied more difficult; abiding by new constraints more demanding. Searching for new sources of gold became as important as mining established ore bodies. Existing mines grew deeper as gold became more elusive. The face of danger changed too because the seething centre of the earth is a far more hostile place than its surface.

One change, in particular, was both significant and almost imperceptible. The very nature of the mining industry changed. South Africa began to lose its dependency on gold as it increasingly acquired the trappings of a modern state. Gold was still important but it was no longer central to survival. The power that the old mining barons once wielded by virtue of their control of the only real source of wealth in South Africa gradually eroded. Today mining is recognised as an important money-spinner for government – but not the only one. The balance in the country is all the better for that.

Weaving its way through the rich tapestry of mining life is the inside story of a fiercely competitive association. To call the long-standing relationship between Gold Fields of South Africa and the Anglo American Corporation a love-hate relationship is to reduce it to an absurdity. Emotive words like 'love' and 'hate' have no place in a businessman's lexicon. Words like 'suspicion' and 'respect' and 'mistrust' and 'mutual dependence' seem more appropriate, and convey better the tensions that arose between these two giants of the gold mining world as circumstances forced them to work together almost as often as they dragged them into rivalry and confrontation. So they knew harmony in their lives, but when they fought, they fought like tigers.

PREFACE

FOR South Africa's most historic gold mining company, Gold Fields, the last quarter-century has meant a roller-coaster ride that took it from high drama to low intrigue in breathtaking swoops. The mother company survived two desperate takeover bids in the 1980s and, 30 years later, its South African offspring fought for its life in a battle that made world headlines. Both companies spent money in Monopoly sums to secure their future and outgun their rivals.

In this blink of a historical eye, Gold Fields experienced underground tragedy and the elation of the country's biggest and most successful mine rescue. It discovered the triumph of long-term investment and the mortification of a massive gamble going awry.

It learnt, the hard way, how to cope with treachery and deception, and how to return the compliment. It survived a merger that brought with it long knives, retrenchments and bitterness. It faced 4 000 angry workers marching on its headquarters and an outbreak of sabotage and arson underground. It not only embraced the South African miracle of transition but contributed to it too, in ways small and big.

Above all, it learned to survive in good times and bad, no matter the odds or the adversary. In the process, it demonstrated why boardroom battles are intrinsically exciting and Big Business is indeed a last frontier for the modern adventurer.

As it entered the 21st century it could boast that it was mining on three continents and exploring on five; that it mined four kilometres beneath the earth's surface – and four kilometres above sea-level too. But the boast was also a tacit acknowledgment that gold was becoming harder to find and its own future was at stake. It was a grim reminder of an abiding truth. Mining was, and always would be, the ultimate high-risk, high-reward venture.

From the start, it's a risky business. The earth resents the intrusion and fights back. The deeper mines go, the riskier things become. Gold Fields has been especially provocative. Its mine in Peru lies so high in the Andes that altitude sickness prevents some of its directors from visiting it. It has sunk shafts deeper into the earth than anyone has ever sunk a shaft before. It has pioneered mining techniques once regarded as impossible, like a single steel rope 3km long to take men and machines down to underground caverns so hot that only tons of ice can make them habitable, and meltdown can make a man's blood boil, literally. It is developing the most advanced mine in the world where robots will operate alongside people.

Capital costs are enormous. While science can determine with increasing accuracy what lies beneath the surface, the element of chance remains. A vein may not be as rich as anticipated, or as consistent, or as easy to dislodge.

The playing field is like a giant roulette table. For the players, the rule is simple: money up front. But the spin of the wheel remains uncertain. Certainty comes only after the croupier has called 'no more bets please'. It is to be found, if at all, underground, at the rock-face, after the bets have been laid. Vast sums have to be committed before a mine comes into production; a decade and more can elapse before a cent is earned. Sometimes the sums are so vast that individual companies, no matter how big, cannot incur the risk alone and seek partners. Even then success is not guaranteed. World prices can change, accidents can intervene, unanticipated difficulties can arise.

It takes strong nerves to make long-term decisions like that.

That's why the business of mining depends on special people with contradictory skills. They must be bold enough to take risks but cautious enough to weigh them carefully; prudent enough to be an accountant but daring enough to be a gambler. They must be careful with money but revel in playing for high stakes. And, at the end of it all, success and failure have one thing in common: they come at a high price. Even so, the producers cannot be sure of a fair reward. Others dictate the price they will get for their product.

Mining is accident-prone. Accidents happen, even when safety measures are meticulous. Nevertheless, Gold Fields has committed itself to an expensive philosophy by which it can be easily judged. It has been spelt out in unambiguous terms by its current chief executive officer Nick Holland: 'If we cannot mine safely, we will not mine.'

The philosophy is controversial, leaving him open to attack by a double-edged sword. 'How can he say that?' say some critics. 'Mining is inherently dangerous.' To which critics on the other side reply: 'The law requires him to mine safely. He's just making a virtue of necessity.' But the simple fact is that Gold Fields has put its money where its mouth is.

It has already sacrificed profit and interrupted production to make work places safer. Not many mining giants have done that.

Viewed from a distance, great enterprises appear to float serenely across untroubled waters. The notion is nonsense. Every great enterprise operates in treacherous seas, pitching and yawing wildly at times. All else is illusion.

'Risk and reward' is not an empty cliché but a precise definition of a business process. So it should come as no surprise that a business like Gold Fields has lurched from crisis to resolution more times than it would care to count in its first 100 years of existence. And then again in its most recent quarter-century. Risk is the single ingredient that is indispensable to success. Mere repetition of someone else's formula won't do. A willingness to take risks – call it vision, if you prefer – separates the giants from the rest.

It is the ingredient that enabled Gold Fields to flourish. It has made for a bumpy journey.

One of its founders, Cecil John Rhodes, came close to destroying the company almost before it started. He allowed its offices to be used to plan the infamous Jameson Raid of 1895–6, a massive political indiscretion. But the company proved sturdy enough to withstand that blow.

It has withstood every blow, every mis-step, since – for 125 years. It intends to go on doing so.

At the time of its centenary it was the second-biggest producer of gold in the world, not far behind its long-time rival, the Anglo American Corporation. It controlled some of the richest mines. At the start of the 1980s the London *Sunday Times* declared it to be 'the best mining company in Africa', and the Johannesburg *Sunday Times* named it 'the outstanding company in South Africa'. It entered the 1980s 'on a rising tide of success', according to its biographer, Roy MacNab.

Now it confronts another enemy. The most daring industry in the world is perceived to be in decline – despite the highest gold price in history. Rising costs and declining reserves signal trouble ahead. Gold Fields is not intimidated.

It has faced down situations like that before.

Acronyms and Abbreviations

AAC	Anglo American Corporation
CCMA	Commission for Conciliation, Mediation and Arbitration
CGF/Consgold	Consolidated Gold Fields
COM	Chamber of Mines
Cosatu	Congress of South African Trade Unions
GFL	Gold Fields Limited
GFSA	Gold Fields South Africa
HSBC	Hong Kong and Shanghai Banking Corporation
JCI	Johannesburg Consolidated Investment Company Limited
MUN	Mineworkers Union of Namibia
NAIL	New Africa Investments Limited
NCE	Notional Cash Expenditure
NUM	National Union of Mineworkers
SADF	South African Defence Force
SIM	Sanlam Investment Management
SRP	Securities Regulation Panel
TCL	Tsumeb Corporation Ltd, a Namibian mining company
WA	Western Australia
WGC	World Gold Council

CHAPTER ONE

A Death in the Family

CELEBRATING a centenary is not just another birthday party. Psychologically, it's so much more than that; a special milestone, a pinnacle attained. Perhaps even a declaration of immortality. You have survived for a hundred years; surely nothing can stop you now?

It's a very human expectation. Unfortunately, it's also wrong. Business doesn't work that way. Big company or small, you are just as vulnerable at 101 as you ever were on your first birthday. Any company that loses sight of that truth is halfway to a fall. Complacency could kill it.

It's a lesson that Gold Fields, the oldest gold mining company in South Africa, has learned the hard way. It has known perilously difficult times itself, flirted with risk, tempted fate and recovered, often gloriously. But more instructive than that, it has had direct experience. It has seen for itself how easy it is to die.

It was a closely involved spectator during the death throes in 1989 of Consolidated Gold Fields of London (CGF), its British parent; aware of what was happening but helpless to prevent it. That's the kind of corporate memory that doesn't go away. So it wasn't surprising to find echoes of that memory in the obituary that Robin Plumbridge, chairman and chief executive officer of Gold Fields of South Africa Limited, delivered in September 1989. Every phrase was carefully chosen, but did not hide the bitterness. He had reason to be angry.

The Gold Fields group was 102 years old when the death of the British parent was engineered; a needless killing. They had been through a great deal together, these two companies: crises, triumphs, disasters. Together they had fought off fierce competitors and hostile takeover bids, wrested wealth from the earth and brought prosperity to entire countries.

The death enabled Plumbridge to set aside, for the moment, the less happy memories of that long association; the times when the South African company had railed against its British parent for milking its profits and inhibiting its growth. One does not speak ill of the dead. Remembered, instead, were the bonds that gave vitality to both companies and eventually saw the offspring grow more vigorously than the parent until it became one of the greatest gold mining enterprises in the world. The bonds were stronger than the bitterness. As Plumbridge recorded in his GFSA annual report:

> Any review of the affairs of Gold Fields for the past twelve months would be incomplete without reference to the demise of Consolidated Gold Fields PLC. For 102 years the affairs of the two companies have been intertwined. The original company known as The Gold Fields of South Africa Limited was registered in London in February 1887 and had as its purpose the discovery and exploitation of gold mines on the Witwatersrand. Although the original company changed its name on a number of occasions as it developed an international character, Consolidated Gold Fields, as it was finally known, retained its substantial investment in South Africa and created our Group in its present form in 1971.
>
> For the past ten years of its existence Consolidated Gold Fields was pursued by an unwelcome suitor which ultimately and tragically launched a no-win hostile bid for the company and finally induced Hanson PLC to deliver the *coup de grâce*. Throughout this period, as relationships with its major shareholder deteriorated, Consolidated Gold Fields remained staunchly supportive of Gold Fields. The fact that the South African company has emerged relatively unscathed from the whole episode is in itself tribute to the support which it received.
>
> Inevitably the events of the past year introduced a series of acute stresses into the conduct of the affairs of the Group. In this context I would like to pay particular tribute to the independent non-executive directors, whose wisdom, guidance and support in providing direction to the Group at a time of serious conflicts of interest, was of the highest professional standard.

I would like to express my sincere appreciation of the contributions made by the senior officials of the group and their staffs in head office and in the operating companies. Many were called upon to undertake work loads which exceeded any reasonable requirement; all played their part in holding the Group together in extremely difficult circumstances.

Pursued by an unwelcome suitor for the past ten years ... tragically launched a no-win hostile bid ... a series of acute stresses ... work loads which exceeded any reasonable requirement ... extremely difficult circumstances ...

The words were biting. Uncharacteristically, Plumbridge was revealing his feelings. What the words did not reveal, however, was the full story. He made no mention of the long-standing feud that had simmered for decades between the two most powerful gold mining companies on earth; a strangely mixed relationship that saw the contesting parties at one moment dependent on each other and collaborating comfortably; at another, at each other's throat.

Neither did he mention that there was a cuckoo in the Gold Fields nest – an intruder. There was no need to. Everyone present at the annual meeting would have known who the cuckoo was.

The non-executive directors to whom Plumbridge paid tribute for their 'wisdom, guidance and support' were Rudolph Agnew, chairman of Consolidated Gold Fields of London, JHA Wood, a Consgold director, and South Africans LG Abrahamse, HP de Villiers, JA Stegmann, PG Steyn and Peter Gush. Admirable fellows all, especially the last named who, like Plumbridge himself, was a former Rhodes Scholar, sometime president of the Chamber of Mines and a mining engineer to boot.

But Peter Gush had one significant defect, which was not mentioned. He was the official representative of that unnamed 'suitor' which had hounded Consolidated Gold Fields to death. By logical extension, he had to share responsibility for the unwelcome plot perceived to have been created to gain influence over the South African offspring.

The suitor was, of course, the Anglo American Corporation. Gush was Anglo's official nominee on the GFSA board. What he thought of the obituary is not recorded. But he wouldn't have missed the irony of being thanked for his support and guidance.

Naturally, Plumbridge's prime concern was the company called Gold Fields of South Africa Limited, with headquarters at 75 Fox Street, Johannesburg. He had been its chairman and chief executive officer for the last eight years. It had been his life. It had been clear to him that significant change in the circumstances of the parent company would have a serious impact on GFSA too. But the situation was complicated ...

To understand the complications it is necessary to go back to the beginning of the curious relationship that evolved between Consolidated Gold Fields and the Anglo American Corporation.

THE FIRST ATTEMPT to take over Consgold (and in so doing to grab a significant chunk of GFSA shares) was orchestrated by none other than the then chairman of the Anglo American Corporation, Harry Frederick Oppenheimer, known to his business intimates as HFO. The attempt came to be nicknamed 'The Dawn Raid'.

In the minds of Anglo representatives, those three words conveyed a tone of approval. In this interpretation, the Dawn Raid was a worthy and swashbuckling attempt to pull a fast one on a rival; and all in a good cause. But in the mouths of Gold Fields supporters, the phrase was seldom uttered without the preface 'notorious'. In this interpretation, the three words were synonymous with calumny, infamy and betrayal.

The Dawn Raid came to symbolise for many at GFSA what they saw as the avaricious nature of Anglo American – a giant corporation that was at once a business associate, a partner, a competitor and a betrayer. Not that Robin Plumbridge would use such harsh language. For him, time has softened the memories of conflict, leaving him with the conviction that the battles were mere 'blips' in an otherwise congenial and collegiate relationship. To accord them a more dramatic status would be to distort them.

In this view he has the support of one of his successors as Gold Fields CEO, Ian Cockerill. 'I was working at Anglo at the time,' he says. 'It wasn't as if there was a secret meeting every five minutes to consider how to take over Gold Fields. It was generally a normal, professional, competitive relationship. I can see why Plumbridge thought that the Dawn Raid and Minorco were mere blips.'

But few of Plumbridge's colleagues see it that way.

Appropriately, the Dawn Raid came into the open on 12 February 1980, two days before Valentine's Day – a day for lovers and, if you were Al Capone, massacres too. It had been brewing for a long time. The official Gold Fields version of events appears in its centenary book, *Gold Their Touchstone* by Roy MacNab. It went like this:

For months, the British Press and the City of London had been abuzz with rumours that someone unknown had been buying up shares in Consolidated Gold Fields. Its chairman, Lord Erroll of Hale, told everybody that he felt as if 'a burglar was creeping up on me in the dark'. Someone was after his company, and no one knew who it was. The situation got so bad that he felt obliged to make a statement to the board in November 1979: 'No approach has been made to us, and the truth, if any, behind the rumour is extremely difficult to establish.' But he wasn't the least surprised that someone might be interested. Consolidated Gold Fields had a 48% interest in GFSA and the two Driefonteins – pride of the South African operations – were producing 15% of South Africa's entire gold production at a cost of under $55 an ounce. This was $30 an ounce less than any other company in the country.

By January the plot had thickened. Fleet Street newspapers had come up with a plausible theory: the Boer War was starting over again, this time on the economic front. Afrikaner interests were at work, they were saying. Having acquired General Mining and tumbled Union Corporation, they were marching on the GFSA fortress.

Enter *The Times* of London, thundering as always:

> If the buyers [of CGF shares] are Afrikaners, whether General Mining, Mr Anton Rupert, Sanlam or some combination, the target is more likely Gold Fields of South Africa. They may not care about Consolidated Gold Fields' other merits, just as they give little heed to the City's gentlemanly rules. The question the City might ask: What price Gold Fields of South Africa when the motivation to buy is partly the settlement of old scores against the English?

Good, rousing jingo stuff – but wildly off-beam.

In early February the British Parliament began to ask questions and Lord Erroll, chairman of Consolidated Gold Fields, asked the British government to intervene when he discovered that 40-million shares – 27% of the equity – was now in unknown hands.

As MacNab records:

> The mystery buyer realised he would now have to break cover. Just after 9 o'clock on the morning of February 12, David Lloyd Jacob [an executive director of Consgold] was in his office when the telephone rang. It was Harry Oppenheimer, informing him officially that he had 15% of the CGF shares and was about to go into the market for another 10%. The famous dawn raid had started. With the aid of brokers, he acquired 13,5-million shares before Big Ben struck ten. It was a masterly performance that proved Harry Oppenheimer to be a chip off the old block. Eventually his companies had 29,9% of the shares of Consolidated Gold Fields, which was as far as they could go without conforming to British rules and making a bid for the entire equity. Later that day, Ian Louw, chairman of GFSA, put out a statement which said: 'Mr Oppenheimer has given me the assurance that his sole objective is to maintain the independence of Gold Fields of South Africa Limited.'

'But,' asked MacNab 'had the gamekeeper, self-appointed, been playing the role of gamekeeper or had the gamekeeper turned poacher?'

It was a question that needed to be asked. Oppenheimer had inadvertently supplied an answer of his own when he had stated publicly: 'Who needs takeovers when you can control with a minority stake?' Who indeed? After all, by obtaining just under 30% in CGF, Anglo had in fact grabbed the leash that controlled GFSA. So the behaviour was consistent with what the *Financial Mail* of Johannesburg had suggested only a few months before: Anglo/De Beers would stop at nothing to lay its hands on the South African company.

Soon afterwards, a British financial journalist painted a rather more vivid picture of Anglo's tactics. In his book *GOLDSTRIKE! – The Oppenheimer Empire in Crisis* [Hutchinson Business Books, an imprint of Random Century Ltd, 1990] Bill Jamieson tells of an elaborate clandestine plot hatched to bypass British company regulations – a plot described by then Consgold chief executive Rudolph Agnew as an attempt 'to build up in secret, and almost certainly illegally, a major shareholding in CGF in defiance of all the known rules'.

This was the plot: De Beers would activate five nominee companies which would each be given the funds to enable them to buy a 4.9% holding in Gold Fields. Wrote Jamieson:

> On no account was the market to be alerted and, above all, on no account was anyone to discover the identity of the buying parties. When the 4.9% level was reached, one company would go to ground and another company would come into play. The companies were to be, in effect, Oppenheimer's grey squirrels in the night: five companies let loose to pounce on a target number of Gold Fields shares and disappear as quickly as they had come; all the discerning ear could ever catch would be the faint rustle of a Luxemburg telex and the click of a numbered account.

Jamieson makes no bones about it. The scheme ignored entirely the British legal requirement that obliged its authors to disclose their activities to Gold Fields if they bought 5% or more of its equity. Section 33 of the Companies Act made it an offence not to disclose – punishable by a fine or up to two years' imprisonment. At an official inquiry later, De Beers agreed that it had breached the rule, but argued that it was done inadvertently. To the end, it insisted that the raid had been defensive, not aggressive; that it had not been an attempt to take over CGF but rather an attempt to prevent others from doing so. The argument was not entirely implausible.

The gold mining giants of South Africa operated in a curiously contradictory arena. When it came to acquiring mineral rights and starting mines they were intensely competitive. But when it came to developing deep mines they were forced to turn to each other for capital; and when it came to selling their product they had no choice but to accept the common price they were offered. In the limited competitive area, Oppenheimer believed firmly that Anglo and De Beers got business because they were the biggest in their fields. They didn't want another big player in the game. General Mining was known to be on the prowl; if it laid its hands on Gold Fields, it would become a serious threat – perhaps even the biggest gold producer. There was heavy irony here. Anglo had in effect created General Mining by giving Afrikaners a stake in the mining industry at a time when they had political but not economic power. Now it feared that its love-child might turn around and bite the hand that fed it.

In the event, the chairman of the London Stock Exchange found De Beers/Anglo not guilty. He concluded that 'nothing nasty' had been done. The nearest he came to criticism was to suggest, with classic British understatement, that though the raid might have been legal it might not have been cricket.

Two months later, in April 1980, the two mining giants decided to declare a chilly truce. After discussions, they made a joint announcement to the London Stock Exchange. It was signed by HF Oppenheimer, as chairman of De Beers Consolidated Mines Ltd and Anglo American Corporation of South Africa Limited and the Lord Erroll of Hale as chairman of Consgold. It said:

> De Beers and AAC [Anglo American Corporation] have made it clear that there is no immediate intention on their behalf or of any of their associates to increase their existing holding and that in any case it would not be their intention to increase their combined holding in CGF beyond 29,9% in the future.
>
> De Beers and AAC have repeated the assurance given at the time that there is no intention to use the holding to bring about any change in the control or management of CGF. De Beers, AAC and CGF believe it is in their interests to maintain a fully-competitive situation in the mining industry in the Republic of South Africa and elsewhere. However they will, where appropriate, seek to co-operate to the mutual advantage of all shareholders.

The statement was bland enough, to be sure. For those who trusted Anglo/De Beers, it put the episode to rest. For those who didn't, three weasel words in the first sentence seemed to nullify entirely the reassurance about Anglo's desire for 'a fully competitive situation'. The words were: 'No immediate intention …'

Rudolph Agnew, for one, didn't believe a word of the statement, even though he had been a co-author of it. From that moment on, Consgold in London and GFSA in Johannesburg remained suspicious of every move Anglo American made. Even so, they could not have guessed how soon the next move would come. If the Dawn Raid had 'not been cricket', the next encounter would owe nothing to the gentlemanly rules of any known game. It would be closer to a brawl.

Curiously enough, it began amicably. With a courtship.

CHAPTER TWO

THE END OF AN AFFAIR

IT WAS an odd affair, this mating dance between Consolidated Gold Fields and a little-known company with fancy offices in London – odd in the way that some Black Widow spiders mate and then kill their partners.

The company, registered as the Mineral and Resources Corporation, or Minorco, tried to pretend for a while that it was more-or-less independent with roots in Europe and a chief executive who looked more English than the English. But everybody who knew anything about the company at all knew it was actually the Anglo American Corporation in offshore drag. And that the very English chief executive was actually born in South Africa.

The dance between Consgold and Minorco became quite intimate. The two companies created the kind of codes that couples might whisper to each other. In the first flush of their infatuation, they called their relationship 'Wedding of the Romans' and invented pet names for each other. CGF was 'Caesar', Minorco was 'Mark'. It was all designed to keep their intentions secret.

In September 1986, after many months of coy flirtation, the two companies went public. Minorco announced the impending birth of a new company in Continental Europe, created by a merger between itself and Consgold. But the course of true love never did run smooth, and quite soon the arrangement was called off, with what seemed a certain amount of mutual sadness. Both parties declared that they still believed that being together made financial sense. But there were obstacles.

Not long afterwards, they decided to try again. Now they called the relationship 'Friends' and Minorco, at least, thought it was going swimmingly.

It seemed that a long-cherished dream of the Oppenheimer family might yet come true. For decades, Sir Ernest Oppenheimer had harboured an ambition to re-establish the empire founded by Cecil John Rhodes. The Oppenheimer empire already had a monopoly in diamonds through De Beers. If it could lay its hands on the company of which Rhodes was co-founder, it would give it the commanding heights in gold too. Harry Oppenheimer inherited the ambition and Minorco chairman Julian Ogilvie Thompson had promised him Rhodes's old company, Gold Fields, as a birthday present. So Anglo's objective in wooing Consgold was fairly transparent. Or would have been had it not been that, in all the troubled times to come, it insisted that all it wanted to do was protect Gold Fields from being taken over by someone else. Indeed, there was a clause in at least one of the agreements reached which obliged Minorco to sell off its GFSA interests the moment the marriage was consummated.

So, in its own eyes anyway, Minorco was playing the role of a white knight – protecting a competitor by reducing its vulnerability to a takeover.

It is less easy, at this distance, to establish what game Rudolph Agnew, chief executive and subsequently chairman of Consgold, thought he was playing. Clearly, he enjoyed the hunting and shooting weekends on the estate called Mells in Somerset, to which he had access. Here he entertained Julian Ogilvie Thompson and other Anglo luminaries while they hunted, shot and discussed joining forces.

But somewhere along the line, the courting became a stalking in Agnew's eyes. And that's where the romance ended, to be replaced by a business negotiation cloaked in misunderstanding, not to say deception. Trying to establish now precisely who said what to whom during those stirring days of nearly a quarter-century ago is hopeless. Suffice it to say that the two parties were not just talking past each other; they seemed to be living on different planets. Not even the vaguely remembered dates can be made to coincide.

Ogilvie Thompson's version is that the idea of a merger had been broached some time in 1983/4. This had led to the public announcement of the 'Wedding of the Romans' – an announcement quickly revoked. But this early setback did not mean the end of behind-the-scenes negotiating. Talks and cosy conversations continued, punctuated by gunshot on the rolling hills of Somerset.

Things came to a climax after only a few months with the 'Friends' proposal – a significant modification of the erotic overtones of the original. There is evidence from both parties that 'Friends' was a deal close to consummation. Consgold advisers had recommended it, and the Minorco board had met in Luxemburg on a snowy Saturday before Christmas 1986 to endorse it. All that was left was for the Consgold board to approve it formally. Then the two companies would climb into bed together to form the most powerful gold mining alliance in the world and would cohabit happily ever after.

If it sounds like a fairy story that is because that, indeed, was what it was.

THE CONSGOLD board was due to meet on a Monday in January 1987. Ogilvie Thompson and Hank Slack, an up-and-coming director of Anglo's American division, felt so confident of success, based on their conversations with Agnew, that they booked newspaper space for an announcement. Then they went to see Agnew – and the new plan fell apart.

Agnew told them 'with a long face' that the foreign directors of Consgold were opposed to the creation of a new company but they could put their proposal to the full board if they wished. According to Ogilvie Thompson, the outside directors 'literally pulled the rug on the deal'. Whether Agnew had put the case for a merger to them as strongly as he had put it to Anglo he could not say. But the reasons given for rejecting the deal were, in Ogilvie Thompson's view, specious. They included concerns like trade union problems.

Agnew, on the other hand, insists today that he never had any real intention of going through with a merger even though he had suggested it. Later, two researchers who interviewed him became convinced that something of the Irish devil had got into Agnew; that he had led Ogilvie Thompson down the garden path. They thought they detected mischievous pleasure. Not that Agnew would have said such a thing in so many words, either before or after. But that's the hidden message he managed to convey, accurate or not.

Harry Oppenheimer, too, concluded that Agnew had led him up (or down) the garden path.

Agnew's version may explain his apparent ambivalence. In his publicised reactions afterwards, there was little indication that he thought the merger intrinsically undesirable. For him, the devil seemed to be in the detail. The fundamentals were wrong. Anglo's offer was too low. It had made the 'despicable' suggestion that if a merger wasn't feasible, CGF should sell its assets to Rio Tinto Zinc so that Anglo could attempt a deal there. The discussions had become ludicrous and Anglo had become arrogant. Besides, the two companies didn't really belong in an alliance. Anglo was a family-dominated business; Consgold, he explained, was more a loose federation of powerful independent companies. There would have been no comfortable fit. However, if those were genuine sentiments, one might have expected them to emerge much earlier on.

Some GFSA executives still believe that Agnew secretly liked the idea of a takeover because he had been promised a job with similar status and he felt that Anglo ownership might add to the prestige. But former GFSA executive director Bernard van Rooyen, who developed a friendship with Agnew, tends to believe the latter's version:

> I knew Agnew when he worked in South Africa. His wife was pregnant and he was short of money and I helped to get her into a maternity home somewhere off Empire Road in Johannesburg. So I had a relationship with him. What he really tried to do was to play a deep, dark game – see if somehow he could fend these guys off. He had Julian Ogilvie Thompson on his board and he liked to lead the life of a country gentleman. He had an expensive lifestyle. There was no doubt he was terribly impressed by the hunting and shooting at Mells.

'You had to see the place to believe it,' says Van Rooyen. 'The woods were just full of shotgun shells.'

Whatever the truth, one thing is incontrovertible: A day came when Agnew invited Ogilvie Thompson to present the case for a merger to the board of Consgold. Four of the most powerful financial advisers in the City of London were invited to attend. Ogilvie Thompson, at least, felt that he was on the fringe of agreement; that the presentation was a formality. Or, as Agnew puts it more coyly: 'Possibly JOT took the invitation to mean that CGF would agree.'

Julian Ogilvie Thompson spelt out his vision: the new company would be offshore and tax free, with headquarters in Switzerland. The company secretary and other staff could commute to and from London as required. Agnew would be given an important job. Did that mean he would be chief executive? Possibly not, 'but he would still run the company'. No one attempted to clarify the ambiguity. On top of everything else, the new company would be created just before Consgold was due to celebrate its centenary. Unfortunate timing.

According to Bill Jamieson's *GOLDSTRIKE!* the presentation was curiously lame and unimpressive:

> JOT began the well-rehearsed presentation. It was not long before he had a sense that the chill outside had settled within. The words and phrases that came so easily 24 hours ago sounded stumbling and hesitant now.
>
> The presentation was falling apart. JOT looked for a reassuring sign from Agnew. None came. Stumbling, unconvincing and apologetic, he fell back on what some at the meeting recalled as arrogance. 'And, of course, you're being offered a fair price. We would really like to get agreement by this afternoon.' Agnew stared ahead and slowly smoked a cigar. Robin Plumbridge, who would have voted against even if he had put on a performance that outshone Lord Olivier, spent most of the presentation staring out of the window.

As Ogilvie Thompson continued, one of the bankers at the boardroom table sent a note to Agnew. It said: 'Rudolph, this one won't fly.' Agnew remained impassive. When the whole thing finally ground to a halt, Ogilvie Thompson and his entourage left the room and the board debated the proposal. Their verdict was unanimous. The decision was 'No deal.' Agnew went to convey the news to Ogilvie Thompson. There was a bleak moment and the Anglo delegation departed.

That was the end of 'Friends.' It was not the end of the battle. It was the beginning. On that day a slow-burning fuse was lit that would detonate a business bombshell that would scar the landscape between the mining companies, precipitate the destruction of one of them and leave a legacy of mistrust in the rubble of the relationship.

NOT SURPRISINGLY, back in Johannesburg, GFSA was beginning to feel like Little Orphan Annie, alone in a storm and helpless. Things seemed to be happening that involved it, but over which it had no say or influence. It couldn't just stand by and do nothing. The glimmerings of a plan began to hatch. And this is where the convoluted plottings of Minorco and Consgold began to mesh with the tortuous machinations of the brains trust at GFSA.

The South African intervention, in the end, had no discernible effect on the outcome of the merger talks. Nevertheless it led to considerable anger between parent and offspring, fierce allegations of improper behaviour and a massive inquiry into insider trading that came to nothing. And all this for what was essentially a sideshow.

The central feature of the South African plan was that it should be executed in secrecy and without the official knowledge of its chairman and chief executive, Robin Plumbridge, or of its board. This was a tall order, since the broad idea behind the plan appears to have originated with Plumbridge himself in a time gone by.

It was further complicated because the reasons for keeping it secret from Plumbridge and some members of the South African board were different. Plumbridge couldn't be told officially because he was also a director of Consolidated Gold Fields and there was little doubt that the GFSA action would present conflicts of interest for him. In a worst-case scenario, he could even be accused of insider trading. As it happened, the worst case nearly happened, but that is a later story. The board, on the other hand, had to be kept in the dark because Anglo American and Consgold were represented on it. The so-called 'secret plan' would obviously go straight back to the predator or the parent company – or both.

And so it happened that the plan, simple but unorthodox, required an element of deviousness that was not out of keeping with anything that was brewing between the main protagonists in London.

GFSA already had a small holding of about 4.9% in Consgold, not enough to block anyone. Very well, then, it would buy a significantly greater interest; increase its holding until it *was* large enough to afford protection. Ten percent should do the trick. It would involve spending tens of millions.

It would make its purchases quickly and secretly, before any predator became aware of the action. The need for speed was self-evident; Anglo was poised to strike through Minorco. All the old fears were rekindled.

Bernard van Rooyen, executive director, was promptly despatched to London to implement the plan.

Van Rooyen had joined Gold Fields soon after completing his BA LLB at Wits. A proud Afrikaner and only 21, he had at first felt something of an outsider in a stuffy company that was at the time widely, but not flatteringly, regarded as 'very English'; that is to say, pin-stripe snobby. His sharp intelligence had quickly made a mark, and he had risen through the ranks to the point where he was in charge of corporate finance and non-technical services. In that capacity he had been responsible for a range of activities from legal services to property development to security services. Working in London had given him an understanding of UK corporate law.

There was something of the rebel in Bernard Renier van Rooyen. Finding himself in so conservative a business environment, he sometimes took an impish delight in pushing the boundaries, using his own initiative when it seemed necessary, cutting the red tape that was supposed to restrict him. As a natural troubleshooter, he 'practically lived on an aircraft' at one stage of his career. Once, when he told his wife he was flying off again the next day, she had said to him in mock rebuke:

'Why did you bother to come home?'

And he had replied: 'London is a very expensive place for laundry.'

He knew his way round the UK's sophisticated world of high finance and could handle the media if need be. He had learnt the lawyer's trick of using the significant pause as a means to convey an opinion or a shade of meaning without reducing it to words. It was a good trick for the media because it left a strong impression while making some statements both unattributable and unquotable.

He seemed to be exactly the right kind of person for such a delicate assignment. Besides, he saw it as his mission to save GFSA rather than Consgold because he was convinced that the British company was not going to last anyway.

'You only had to work there and see some of the goings on,' he said years later. 'When I was transferred to the UK for the first time I was amazed. London sort of opened at 10.00 in the morning. Lunch started at 12.00 and might go on until 15.00. Generally I felt it was a very unprofessional place.'

So he felt confident of being able to handle Consgold if anyone there became suspicious of his activities. First step, however, was to get Reserve Bank permission to take money out of South Africa. Luck was with him.

'As it happened, the financial rand had just been abolished,' says Van Rooyen. 'I remember the guy running exchange control saying to me: "There's a gap here. The regulations are in a state of suspense. It'll be two weeks before they're up and running again. I don't really mind what you do now." So we moved money into Switzerland and proceeded to buy up a significant chunk of Consgold.'

Only the 'significant chunk' was not in shares. Arriving in London he quickly discovered a smarter alternative. Stock exchange rules demanded that share purchases on any scale had to be disclosed immediately. Such disclosure would quickly blow the whole operation. But the new black art of derivatives was being introduced to the market, and a local expert suggested he look at buying options instead. Options allowed more time; they did not need to be disclosed until a week after purchase. So options it was. By chance, the options were on offer from Barrick, an American gold mining company with links to Anglo American and Consolidated Gold Fields. Van Rooyen thought there was an element of poetic justice about that. Acting CEO Dru Gnodde authorised the purchase.

Companies that sell these instruments do not expect that the rights they embody will be exercised forthwith. At some stage, yes; possibly if there is a significant change in the share price. But not immediately. So it came as an unpleasant surprise to Barrick when GFSA promptly demanded to convert their new options to shares. But there was nothing the American company could do about it.

GFSA had taken a big step towards its target with the greatest amount of secrecy allowed by the rules. There was widespread suspicion – in Consgold, in Minorco – that the South African company was up to something. But what? No evidence could be found; not immediately, anyway.

CHAPTER THREE

BATTLE STATIONS ALERT

THE STORY behind the story of the Secret Consgold Purchases is best told by the central characters themselves. First, deputy chairman Dru Gnodde, the man charged with implementing the GFSA strategy and acting with full responsibility under the delegated powers given to him by chairman Plumbridge, who insisted on staying in the background.

Born in Johannesburg in September 1928, Andries Michael Drury Gnodde, known since childhood as Dru, ended up in mining by chance. He was schooled at St John's College, did a BA at the University of Cape Town and then an LLB part-time at the University of the Witwatersrand while serving articles. After that he was sent by his parents to Cambridge, where he earned an MA LLB with first-class honours. He was equipped to practise as an attorney or to turn his attention to the bar. But he did neither.

'There were enough problems in the world without taking on the problems that clients bring to their lawyers,' he explains cheerily. So, at the age of 27, he joined Gold Fields instead.

The notion of him 'avoiding problems' doesn't quite hold water. In time to come, he joined the Council of St John's College where he became chairman. Then he joined the Association of Private Schools, where he was elected chairman. And this, in turn, led him into a very problematic situation: trying to persuade the then Minister of Education, FW de Klerk, that despite apartheid, private schools should be allowed to admit pupils of all races. De Klerk was reluctant. Eventually Gnodde decided on a more spirited approach.

'Come on,' he urged De Klerk at one of their private meetings, 'Why not let the bloody stupid English educate the people you are going to need in the future?' To his credit, De Klerk lent back, laughed aloud and said okay. He also agreed to continue the Government grant.

So Gnodde was not exactly your typical problem-ducker; not even when he finally left GFSA after 33 years of service. He immediately became chairman of five JSE-listed companies, chairman of the Rand Water Board and chairman of Lloyds Names in South Africa.

He was certainly not ducking problems when he assumed the responsibility of implementing the unconventional and audacious strategy of buying up shares in GFSA's parent company. Indeed, he seemed to relish it – even though the then vice-chairman of Anglo American, Julian Ogilvie Thompson, was later to describe the action as outrageous and unacceptable.

Plumbridge was in a tricky situation. Not only was he chairman and CEO of GFSA, he was a director of the British company too. With a foot in both camps, there was a high risk of conflicts of interest. Buying shares in either company might be considered insider trading. The executive determined to keep him out of the loop, which meant that it had to devise a way to keep its actions a secret from him. This was easier than it sounds, since Plumbridge had anticipated such a necessity some time before, and had authorised his team to carry out the strategy if need be.

Came the day when formal approval had to be obtained from the GFSA board for a fait accompli: the purchase of the share options. Gnodde was in the chair, explaining to members that Plumbridge was 'unavailable'. Some round the boardroom table found that hard to swallow. They could have sworn that they had seen him lurking in his office a few doors away.

'Of course Plumbridge knew all about the share purchases,' Gnodde recalls, 'but at his own request he wanted it put out that he was in the dark.'

'That's not right,' insists Plumbridge. 'Yes, I fathered the idea, but I didn't even know my deputy was implementing it. I didn't need to know. I believed firmly in the principle of delegating authority when I was away.'

In any event, the arrangement achieved its goal; it separated Plumbridge from the strategy that Gnodde was adopting as the authorised stand-in for his boss. It was a novel approach. It was matched by an equally novel strategy for dealing with the Gold Fields' board.

Gnodde had taken care to keep all committed GFSA board members unofficially informed of what the company executives were doing behind the scenes. So the look of studied surprise that some members tried to adopt was false in all but one case as the board heard the official explanation. 'We felt we had to act quickly,' Gnodde explained to board members. 'Consgold was vulnerable to a takeover or merger that might not be in the best interests of GFSA. It would have been irresponsible for the executive to have done nothing.'

Heads nodded, then eyes swung to one man at the table who had been deliberately denied knowledge of what was happening. That man was Peter Gush, Anglo American's representative on the GFSA board. He suddenly found himself in a dilemma to match Plumbridge's. But with less time to plan for it.

Effectively, as a Gold Fields director, Gush was being asked to approve a strategy that all other directors agreed was in the best interests of the company. But, in his primary capacity as an Anglo American director, he had a duty to protect Anglo interests, and that didn't include thwarting its desire to buy up a significantly larger share in CGF. Which 'best interest' trumped the other – Anglo's or Gold Fields'?

When it came to a vote, there were nods all round. Gnodde turned to the minute taker. 'Please record that the board has agreed to accept the actions of the executive in purchasing the shares,' he said.

'Without dissent,' he added for emphasis.

Problem resolved. But the episode served to heighten Gnodde's long-held fears about Anglo's intentions over Gold Fields. Those misgivings were deep-seated. Way back in the Sixties, when he was personal assistant to GFSA's legendary genius, Dr William 'Bill' Busschau, he had witnessed a curious incident. Sir Ernest Oppenheimer had come marching into Busschau's office one day when he was senior manager, before he became resident director.

Sir Ernest demanded the books of West Witwatersrand Areas Limited (West Wits), a pyramid company created to finance the gold mines of the West Wits line. This company was the vehicle used to house the South African assets of Consgold. The mines that it controlled included Venterspost, Libanon, Doornfontein and West Driefontein. The last was the jewel in the Gold Fields crown and, at that time, the richest gold mine in the world.

Sir Ernest insisted that Anglo now owned more shares in West Wits than GFSA and was entitled to management control of the West Wits company. The crown jewels.

Busschau reminded him, politely, that he had overlooked the small matter of a holding by a GFSA associate company, which swung the balance back to GFSA. Sir Ernest was infuriated. Gnodde was left with a lasting suspicion: that Anglo would grab what it could, when it could, if it could. It wasn't always a rational fear, especially at times when the two companies combined amicably on joint ventures. But there it was, embedded in his consciousness.

Try as he would, he could not shake it loose.

ROBIN PLUMBRIDGE'S problem of conflict of interest came back to taunt him. But his ingenious explanation carried the day. On 18 December 1990 – more than three years after the events in the GFSA board room – he was called to give sworn evidence to a formal Companies Act inquiry in London into the 'membership and securities' of Consolidated Gold Fields PLC. There he told for the first time his version of the GFSA plan to buy a significant holding in its former parent company and his role in it.

To their credit, the inspectors appointed by the Secretary of State – Phillip Heslop QC and Richard Levy FCA, assisted by Peter Brown – listened without comment. If they were surprised by aspects of it, the record does not show it. Only once does a note of incredulity creep into the voice of the interlocutor. It is a passing moment. Heslop QC set the scene:

> HESLOP: The starting point would be the acquisition by your company of a stake in [Consolidated] Gold Fields which was conceived, as we understand it in the latter part of 1982. Could you tell us what your thinking was behind that acquisition?
>
> PLUMBRIDGE: Yes. Can I start in 1980, which was more specifically

> after the dawn raid, after the public statement by Harry Oppenheimer and Lord Erroll in which they indicated that they had no intention – Anglo, De Beers, Minorco, whoever – of moving their interest above the 29% or interfering in management. When that statement was made, which was more or less concurrent with my nomination as chief executive, a lot of time was spent firstly by myself and secondly by Bernard van Rooyen on analysing the course of action which Anglo American were likely to take. ... We came to the conclusion that the verbal undertakings were unlikely to be honoured in the time-frame; that Anglo American's intention was to go through the 30% one way or another. ... The consequences of Anglo American obtaining de facto control of Consolidated Gold Fields was inevitably that they would acquire de facto control of ourselves. We believed that if anybody wished to make a bid for GFSA, it should be a front-door bid.

As a result of that analysis, Plumbridge said, GFSA had created a company called Asteroid to protect GFSA and to guarantee the South African company some sort of seat at the bargaining table if Consgold's independence were ever threatened again.

> QUESTION: As we understand it, it is a scene which seems to go right on. The fear of Anglo acquiring control without paying the appropriate premium through a front door offer is something which throughout this period, and all the way through, has concerned your board?
>
> PLUMBRIDGE: Yes.

Plumbridge ended this phase of the inquiry with a little dig of his own: 'I think the relationship between Anglo and ourselves – if I can jump backwards to before all the investigations – it would be my belief that they had hoped they would not have to sell the GFSA interest. My belief there is based on the fact that they had, as long as I can remember, always coveted GFSA.'

QUESTION: The implications of control in terms of what would happen in the Chamber of Mines and the union implications and so on were also regarded by you as contrary to the interests of the people you were representing?
PLUMBRIDGE: That is correct. Yes.

Soon thereafter the inquiry fast-forwarded to December 1986: the *Romans* deal with Minorco had lapsed and now the *Friends* deal was on the table. It was that critical weekend before the board of CGF met. Plumbridge, despite not having seen the board papers, nevertheless was convinced the Consgold board was going to consider the merger proposal. Back in Johannesburg, GFSA was weighing up its own options. This included lobbying the South African Competition Board to stop Anglo.

QUESTION: As we understand it, Mr van Rooyen did approach the [South African] competitions board and the board confirmed that anything involving a deal between Minorco and Consolidated Gold Fields would be of concern to it. The upshot seems to be that the Anglo interests do not seem to have appreciated it, or anyway gone to the competitions board, and you in a sense got there first?
PLUMBRIDGE: Correct.
QUESTION: The board was very concerned at the implications of any offer. Is that a fair summary?
PLUMBRIDGE: That is a fair statement. The Anglo American interests variously controlled of the order of 50% of the market capitalisation in South Africa, the stock exchange. At that time we were about 10% stock exchange equity; all the group companies together.

	The competition board's position was that putting together two companies with that size of interest in the economy was a prima facie case of not being in the national interest.
QUESTION:	Looking ahead to the [Minorco] bid which ultimately emanated in September 1988, do you think that by then the Anglo interests had sorted out the competitions board?
PLUMBRIDGE:	No, once they made their bid our competitions board did start its investigation. It came to the conclusion that it was not in the national interest for the two companies to be brought together and it negotiated an arrangement with Anglo American that if the Minorco bid was successful they would divest [themselves of GFSA]. Subsequently, of course, Anglo American has purchased additional shares in our company, which was not altogether a surprise to us.

At this point the inquiry became more pointed. It wanted to know about a statement by Plumbridge that GFSA 'now had a mechanism in place to move to 10% [of CGF] and possibly beyond it at short notice'. How much did he know of the share-buying when he met CGF executives and others on December 23?

QUESTION:	By December 23rd what did you know about GFSA's intentions, and indeed what it had already done in relation to its shareholding in the company?
PLUMBRIDGE:	There were no intentions at that stage. It was a general statement of support. It should be seen in the context that over quite a prolonged period I had been of the view, which I expressed to the Consolidated Gold Fields' executive, that the best way of their protecting the status quo would be for the associates to acquire a back holding into CGF. A holding in the range of 25% or so would, in my view, have

neutralised the Anglo American/Minorco holding. That proposal had not found any favour, and particularly with [Consgold MD] Anthony Hichens who was philosophically very opposed to the concept of reverse holdings.

QUESTION: Had there been, beyond that general thinking, any contact between yourself and Mr van Rooyen as to setting up the mechanics to take your holding over the existing 4.9%?

PLUMBRIDGE: No.

QUESTION: One thing that does strike us is this. As we understand it you came back [from London] on Christmas Eve and then you went away on leave. While you were away Mr van Rooyen, consulting first of all the deputy chairman and then in due course such non-executive directors as were thought not to have an involvement one way or the other, arranged a substantial line of finance with Standard Chartered Bank and procured that GFSA started a programme of acquiring traded options in Consgold on the London market. All of it, it is being said, was done without either tipping the company's hand to the Anglo interest – and we understand that – or to the Consgold people on the board of GFSA – and we understand that – and also throughout all of that without you being involved.

We would like to hear what you say about that. It seemed to be a great deal of money. It did involve, we would have thought, a major strategic move by GFSA. It was self-evident it would have repercussions with Anglo in particular, which one might have thought you might have very strong and clear views on. Without the benefit of your views the whole thing, it might be said, would be a very tricky transaction to go into. What do you say about that?

PLUMBRIDGE: I think if one goes backwards first, to the development of the original strategy to buy the 4.9% – that was part of a strategy which envisaged going to 10%, so the concept of going to 10% had been in place from a very early stage.

It was also acknowledged at that time that the decision to go from 4.9% to 10% could well have to be taken without my knowledge because of the conflicts that arose – because I was a director of Consolidated Gold Fields.

If one moves forward to the December weekend when I sat with the financial and legal advisers, we spent a great deal of time going through the options and going through my particular position, the conflict of interest which existed. We exposed all the options, and the advice that I got was very clearly that as far as any sort of acquisition programme was concerned ... it was an absolute no-go. The advice that I got regarding my own position was that, while it was not as clear, it was negative, and in the light of everything that transpired on the Monday and Tuesday in London [when the merger was rejected], when I got back to Johannesburg I informed my colleagues that I had to abstain from any consideration of any short-term issues.

In addition, the ethic which we have which relates to people's absence is that the deputy assumes full responsibility for his actions, and at executive level everybody has a deputy, whether you deputise upwards or downwards. All my responsibilities at that point were assumed by Mr Gnodde, who was my deputy.

QUESTION: We quite understand that a lot of care and a lot of advice was taken to ensure that you were not exposed to any criticism for breach of any legal or other requirement. But are you really saying, Mr Plumbridge, that from the time the initial stake was taken it was implicitly, if not expressly, understood by the board of GFSA that if and when it may prove necessary, by means which may not at that point have been understood but could be organised by the executive, a stake could be taken up as and when required? Is that really what it comes to?

PLUMBRIDGE: I think firstly it was not the board. The executive directors were the people who were essentially involved. We knew that if we wanted a seat at the table the 10% was the mark we should aim for. It was also quite clearly agreed that we did not wish to provoke Anglo American, and that going through the 4.9% would provoke Anglo American. The question of if and when one went through the 4.9% was always left as totally open, and the issue of whether or not I could participate was left as totally open, to be judged in terms of the circumstances then prevailing.

QUESTION: Would it be fair to say – because this, I think, is the impression I have formed from the papers – that whilst you took steps to ensure that you were not involved in the decision to increase the stake, nevertheless the decision taken by your executive directors (when you found out about it) was no surprise to you because it was consistent with possibilities that had been on the agenda for some time?

PLUMBRIDGE: The timing was a total surprise. The concept that they would have gone through the 4.9% was something that I judged could have happened, but I was surprised at the timing.

QUESTION: Perhaps you could just tell us when and in what circumstances you learnt what Mr van Rooyen and the executive directors had been up to?

PLUMBRIDGE: I came back from leave and I must get the days right because I am terrible on dates ... I was contacted in London by Van Rooyen on the Wednesday, I remember, and asked to go to Hill Samuel with him. When I actually saw him before we went across to Hill Samuel, he told me.

QUESTION: [Having established that the meeting with Van Rooyen took place before the Consgold board meeting]:

The summary seems to be that you were being told the progress on the option front and at the same time there was a considerable amount of discussion as to what might happen at the board meeting and the implication in terms of what you and your company could do. It is clear that at this particular meeting you very deliberately kept clear of reading the board papers?

PLUMBRIDGE: Yes.

QUESTION: Could you tell us how you recollect being told about what had happened? Would you be staying in the same hotel and Mr van Rooyen came round to your room, or did he tell you on the phone? What was your reaction to what you were told, because plainly it was a frightfully important step to your company?

PLUMBRIDGE: I cannot remember exactly. We normally stayed at the same hotel, so it could well have been phoning in.

QUESTION: The Hyde Park?

PLUMBRIDGE: It was the Hyde Park, yes. My main recollection was that I was absolutely shot. I had left the coast at four o'clock in the morning and it was now somewhere around ten or eleven o'clock the following morning. I was not exactly in the frame of mind to absorb anything. I think I went to bed and it could well have been after lunch that he phoned me, or lunch time. I guess he would have come around to my room and just said: 'Look, this is the situation. I have arranged a meeting.' I cannot be specific.

QUESTION: I think you said earlier that you were very surprised.

	Was this surprise that a decision had been taken with which you were very pleased, or the contrary?
PLUMBRIDGE:	No, I was surprised that they had chosen to do it at that particular point in time, but that was their judgment ... It has always been my philosophy that if you delegate or hand over responsibility, those that are responsible are accountable for their decision and I accept their decision. I might grumble about it sometimes but I would generally not say anything.
QUESTION:	We know that you told Mr Agnew afterwards about the increase in the stake?
PLUMBRIDGE:	No, it was my judgment that unless I was asked a question, the disclosure should come in the normal way. In the case of Mr Agnew, he came out of hospital immediately before the meeting and I had not had the opportunity to inform him personally. I would have had a problem if anyone had asked me a direct question.
QUESTION:	Presumably also, if you had told Mr Agnew beforehand, he would have had a problem as chairman in allowing speculation about who might be behind the build-up if he knew your company had increased its stake?
PLUMBRIDGE:	Yes.
QUESTION:	We have seen the correspondence between Mr Agnew and Mr Ogilvie Thompson, and the correspondence with yourself ... As we understand it, Anglo were simply very cross and regarded it as something that should not have happened. Pressure was put on you by Consgold to cease the share-buying programme?
PLUMBRIDGE:	Correct.
QUESTION:	Without accepting that they were entitled to do that, to allow the dust to settle – I think that was the phrase used – you agreed to do that.
PLUMBRIDGE:	Yes, it was done on the basis that any reactivation would be subject to board approval.

But of course the dust was not allowed to settle. It got worse. And, as is often the case with wars and battles, many claimed victory but no one actually won in the end.

Chapter Four

A Tiff in the Family

ON THE face of it, Gold Fields South Africa would have been well advised to steer clear of the looming battle between its one-time parent and an Anglo proxy. But that would have been to evade reality.

It is true that for most of its life, GFSA had been merely a subsidiary of the British company and would have been expected to know its place. But it had fought to free itself from its British apron strings in the days when apartheid was making South Africa the world's polecat and the SA government tended to view being beholden to Britain as treachery.

However, its motive for asserting independence was commercial rather than political. While Afrikaner nationalism was rampant and the political climate was clearly more favourable to a company rooted in the country, GFSA's real motivation was to be free of a family which it felt it had outgrown. It resented repatriating its hard-won profits. It wanted to grow without external constraints.

Nevertheless, there was no getting away from it: what happened to Consgold would impact on GFSA. Consolidated Gold Fields was by far its major shareholder. In a 'worst-case' scenario, a takeover could mean that GFSA, willy-nilly, would fall into other hands. Harry Oppenheimer's famous question – Why take over a company when you can get control with 30%? – seemed to hang in the air.

To GFSA, it was intolerable to have events unfolding that would affect it directly, but about which it could do nothing.

IN FEBRUARY 1987, Plumbridge finally disclosed to a dismayed Consgold board in London that its long-time fledgling, Gold Fields of

South Africa, had secretly increased its holding in the London company to 8.4%, and was planning to go to 10%.

The revelation came as a shock to Consgold chairman Agnew and MD Antony Hichens. Neither believed that Plumbridge was simply an ignorant bystander. Both felt that he had not 'played ball' with them.

They had sensed that something was going on but could not put their finger on it. Normally, they might have picked up the expenditure on shares and options in the GFSA accounts but Bernard van Rooyen had been cunning enough to block that avenue. As he describes it:

> I told our audit partner that I had a small problem. I had to find a way of getting these transactions into the books. He said: 'Well, what did the shares cost?' and I said something like three pounds six shillings. And he said: 'What are they worth now?' and I said about six pounds. So he said: 'Ok, we'll stick it in current assets.' You wouldn't get away with that today. But that's what puzzled the Brits. They couldn't identify any expenditure on shares.

Meanwhile, the fall-out from the proposed merger and GFSA's attempted counter continued to make waves. Plumbridge told Agnew that the South African Competitions Board was now taking a very active interest in what was going on:

> The chairman of the competitions board, as I understand it, had reported to his Minister, who got very agitated. The intelligence that we got was that he had informed the State President of what was involved. Between them, they got into a fair state. It came back to us and we sent a message back simply saying 'For heaven's sake, this is not a matter that requires the State President to get involved.' It seemed to us to be a total over-reaction.
>
> Whether in fact the State President was informed I do not know. But that was the message we were getting back from the chairman of the competitions board.

Later, Plumbridge was asked to elaborate to the British inquiry. Was the reason for the agitation because Oppenheimer's interests were so large that the government did not want to upset him? Not at all.

Plumbridge explained:

> If you go back to the origins of the National Party, they were always against big business. Therefore there was resentment towards what was perceived and described as the Oppenheimers. Over time this had moderated but it had been reactivated when Anglo American did deals with Southern Life and then with Barclays to acquire the South African interest of Barclays. The government were very unhappy that there should have been created a linkage between Anglo American, Southern Life and the bank now known as First National. It had been blessed on a regulatory basis, but at Cabinet level it reached them effectively as a fait accompli, and there always has been a lot of unhappiness about that because of the aggregation of power which arose.

WHEN PLUMBRIDGE made his disclosure to the Consgold board, Agnew felt unhappy about the share-buying and unhappier still at the thought that GFSA's action would offend his most powerful shareholder, Anglo American. He had no desire to do that. If Agnew felt aggrieved, Anglo's representative, Neil Clarke, felt thoroughly put out. But their objections were left in the shade when Anglo deputy chairman and Minorco chairman, Julian Ogilvie Thompson, heard the news after the board meeting. Informed of the GFSA revelation, he said angrily that it was unheard of for a subsidiary company to buy secretly the shares of its parent. The whole idea was outrageous. And he wasted no time in saying what he thought of Plumbridge's ignorance, which he assumed to be feigned.

'In the court of public opinion,' he declared, 'Plumbridge is guilty of insider trading. Anglo will find it extraordinary if CGF fails to intervene.'

Agnew heard the message. He instructed Hichens to tell GFSA to stop buying CGF shares immediately. Hichens fired off a peremptory fax to Gnodde: 'We have received information that you plan to increase the GFSA interest in CGF to 10%, and that you have arranged the necessary finance to do this. We understand that Mr Plumbridge has no knowledge of these purchases. CGF requires your immediate assurance that you will immediately cease purchasing CGF shares.'

But that was not vigorous enough for Agnew. Before Gnodde had even had time to consider how he should respond, he received an agitated phone call from CGF executive director Humphrey Wood. Wood wanted to know when Consgold could expect a reply to its demand. Gnodde was taken aback.

'I believe the announcement has caused some fury in certain quarters,' he said. And Wood relied: 'Fury? That's a gross understatement. Fury is far too mild a word.'

Wood explained that GFSA's action had created a tricky situation: 'Its put CGF in a box which will force it to press on down the line until it finds some suitable place to exit.' It was an extraordinarily opaque statement, almost gobbledegook, but Gnodde thought he knew what it meant. Decoded, it meant that GFSA's 'protective' strategy had effectively scuppered the unspoken hopes of at least some of Consgold's directors. Secretly, they had liked the idea of an Anglo takeover; hence the prolonged mating dance. They had been told their old jobs would be secure, and they thought they could improve both their status and their income under Anglo's more generous regime. And now their subsidiary had come along and destroyed their hopes by 'saving' Consgold from that fate.

Wood went on to say he realised that the South African company needed to ensure a place at the Consgold table in case there were 'nasty moves' in future. But surely Gnodde could recognise that it was close enough to a blocking situation to allow it to sit back and wait? Gnodde thought not. He believed it was in GFSA's interests to get up to 10% as soon as possible. Wood thought that was not very reassuring.

Agnew was even less reassured. Before the afternoon was out he phoned from New York and found Gnodde in Plumbridge's office. Executive director Van Rooyen was with them. Agnew did not mince his words. He said he wanted to reinforce Hichens' message. He needed an immediate positive answer. Failing this, he would take all the constitutional steps necessary to see that he got what he wanted. Gnodde said the GFSA board had ratified the decision to buy more Consgold shares and he 'could not act merely on the wishes of a large shareholder.'

That did it.

'Don't play it by the legal niceties,' said Agnew. 'Our major shareholders own our company and they are entitled to get their way. Your actions have unleashed many pressures and conflicts in the northern hemisphere – and don't assume it's just pressure from 44 Main Street.'

Gnodde said: 'I hear what you say and I will consider it before replying.'

'Good,' said Agnew, 'But I want you to know that I won't stop until I get what I need. Refuse me now and I will use all my powers to see that you and Robin Plumbridge are removed.'

Gnodde's first instinct was to reply: 'Really? Don't you realise that you have a legal obligation to explain why you're firing a director? Are you really going to tell the world you're firing me for trying to protect you?'

But he decided to be more diplomatic. 'We will give full consideration to what you have said and I will send my written reply to London,' he said.

Plumbridge, Gnodde and Van Rooyen looked at each other. They were dealing with an ultimatum from their largest shareholder. Could they ignore it? The three men went through the proposed response line by line. They decided to tone down the draft by deleting some paragraphs which might be considered provocative. Then Gnodde made his last official phone call of the day. He read the final version to Agnew.

This version said GFSA agreed not to raise its existing stake and would buy no more. That seemed to placate Agnew. It was just as well that he couldn't see the knowing smile on Gnodde's face. GFSA would buy no more – but it had no intention of selling the 8.4% it held already. Gnodde had calculated that, under a complicated stock exchange formula, 8.4% was effectively enough to block Anglo American from laying hands on the GFSA assets; enough to block any full takeover. And it didn't really need the 10% anyway. Agnew didn't seem to know that.

And so the stand-off was resolved and Gnodde kept his job until he reached retirement age in 1988.

For Robin Plumbridge, it was a time of frustration. Forced into the role of an observer because he inhabited this no-man's-land of potential conflict of interest, it consigned him to the role of onlooker. It was not a role that suited his style and temperament. By nature, he was not just a participant. He was a hands-on leader. And a brilliant one at that, according to many of his peers.

BORN IN Cape Town on 6 April 1935, Robin Allan Plumbridge matriculated at St Andrew's College in Grahamstown, Eastern Cape. He wanted to be a farmer, but his family couldn't afford to keep him in an occupation like that. So he went to the University of Cape Town to do a land surveyor's course because it promised an outdoor life. Eighteen months later he was told that he was St Andrew's nominee for Rhodes Scholar.

In those days, before political correctness had been invented, the criteria for being chosen were as stipulated in Cecil John Rhodes's will. Candidates had to be white, male and gifted academically and athletically. The chosen ones would be sent to Oxford University to study and play sport. Plumbridge did both with fervour, reading mathematics, earning a Master's degree and representing Oxford at rugby for three years. He also played three games for the Barbarians. Cricket was another love – 'but you can't play two major sports equally seriously, so I confined myself to playing for the Authentic, which is the Oxford second team.'

After graduating, the only company that was prepared to offer him a job and pay his way back to South Africa was Gold Fields. He believed that was because then chairman Busschau had 'a great understanding for the problems of an impecunious Oxford student'. He started as a general trainee at the age of 22, and stayed with the company until the day he finally retired in October 1997. Not for a single moment in those 40-odd years did anyone have cause to doubt his loyalty to Gold Fields and his dedication to its interests.

In the early Eighties, the *SA Mining Journal* painted a glowing picture of the 45-year-old new chief executive of GFSA. It quoted a colleague as saying:

> Robin is a very balanced individual who has always progressed

beyond his years. He is a man of enormous patience who is well-liked by people with whom he works. He handles people – whether subordinates or equals – extremely well and is always very approachable and pleasant. He never looks ruffled by a crisis. I have seen him in some hot spots with trade union leaders – he keeps his cool, is always prepared to listen, but maintains a firm stand himself. It is better to have him as an ally than an opponent on any issue.

The article quoted him on his management style:

> I favour a system that involves a high degree of delegation. Perhaps this is the most difficult to achieve, people are reluctant to delegate. One has to consciously sit back periodically and encourage oneself and others to take stock of this question of delegation. One must make sure that the greatest possible degree of delegation has taken place.

Ironically, it was a perceived reluctance to delegate that became the single biggest source of irritation to some of his colleagues in later years.

Nearly all acknowledged his mathematical bent and forceful presence. Most interpreted his distant, almost forbidding, manner as being brought on by shyness rather than arrogance. But some claimed that his cleverness and occasionally caustic tongue had intimidated them.

Interviewing him in retirement on his grape-growing smallholding near Somerset West – dressed in a farmer's outfit of rough open-neck shirt and worn trousers, a man content – it is hard to reconcile this benign presence with the austere figure described by some colleagues. It provides a salutary reminder that everyone has multiple personalities: a work face and a home face; the way others see them and the way they see themselves.

Besides, criticisms can be two-edged swords. Sometimes they say as much about the critic as they do about the target. Such was his influence and dominance that he was widely seen as 'Mr Gold Fields' during his tenure. Even today he is irritated by the title. 'It was not my company,' he insists. 'It belonged to the shareholders. I was an employee.'

As happens, there is a significant difference between his perception of his leadership style and the perceptions of some others. The issue of delegation is one example. There are others. Some subordinates found him difficult to approach. Men who were summoned to his office instinctively put on their jackets. 'That's odd,' says Plumbridge. 'I never wore a jacket in the office. I was a shirt-sleeves man myself.'

He had a reputation for being formal in his relationships. Some insist that he tended not to greet people in the corridors and was perceived to discourage unplanned visits to his office. Yet he says of himself: 'I had an open-door policy. And I enjoyed arguing with staff who had given proper thought to their opinions.' Perhaps it was the existence of a charmingly formidable secretary guarding his lair that accounted for the differing perceptions.

Even among staff, opinions differed. In his 27 years at Gold Fields, says Peter Janisch, a retired executive director, he never felt overwhelmed. Nor did he feel that he was being frustrated in achieving his own goals and developing his talents. He felt he had enough delegated power to do his job satisfactorily. He has an abiding memory of the boss stopping off at his desk from time to time for an informal chat.

But others found Plumbridge more forbidding. A former senior executive cannot forget one particular incident. He had been acting as CEO while Plumbridge was overseas. He took what he thought was a perfectly straightforward decision on a technical matter. When the boss returned, he countermanded it. From then on, say colleagues, the executive decided that he wasn't going to stick his neck out – not if it was going to be chopped off on a whim.

There was another area of criticism. Plumbridge was a man who believed in gold. That, to him, was central to the future of Gold Fields. Gold, and other metals. In time, some critics and some shareholders came to see the lack of diversity as a danger to the company.

Plumbridge offers an effective counter:

> I wasn't against diversifying as far as natural resources were concerned. We had carefully assembled an excellent team so that we could tackle the technical issues associated with all forms of mining and metallurgy. Rembrandt saw Gold Fields as traditional deep-level Witwatersrand gold miners and were not enthusiastic supporters of

our ambitions to diversify as and when possible. The reality was that SA gold mining was in decline and the future lay in coal and platinum and that we had to look internationally to survive.

That last sentiment was to be echoed time and again in the years to come.

IT SEEMS almost as if Plumbridge had two phases in his working life. For most of his years in the top job, he was every bit the successful businessman, growing the company, playing his role in the Chamber of Mines, winning influence in international circles, marketing his favourite product, gold, with extraordinary success. The Plumbridge of the first phase thought he had the best lieutenants in the industry and was confident they shared the same vision.

And then came the latter years, when good staff seemed to be filtering away, when the gold price seemed mired, when critics began to say: 'He's stayed too long.'

They may be surprised to find that Plumbridge agrees with them. He always thought ten years should be about the limit for a top executive. He was persuaded against his better judgment to stay longer. But that was something in the future.

At this moment, with the future of Consgold in the balance, he had other thoughts on his mind. It was thoroughly frustrating that he was precluded from playing a more active role in fending off the 'unwanted suitor' who was trying to steal not just the hand but the entire reluctant body of GFSA's British parent.

CHAPTER FIVE

GLOVES OFF

ACTUALLY, the storm over the share purchases by GFSA was a sideshow. The real drama was building in the wings. It became public in 1988 when the jilted Minorco decided to abandon attempts at negotiation and embark instead on a hostile takeover bid. In so doing it created a situation that would transfix the world of business on three continents, not least for the sheer mutual ill-will it generated.

Newspaper readers everywhere would hang upon every spiteful word of public dialogue between the warring parties.

As the melodrama of the Minorco bid played itself out over eight fraught months, Gold Fields of South Africa did its best to vanish into the background. It could hardly have been otherwise. The share-buying incident had left burnt fingers and scorched relations. Besides, Plumbridge found the public spectacle distasteful. It was a battle that lacked both dignity and decency, two qualities he considered indispensable to a gentleman.

But there was a far more important reason for GFSA's discretion. Any overt role would simply have reminded the world of the fundamental flaw in chairman Agnew's defence strategy.

Agnew had decided that his best way of winning public support was to label Anglo American as an apartheid Trojan horse and Minorco as its secret love-child. In this scenario, Minorco was going to help Anglo to help South Africa to lay its apartheid-tainted hands on most of the world's gold. This, he was convinced, would unite the anti-apartheid lobby in rejecting the South African link and, by extension, supporting Consgold.

It was grotesquely unfair. But what it lacked in intellectual weight it made up for in emotional clout. Sanctions had been imposed on the country to wide external acclaim. Any business organisation trying to prevent a moral pariah from holding the world to ransom by acquiring a near-monopoly of gold would surely win applause. Turning the battle into a moral crusade could bring victory.

'You can deny your bastard sons,' he thundered at Anglo/Minorco, 'but you can't deny your children.' And: 'You can take Minorco out of South Africa but you can't take South Africa out of Minorco.'

The quotes were outrageous – and typical. Agnew was a fiery Irishman with great personal charm. On top of that, he looked like a Fifties matinée idol with his clean-cut features, slicked-back grey hair and intense greenish-brown eyes. A fellow-director of Consgold, Michael Beckett, summed him up like this:

> He had never had any money so Consolidated Gold Fields gave him great comfort. He had an apartment, two chauffeurs and unlimited expenses. He turned Mells Park in Somerset, a converted lime quarry, into a country estate. Shooting parties were ostensibly to bring in construction deals. He moved Consgold from Moorgate to Charles II Street to a listed building that Anglo sarcastically called Versailles. The building had to be restored to its original specifications, which were very grand. When Minorco made its bid he saw all this stuff disappearing from him.

To be fair, Agnew didn't invent the high-flying style. His predecessor, George Harvie-Watt (born George Watt) did. As Beckett puts it, Harvie-Watt wanted to lead the good life without having to spend his own money. Once a year he would take a Union Castle liner from Southampton to Cape Town, accompanied by his wife, a secretary and a management assistant because they needed a four for bridge. On arrival they would stay at the Mount Nelson for a few days before taking the Blue Train to Johannesburg. The Daimler, shipped from Britain, would be driven up to meet him. On the Highveld he would hold court for a month, visiting mines, wining and dining, and holding intimate lunches. He would shop in Johannesburg using the travel allowance that GFSA paid to him. Eventually GFSA made a mild protest and he toned things down.

WHAT AGNEW didn't bargain for was that his attacks on South Africa would enrage an important player enlisted to protect Gold Fields of South Africa from hostile takeover bids. Rembrandt, a South African company, was about to take a significant holding in GFSA. Johann Rupert, a staunch South African and a rising star in the Rembrandt group, let it be known that if the Agnew attacks persisted, this deal was off. Agnew modified his strategy but not before the link with apartheid had been made indelible.

The fact that Anglo American had decided, quite deliberately, to let Minorco present itself as a separate Europe-based entity helped Agnew considerably. He wasn't about to spoil the rhetoric because another fact was also true: within South Africa, Anglo was widely perceived as a liberal employer opposing apartheid. It didn't deserve to be painted as an apartheid supporter, but this was a consideration that didn't weigh heavily with Agnew. As in any fight to the death, he reasoned, no one demanded that all facts be given the same weight. Or any weight at all. All's fair in love and war, isn't it?

But if GFSA were to join the fray overtly, why – that might reveal Consgold as being tainted too. Consgold also depended heavily on earnings from a mining company operating in apartheid South Africa. What gave it the right to the moral high ground? Best that GFSA didn't become too visible as the most expensive corporate defence in British takeover history was launched.

It was a campaign marked by bitterness, intemperance and dubious activity on both sides. Julian Ogilvie Thompson, who was persuaded against his better judgment to make the bid hostile, called it 'a worldwide programme of vilification and abuse'. A Consgold director, Antony Hichens, called it a campaign of 'articulated abuse towards Anglo', and concluded: 'People enjoyed this, and it became the daily soap opera.' Anglo didn't enjoy it. 'They were thin-skinned and they had never been abused like this before,' said Hichens.

Consgold director Beckett peered out of his home window one day to see two men burrowing in his dustbins. They turned out to be private detectives hunting for information. Later, he found a tape on his office desk with a message saying 'Play me.' It was a recording of a phone conversation in which Ogilvie Thompson and Sir Michael Edwardes planned their takeover tactics. Beckett never did find out who had sent it to him.

By the time the takeover war had come to an end, relations had been so soured that Ogilvie Thompson and Plumbridge never spoke again. Or, at least, so the legend has it. But Plumbridge insists it is just folklore.

The hostile bid was launched on 21 September 1988. Before it was resolved, it dragged in regulatory bodies in Britain and a court in the United States. President Reagan was urged to block the Minorco bid on the grounds that concentrating too much gold in the hands of a company operating in a polecat country constituted a threat to the national interest. Consgold hired an international detective agency which set 45 legmen on the task of digging up dirt about Anglo. It gripped the media on three continents. It provoked investigations by the South African Competition Board, the Department of Trade and Industry in London, the British Monopolies and Mergers Commission, the Office of Fair Trade and the British Takeover Panel. Findings alternately encouraged one party, then the other.

Part of the public attraction was that Agnew revelled in being outrageous, which offered an intriguing contrast to the studied and often exasperating coolness of Anglo/Minorco. A counter-attraction was that Minorco was headed by Michael Edwardes, who looked the very image of a proper Englishman but who actually hailed from East London, South Africa. His claim to fame was that he had earned international headlines when he broke the power of British trade unions at British Leyland. He was no pushover; the new war was bound to be a great and prolonged spectacle.

Agnew called Edwardes 'a pipsqueak making the pips squeak'.

Ultimately the battle was resolved not by the parties themselves, not by the regulatory bodies, but by an unlikely participant on a different continent. Here's how it came about.

An American company, Newmont Mining Corporation, was 49% owned by Consgold. Like GFSA, it feared that if Minorco were to succeed, it would gain control of both companies and have the power to influence Newmont's production and even shut down its mines. Accordingly, Consgold and Newmont joined forces to apply to a US District Court in New York for an injunction to stop Minorco.

The injunction was granted provisionally in October 1988 and confirmed on 22 March 1989. (Later, in a different forum, Consgold argued a contrary view equally fervently. It insisted that its 49% share of Newmont didn't enable it to tell Newmont what to do.)

In between those dates the adversaries bobbed in and out of court no less than four times, either making or refuting new claims. At one point, Minorco made a firm offer to sell its acquired interests in both GFSA and Newmont Mining if the court would only allow it to continue buying the shares it needed to make good its takeover bid. Judge Michael Mukasey was not persuaded.

Anglo, he insisted, had a reputation for finding ways around such undertakings. His court could not monitor whether Minorco/Anglo kept faith. Mukasey put it bluntly. 'The one reliable constant here,' he pronounced, 'is the interest and incentive of the Anglo group to control its direct competitors.'

Agnew, never one to miss an opportunity, added his own reinforcing sally in a press release:

> Minorco has tried and failed in its attempt to present itself as something that it is not. The United States federal district court has delivered a resounding judgment against Minorco and its parents. Our shareholders should shortly do the same.

On the final occasion in the New York district court, Minorco offered an ingenious argument: it asked the court to reconsider on the grounds that Minorco had launched a search for a buyer for Newmont even before it had acquired it. What could better illustrate its good faith? It was a novel approach but it moved the judge not one jot.

Mistrust of Anglo American was probably born 15 years previously when an American grand jury indicted De Beers and two other companies operating in the United States for conspiracy to rig prices and share markets – and De Beers took refuge back in South Africa and avoided going to trial.

THE FIRST New York district court ruling hit Minorco with a double whammy. Not only was it prevented from buying any more Consgold shares, it was effectively prevented from meeting the deadline to make its offer unqualified, as required by the London Stock Exchange. There was no escape from this cleft stick. The only way it could meet the conditions of the takeover bid would have been to defy the US court and make an offer to all shareholders; something it couldn't do without incurring the risk of legal action against a United States company in which it had a significant interest.

The battle descended into a war of words in different forums. Consgold bought handsome advertisements in British newspapers to declare: 'Stay with Gold Fields.' Whereupon Minorco bought ads to say: 'Don't let Gold Fields pull the wool over your eyes.' Shareholders from both camps were bombarded with glossy publications warning them of the dire intentions of the other party. Neither side seemed to care too much that their arguments not only contradicted each other but sometimes contradicted their own as well.

Some idea of the flavour of the debate can be gleaned from these extracts:

> **Consgold, 9 March 1989:** Don't trust Minorco or its shares.
> * Poor management, poor record and poor prospects.
> * Damaging South African control – at least 71% now, at least 48% if the bid succeeds.
>
> Minorco is a South African controlled company. Luxembourg is highly beneficial for the Anglo American grouping, both to avoid tax and to keep the details of its organisation secret. Minorco has said that it can pay its dividends gross. Do not be misled by Minorco.
>
> **Consgold, 4 April 1989:** MINORCO – POOR PAST AND NO FUTURE.
> - Poor management, poor record and poor prospects.
> - Minorco's miserable record is the responsibility of its present management. They now seek to manage Gold Fields. Why should you back them?
> - Poor value now, even worse once 80-million new shares flood the market and unwilling holders sell their shares.

Minorco, 8 April 1989: Questions for the board of Gold Fields:
- How can the board deliver value to shareholders if it does not itself know the value of the Gold Fields group?
- Why does the board imply that Gold Fields controls assets which it does not own; that Gold Fields has direct access to cash flows which it does not control?
- Central costs reduce the value of Gold Fields – why have they not been disclosed?

The [Gold Fields] board has presented you with a mine of misinformation and expects you to construct your own valuation. Have the directors adopted this approach because they are frightened that the resultant valuation would be too low to justify rejection of Minorco's offer? Beware misleading illusions.

Minorco, 10 April 1989: The phoney war ended this morning at 7.30 am London time. Our bid of £15.50 is final. It is final too in the sense that it cannot be increased by negotiation between the parties. Nobody will pay more. Gold Fields deliberately chose to forfeit any opportunity of influencing our offer price. Right to the end their actions call into question whether the Gold Fields management has focussed sufficiently on the interests of their shareholders. Their private court action in the States is the last in a long line of frustrating tactics ...

Consgold, 1 May 1989: The US courts have held that Gold Fields is threatened with irreparable injury by a Minorco takeover ... and that the acquisition would be likely to lessen substantially competition in the world gold market.

Meanwhile, further complications arose. Minorco gained acceptances of the bid offer that, added to its own shareholding, gave it control of 54.8% of CGF's equity. 'We've won!' proclaimed Minorco. But Agnew, stubborn as ever, wouldn't concede, and came up with his own calculation. As Agnew explained: 'I am anxious to keep all shareholders fully informed following the announcement by Minorco that it had received acceptances of its hostile offer of 24.9%. Disregarding Minorco's holding of 29.9%, holders of 64% of the balance of Gold Fields issued shares rejected the bid and stayed with Gold Fields.' Yes, well ...

Earlier on, Minorco had tried to fashion a second string to its bow by appealing to the British Panel on Takeovers and Mergers. It argued that Consgold's attempt to block Minorco without consulting its own shareholders infringed a basic principle of the takeover code. The panel was acutely conscious that it was being asked to intervene in an extraordinary situation. It ruled:

> The present case is very exceptional. It has been Europe's largest takeover bid and has been bitterly contested between two major international groups. One protagonist is associated with the world's largest producer of gold. The other protagonist is the second largest producer. Over half the assets of Consgold are in the US. It is said by Newmont that the proposed bid could seriously affect the trading activities and interests of a major US public company which has its own interests separate from Consgold and which, on the evidence before us, has acted independently of Consgold. We consider that a situation of this kind, although it may arise again, will not frequently do so. Offeree companies should realise that this decision should in no way encourage them either to use foreign subsidiaries to commence frustrating proceedings, or to try to procure third parties to do so.

And what was the decision? Said the Takeover Panel: 'The continuance of the US proceedings without shareholder approval clearly has the effect of frustrating the offer. The majority view of the shareholders should be respected.'

'We've won!' proclaimed Minorco. But again Agnew had different ideas. Disarmingly, he agreed to withdraw Consgold from the action in the New York court forthwith. And what about Newmont? 'No,' he said. 'We can't tell Newmont what to do.' And Newmont was determined to go ahead. How did that jell with his earlier argument that a significant shareholding constituted de facto control? The answer seemed to be that sometimes it did, and sometimes it didn't. Agnew seemed airily unconcerned by such trifles. But it was precisely this apparent contradiction that created the neatest Catch-22 in British business history – and stymied Minorco in the process.

THE ORIGINAL Catch-22 is the title of Joseph Heller's novel set in the last days of the Second World War. According to Heller, it went like this:

> There was only one catch and that was Catch-22, which specified that a concern for one's safety in the face of dangers that were real and immediate was the process of a rational mind. ... Orr [a character in the book] would be crazy to fly more missions and sane if he didn't. If he flew them he was crazy and didn't have to. But if he didn't want to, he was sane and had to.

In the great takeover war, a similar bind developed. In essence it boiled down to this:

Minorco gained acceptances of its takeover bid from 54.8% of the voting rights of Consolidated Gold Fields PLC. It was now obliged to meet a specific deadline for extending the offer to all other Consgold shareholders. Without that, the bid would fail. But an American court had issued an injunction preventing Minorco from buying any more Consgold shares – and showed no sign of relenting. So Minorco couldn't fulfil its obligation. Result: Catch-22.

The situation was complicated by a further issue, call it Catch-23. The British Takeover Panel ordered Consgold to get the approval of its own shareholders before pursuing legal action to stop Minorco. Consgold evaded the order – and the confrontation with shareholders – by withdrawing from the legal action. But an American company 49% owned by Consgold continued the action and kept the injunction alive thanks to a Takeover Panel ruling that it was an independent entity not beholden to Consgold.

That ruling, together with the US court injunction, became the last nails in the Minorco bid coffin. Confronted by stalemate, Minorco finally gave up. Catch-22 and Catch-23 had triumphed.

Puzzled, the *Wall Street Journal* asked:

> What is this case doing in a US courtroom in the first place? Everyone agrees that Britain is the location of the takeover fight ... The only true loser so far is the costly and erratic US court system, which has proven once again why its reach does not deserve to extend the world over.

On 16 May 1989, Mukasey's ruling on an appeal by Minorco was made public. It came a mere 24 hours before the takeover deadline expired. It was widely believed that the judge was partly influenced by the need for an anti-South African political stance. He had decided, yet again, that the injunction should not be lifted. He was not convinced by a further offer by Minorco to 'hold separate' the interests in Newmont. His scepticism shone through: 'Problems of enforcement and detection would remain. Unidentified members of the Anglo group remain free to acquire shares. Many of the Anglo group members are not subject to this court's jurisdiction and thus could easily evade detection.'

For Michael Edwardes and his team at Minorco, it was a death knell. Their final statement said: 'We tried our best. We felt our latest position was powerful but Mukasey threw it all out.' They could do no more.

For Agnew and the Gold Fields crew, triumph was tinged with melancholy. It was almost as if they knew that their days were numbered.

Less than seven weeks after Mukasey's fateful ruling, another predator came knocking at Agnew's door, egged on by the disappointed Edwardes. His name was Lord Hanson and he seemed to have an uncanny ability to identify companies that were performing poorly yet sitting on assets of enormous potential. Both he and his company, Hanson PLC, had grown rich by masterminding such asset-stripping.

Boldly, he made an offer that was significantly lower than Minorco's final offer. Once again, Agnew picked up pen to write to his shareholders. Was the old fire still blazing in his soul? At first, it seemed it might be: 'You may have read in the Press,' he wrote, 'that Hanson PLC has announced an offer for the whole of the issued share capital of Consolidated Gold Fields PLC at a cash price of £14.30 per share. The value of this offer is substantially below that of the recent offer by Minorco and falls well short of the value of Gold Fields. The directors and their financial advisers recommend you to take no action and not to sell your shares in the market.'

Then, suddenly, the tone changed: 'Unlike Minorco,' he stated, 'Hanson is a serious company and any approach from it has to be carefully considered. I intend to meet Lord Hanson to impress upon him the true worth of Gold Fields.'

For a final time in this sorry saga, Plumbridge decided to play no role, to present no opinion, on the Hanson offer. A small-print statement in the letter to shareholders said Plumbridge had received legal advice that he had a conflict of interest which prevented him from allying himself with any recommendation by other CGF directors.

By mid-July 1989, Hanson had upped his offer – a smoke-and-mirrors arrangement that didn't mean more cash for Consgold – and Agnew surrendered meekly. Why? Plumbridge thinks he knows: 'The only explanation was exhaustion after months of fighting Minorco. He'd given his all, and he had no more to give.'

Within days, Consolidated Gold Fields was sold and almost immediately broken up for disposal. The 102-year-old company was dead, its head office shuttered, almost all staff dismissed and its 38% holding in Gold Fields of South Africa ready to be sold off.

Hanson paid a last visit to the Charles II headquarters, asked to be left alone and began an inspection tour. Then he put stickers on those pieces he wished moved to his own home. Beckett phoned Hanson and asked him what should be done with the Consgold treasure trove of 4 000 bottles of wine, many of them rare. Hanson said: 'Sell it.' So Beckett called in wine merchants Justini & Brookes and they came round within an hour with a truck. Three van-loads and £32 000 later the deal was done. But then Hanson changed his mind and said: 'Send the wine to me.' Beckett phoned J&B again and they said: 'Sure you can have it back, but it will cost you the full retail price – £84 000.'

It was poetic justice. There were no winners at the end of the protracted takeover war, save Lord Hanson. So it seemed only fair that he should miss out on something too. Minorco had failed to achieve its objective, Consgold had failed to survive its triumph and shareholders of both companies had seen a total of £60-million go down the drain in pursuit of a pyrrhic victory. Surely now things could return to normal?

But no – that wasn't the end of the matter. The feud ran too deep for that. There was still one more round to be fought.

CHAPTER SIX

Cloak and Dagger

ONE OF THE LAST – and noblest – actions taken by Consolidated Gold Fields, in the days when it was fighting for its life, was destined to remain unreported for more than a decade. The company was party to an under-cover drama that helped to determine the fate of South Africa in the darkest days of apartheid. The hero of this remarkable episode – and he would shudder at the word 'hero' – was a thoughtful, quiet-spoken head of communications at Consgold by the name of Michael Young.

The drama played out in an unlikely setting: an English country mansion in Somerset. It might have remained untold had not author Robert Harvey referred to it in the final chapter of his 2003 book *The Fall of Apartheid*. It might have been lost to a wider audience if British television director Pete Travis hadn't spotted the dramatic potential and made a television movie called *Endgame* which was aired internationally in 2009. It had some of the elements of a James Bond adventure, though Young would certainly shudder at that allusion too. He was nothing like an 007.

When the background to South Africa's memorable transition to democracy was at last fully revealed, it was to British and international TV viewers, who saw it long before most South Africans even knew it had happened.

The revelation of how ANC exiles began secret peace talks with emissaries of the apartheid government while the flames of revolution were being fanned in South African townships reads like fiction. But it was very real. It was so unexpectedly successful that it would come to provide a model for resolving apparently intractable disputes. When the IRA wanted to open negotiations with the British Government it approached

53

the ANC to find out how that organisation had done it. Hamas approached the IRA for similar advice in its war with Israel. And, most recently, the United States revealed that it had secretly opened negotiations with the Taliban in Afghanistan.

Perhaps the impact of what came to be nicknamed 'Glenfiddich Diplomacy' was heightened because the movie *Endgame* rang so true. It was shot in real locations: PW Botha's former office in Parliament; Pollsmoor Prison near Cape Town, where Mandela was held after his move from Robben Island; and the gilded cage of Victor Verster Prison, where Mandela was held (and spied upon) until his release in 1990. Its star, William Hurt, gave a credible performance as Afrikaner academic, Professor Willie Esterhuyse, accent and all.

Says Mark Strong, the British actor who played the role of Dr Niel Barnard, former head of South African Intelligence – represented as a sinister character in the movie: 'It was really quite eerie. The furniture at Victor Verster is the furniture that Mandela used. There's an umbrella in the garden and you can still see the holes where the secret cameras were. In the corner of Mandela's bedroom there's still a hole where another secret camera was planted.'

MICHAEL YOUNG'S early career would have placed him squarely as British Establishment, the very model of pin-stripe respectability. An interviewer from *The Times* of London wrote of him: 'He has the smooth manners of a senior civil servant.' But the reporter didn't notice that this dignified façade hid a daredevil spark.

An early job after graduating from the University of York was at 10 Downing Street in the days when the Conservative Party's Edward Heath was Prime Minister. Young admired his boss's flexibility of thinking. In the 1970s, at Heath's request, he worked on one of the first contacts between a major British political party and the IRA in an attempt to bridge the divide fuelling the civil war in Northern Ireland. Young also advised political leaders in Portugal and Spain as they moved from dictatorships to democracies.

Working under Prime Minister Margaret Thatcher wasn't quite as satisfying. He became disillusioned by some of her hard-line attitudes.

In the Eighties he accepted an appointment from Rudolph Agnew, chairman and CEO of Consgold, as the company's head of communications. Young had an intriguing understanding of his job. Later he was to say: 'My best work is done quietly. As a licensed liberal in this fairly right-wing company, it was my job to think the unthinkable thoughts.'

He didn't stop to consider that unthinkable thoughts might lead to unthinkable actions.

It was no secret that Consolidated Gold Fields was in a tricky position politically. It had a bigger investment in South Africa than any other British company. Its fortunes were inextricably bound up with the country's future. It made business sense to try to play some role in finding solutions. But what? Strongly opposed to apartheid, Sir Rudolph nevertheless believed that the best way to destroy it was to feed it, not starve it; in other words, to engage rather than boycott.

One day in the mid-Eighties Young came to Agnew with a curious proposal. It was all very well wringing hands and deploring apartheid; the real question was: What can we do about it? He had some ideas.

As a first step, he needed to find out for himself what the ANC was about, and what it really wanted. Could revolution be avoided? Was there another route to be taken? Could peace be negotiated without gun barrels? He wanted to detach himself from his normal duties and devote himself to the task.

To some it might seem an impossibly naïve idea, but to Young it made complete sense. Agnew gulped – and agreed to let Young try. He made just one stipulation. Gold Fields was not to be publicly involved. If Young's activities leaked and political embarrassment ensued, Young would be disowned and thrown to the wolves.

'That's the way the game is played,' says Young, 'and I accepted it.'

In the meantime, the exercise was to remain top secret. Not even Gold Fields of South Africa could know about it; especially not GFSA. He couldn't be sure that the South Africans were able to 'think outside the box'.

He explains his thinking on the ANC:

> Things were definitely going to change in South Africa; it was simply a matter of how long the regime could last. My job at Gold Fields was a strategic role, where I had to try and work out how our

gold-mining house could remain in South Africa for the long haul. Other companies were throwing money at black education, hoping to build up a black entrepreneurial class, and see if that could be the salvation. I took the view that there was only one issue, and it was this: how do you get from a rigid, totalitarian, white-driven state to a black state through the process of the ballot box?

Intellectually and ideologically, the status quo couldn't be maintained. If there were to be a democratic transition to black majority rule, it required that you actually engaged with the people who represented the bulk of the population. Whether the political and business classes in the UK, Europe and America liked it or not, that meant talking to the ANC. My chairman agreed that I should try to forge links with the ANC in exile, just to see what they were like and what they wanted. So I met the ANC, and we began to discuss what needed to happen.

Young asked ANC leader Oliver Tambo: 'What does a British company need to do to help resolve the South African situation?'

Tambo replied: 'Please help me build a bridge. I need a bridge built to the regime in Pretoria.'

THIS IS WHERE the unthinkable became the implausible. Getting to know the ANC involved visiting South Africa and meeting local leaders secretly. Five or six times, Young was smuggled into townships, hiding in the back of cars. The country was in a semi-permanent state of emergency and violence was rife. The feared security police became aware of his activities and began to hound him.

Raising the political temperature generally in 1985 was a daring visit by a group of mostly Afrikaners to meet ANC leaders in Dakar. The group was led by former leader of the opposition Dr Frederik van Zyl Slabbert. The trip was successful in that it opened an avenue of communication – but the aftermath was ferocious. Government media denounced the delegates as traitors and right-wing whites were appalled. Delegates' lives were threatened, their homes guarded. It was not an encouraging omen for Young.

Later he explained how his situation had come about:

> The state as a whole wasn't homogenous. What PW Botha had done was marginalise the cabinet and parliament, and set up a state security council which actually ran the country. Had the police and their intelligence forces – who were very much more redneck and untutored and right-wing – been the people that were following me, I think I'd have been found in a bush, dead. The people who were following me belonged to Niel Barnard's National Intelligence Service (NIS). These were people who didn't like the options they saw ahead, but realised the status quo wasn't possible. I think they felt: 'He's doing something interesting. Let's just watch this. If it gets out of control we can jump on it.'

Young was very conscious that, since only chairman Agnew and his deputy chairman knew what he was doing, he could easily 'disappear' at any time. He says:

> Most telephone lines between South Africa and the UK were intercepted. It was clear to me very early on that they would discover that something unfamiliar was happening. Normally when British businessmen like myself went to South Africa, we'd fly in, we'd be met, we'd go to our subsidiary company there ... and the first question we would be asked at the airport was: 'When are you leaving?' So the notion of me wandering around outside the business environment would have been very odd.
>
> Apart from tapped phones, it was very clear that I was being followed. I received phone calls from the security police telling me they knew what I was doing and I had better watch my back. I was taught how to check under my car for booby trap devices and so on. Yes, I was frightened, but it seemed to me that this was such a potentially important initiative that you just needed to get on and do it. You don't discount the danger, but I think you sublimate it when you're younger in a way which you might not when you grow slightly older.

President PW Botha turned a blind eye to Young's activities just as he did to the Dakar trip. Young is convinced that Botha sanctioned what he called 'this little adventure in the United Kingdom' because he had his own devious plan for Mandela. The ANC icon had been locked up for a long time. Botha hoped that might make him more amenable to doing a deal on his own. 'They wanted to isolate him, and see if they could nurture him and do that deal. It was quite clear to me that could have led to the most almighty schism within the country, which would have created precisely the kind of bloodbath we were trying to avoid.'

HAVING ESTABLISHED that the ANC was ready to talk, Young set about finding the right people to talk to. It wasn't easy. He says:

> I tried a whole range of people. I couldn't just go and knock on PW Botha's front door and suggest to him we needed to be talking to the ANC. What one had to do was look at the power structure and determine who were the people close to the centre of power, who took a view that the status quo was not maintainable and realised something needed to be done and had the courage to follow that through. That meant, for the most part, going to Afrikaners. But I had to be careful who I spoke to. If I'd been careless, I could have been picked up and sent packing very quickly. I had to give quite a bit of thought to who might be willing to enter into discussions without denouncing me. I happened upon Willie Esterhuyse, a philosophy professor and Afrikaner social reformer. Willie was the man who actually gave me a fair hearing, and had the courage to say 'Yes, I think what you're doing is probably right, and yes I'll come along on the journey with you.' All the South Africans who agreed to take part were brave, very brave.
>
> The template we used was to identify players who were serious and not always visible, to bring them away so that they could begin to understand one another as human beings. You're not operating on this global platform with lots of spotlights. It's silent, it's long term and if you want cheap thrills and brownie points, then you've lost it.
>
> I told both sides at the start there were two pre-conditions. If they

wanted to play games with this, I wasn't their man. It would be a secret process, and to ensure secrecy we would take it away from the main theatre and to a place that allowed secrecy.

There was to be no playing to the gallery.

He chose an unlikely venue: Agnew's grand English country house called Mells Park in Somerset. Over five long years, a series of 12 meetings took place; meetings between avowed enemies who dared not be seen together, while President Botha continued to rail publicly against the ANC –what he called the communist terrorists who were threatening to destroy the decent, God-fearing white government of the day.

Gold Fields supplied the fine food and wines; Young supplied the early discipline. He was a quiet but firm chairman, refusing to allow Thabo Mbeki – more cosmopolitan than the South Africans – to dominate proceedings. Outside the formal negotiation he used subtle tactics. Opposing players were given adjacent rooms, increasing the prospect of chance meetings, of walks in the grounds. In the evenings, Glenfiddich helped to oil informal conversations.

Gradually included were whites like top Afrikaner businessmen Marinus Daling and Willem Pretorius, and academic and author Sampie Terreblanche, who was becoming disillusioned with the Nationalists. Jacob Zuma joined the ANC delegation in the latter phases and made a significant contribution.

Young remembers:

> At one point during the Mells Park process the external world was beginning to get in the way – Mrs Thatcher would make some silly remark about terrorists and it would cause a frisson in Pretoria, where it was taken as a sign that Britain was coming around to accepting apartheid.
>
> So I was asked to go and see Mrs Thatcher, to see if we could bring her into a more ordered relationship so that the government didn't get in the way. She wouldn't see me. But I saw her chief of staff and it was clear from the conversation that she would not engage with the ANC because they were terrorists.

He thought it a short-sighted response.

IT WAS WHEN the delegates began to tell jokes as they shared drinks in the evening that the breakthroughs happened. They stopped being frightened of each other and came to trust instead:

> More often than not I made myself scarce in the evenings because I wanted them to feel safe together. I had to be careful that it didn't appear to be a sort of neo-colonial situation with the white guy saying 'This is how it's going to be, fellas.' They would have shown me the door quickly if there'd been a hint of that. That's one of the reasons it was successful, it wasn't a government intervention. I didn't have an election to fight in five years and have to display some goodies. I had a process that would take as long as it took.

Key to this process was the emerging friendship between Mbeki and Esterhuyse that endured long after 1994. Between 1987 and 1990 attitudes softened on both sides. What Esterhuyse called Glenfiddich diplomacy worked its subtle magic. When delegates began to think of themselves as South Africans first and politicians second, greeting each other with friendly hugs, Young realised that the strange alchemy was working at last. He could safely leave them to resolve their own problems. It was to be the saving of South Africa.

They also came to understand that a settlement would not involve one-sided capitulation. This led eventually to an agreement to negotiate without preconditions. Throughout, Nelson Mandela was informed of progress by secret messages passed by his lawyer.

Once the opposing parties had taken ownership of the process, Young could play a more passive role. 'They were the South Africans. It was their problem. I was now the outsider,' says Young. 'My job was over. I wanted it that way.'

Ironies abounded. Young, the honest broker, was a quintessential Englishman, not a characteristic highly admired by either side. The leader of the government delegation, Professor Willie Esterhuyse, a pillar of Afrikanerdom, established a lasting friendship with ANC delegate

Thabo Mbeki, a terrorist by official government definition. Big business has seldom been admired for its political adroitness, yet here was a giant corporation with the largest single investment in South Africa of any British company helping to bring enemies together while ready to disown Young should his secret activities be exposed. Seldom has a company played a more crucial role in what the world came to see as a South African political miracle.

Years later Mbeki told Young that one of the ANC's greatest fears was that, when Pretoria became ready to talk, the ANC might not recognise the moment. Glenfiddich Democracy removed that fear.

Michael Young remains ever the backroom boy. He returns to South Africa from time to time, has occasional meetings with President Zuma. He remains optimistic about the country's future. 'I'm a half-full glass sort of guy,' he says. 'What you have to remember is that South Africa is a very young democracy. It takes time to mature. There is not a country in the world that doesn't face challenges. All that is needed from its leaders is clarity of purpose and a commitment to transparency.'

The final irony, of course, is that Consgold did not survive long enough to enjoy the accolades that history would undoubtedly have accorded it. And that, when Consolidated Gold Fields died, its executioner – Lord Hanson – was persuaded by Young to continue to contribute to the Mells Park process. Perhaps he got the kudos.

Agnew received a knighthood for 'services to international human rights and conservation' and became Sir Rudolph.

CHAPTER SEVEN

'Friends' Fall Out

JUST WHEN GFSA thought it could relax its guard, a new attack materialised. It came out of the blue and, at first, from unexpected directions, but there was no doubt who was behind it. News of this new bout of hostilities had the shock effect of a shot fired at the winning tape rather than the starting line. For the South African company, it seemed the last straw, and it released all the pent-up tension that it had more or less bottled up while the Minorco saga ran its course.

Almost without a backward glance at the smoking ruins of Minorco's failed bid, Anglo was back to its old tricks. It was the effrontery of it all that provoked the outrage.

Evidence of the renewed attack came into the open only a few weeks after Minorco had conceded defeat and Consolidated Gold Fields had celebrated pyrrhic victory with a champagne party at London zoo; almost while Europe's arch asset-stripper, Lord Hanson, was still calculating the value of the loot he had acquired from Consgold and trying to believe his good fortune.

In short, at a time when affected parties were off-guard.

GFSA was alerted by Lord Hanson. Among the valuables he acquired in taking over CGF was a 39% stake in the South African company. By arrangement, most of this holding went to the Rembrandt Group and a company called Asteroid, created by Gold Fields to protect itself from any future unwanted takeover. That still left 6 479 695 shares in the kitty, or 7.9% of the issued capital – a handy little parcel.

Anglo wanted it. It would take its holding to 30.9%; something like the figure Harry Oppenheimer once suggested made takeovers unnecessary. Gold Fields erupted. Its petition to the Competition Board for the deal to be disallowed appears to have been written in white heat. It ran for 68 pages with a further 30 annexures. It sought to persuade the board that Anglo's purchase could create a monopoly.

As a first step, it tried to demolish any suggestion that it was a portfolio investment, acquired to enjoy dividends and watch its capital grow:

> An investment by one company in the shares of a competitor company will naturally arouse suspicions that the acquiring company has set about making an acquisition. The motive immediately comes under the spotlight. Any attempt by the acquiring company to say that its motive is to make a portfolio investment sounds false. It is therefore not surprising that Anglo and De Beers have in the past repeatedly offered other motivations in explanation of their conduct. One such motivation is a desire to keep the target company independent, or out of the hands of competitors. It will be submitted that these motivations demonstrate that the purpose and effect of such investments is to confer upon the Anglo/De Beers Group some degree of control over the target company.
>
> Anglo and De Beers have in the past frequently acquired control of target companies gradually, starting off with small shareholdings. These 'creeping acquisitions' have in many instances been conducted anonymously and clandestinely by using nominee companies and/or blind trusts. Often, Anglo and De Beers have at the outset given assurances that they have no *present intent* to acquire control. This has become the typical pattern of an acquisition by the group.
>
> Anglo/De Beers Group should not be permitted to get away any longer with the giving of assurances and solemn undertakings which are expressed in such terms or given in such circumstances that they are not legally enforceable.
>
> It has been an abiding passion of successive chief executives of Anglo and De Beers for at least the last half century to acquire Gold Fields. Because of the opposition to the Minorco bid in England and the USA, Anglo and De Beers gave assurances that they had no wish to acquire control of Newmont or Gold Fields. In order to fend off the New York action, an undertaking was given that if Minorco succeeded, Consgold would divest itself, inter alia, of all its shares

in Gold Fields. Against the background of these assurances and undertakings, Anglo/De Beers Group not only retained all of its shares in Gold Fields but commenced an aggressive programme of buying additional shares through undisclosed nominees during the second half of 1989.

The acquisition by Anglo/De Beers Group of de facto or de jure control over Gold Fields would, by virtue of the size of the two groups, without question be against the public interest.

The belligerent tone was unmistakeable. Gold Fields had had enough. It hammered away at 'greedy Anglo' for another 50 or so pages. Anglo's gold mines were 'ageing and operate at significantly greater and progressively increasing depth'. Gold Fields, on the other hand, had discovered a major new resource in the southern Free State which could be developed at relatively low capital and operating cost. Of course, it was in Anglo's interest to 'hold its competitor's head under water'. As in platinum and coal production too.

TWO REVEALING letters in an annexure gave an insight into relations between the two great mining companies. They dealt with a row that flared when Anglo discovered details of a deal that Consgold had made with Rembrandt some years before. Nobody made any bones about it: the issue was control – and who might exercise it.

FOR: RIJ Agnew
FROM: J Ogilvie Thompson
10.7.1987

It seems necessary for me to spell out the exact nature of Anglo American's position. As you know, we welcome the idea of Rembrandt becoming a shareholder and indeed we encouraged you and them to come together. However throughout these last months this has been on the basis that they were not looking for more than 20 per cent and I thought we had specifically agreed between each of the three parties that no two would gang up on the third. Initially, you and subsequently Johann [Rupert] had kept me in touch with discussions which seemed to be going along the lines we had discussed.

In the event CGF has entered into an agreement with Rembrandt which, should CGF decide to or be forced to sell more, could put Rembrandt in a position of control or the ability jointly to arrange control with another.

This is so clearly contrary to all our discussions over this decade and earlier this year including the meetings in Johannesburg re GFSA that Anglo American Corporation can only look upon this as a hostile act. I do hope you will speedily find a way to remedy this situation.

TO: Julian Ogilvie Thompson
FROM: Rudolph Agnew
13.7.87

Let me state our position quite clearly.
1. CGF has arranged a sale of part of its interest in GFSA at a highly advantageous price; the market has acknowledged this and I gather you, from a CGF standpoint, agree that this is so.
2. The sale is effected in such a way that CGF's ability to influence GFSA has not altered.
3. In order to achieve the best price it was essential to the transaction to add first-refusal pre-emption rights on a reciprocal basis. A 40% block has a premium value as this deal underlines.
4. Neither is CGF a planned seller of further shares of GFSA nor does Rembrandt, as a matter of publicly stated policy, wish to become 'the largest' (let alone controlling) shareholder.

On the broad matter of consultation, we have made strenuous efforts to involve Minorco closely in our deliberations. You have refused extra CGF representation and membership of the Strategy and Finance Committee. You personally have not, I am sure for good reasons, attended formal or informal meetings of CGF in recent months.

In summary, our position is that we are convinced that CGF

has achieved a first-class transaction which has been unanimously approved by our board. CGF has no intention of 'ganging up' on Anglo American. On the contrary, the value of not only CGF but also Minorco appears to have improved significantly as a result. The interpretation of all this as a 'hostile act' seems to us an extraordinary statement.

I am sure that you will agree that we must continue to run CGF in the interests of all CGF shareholders. Within this constraint we will do everything possible to take account of the special interests of particular shareholders, if for no other reason than to promote genuine co-operation. It is in this spirit that I suggest we offer to inform you in advance if we should ever intend to approach Rembrandt under the pre-emption provisions of our agreement. Regards.

It was an elegant example of a brush-off with an escape hatch. Agnew was not going to be bullied, but he wasn't about to offend Anglo too deeply either. And so it transpired.

FOR: Rudolph Agnew
FROM: Julian Ogilvie Thompson
17.7.87

Thank you for your message of 13th July which is indeed of some help. The deal may well be in the interests of CGF shareholders and certainly the market and the Press have so concluded. However neither your fax, nor the action that CGF has taken, addresses itself to what we understood were the arrangements between CGF and Anglo American (rather than Minorco) regarding the future of GFSA. Just as Rembrandt has stated (publicly) that it is not seeking control of GFSA but (privately) wants to be in a position to prevent control from passing elsewhere, so also had Anglo American thought it had made just such an arrangement with you as underlined by our February discussions. (Indeed it is Anglo's apparent exclusion from any process of determining where future control might lie that the South African Press, at any rate, has harped on.)

Our objective in all of the discussions was to welcome R as a shareholder up to 20% and to ensure that, if CGF ever decided or was forced to dispose of more GFSA shares Anglo American/Amgold would be consulted well in advance and would expect to have a say in where the shares went. All this seemed only reasonable in a 48/22 relationship that flowed from a partnership in West Wits over decades. The agreement is in conflict with this.

Our concern now is twofold:

a). Notwithstanding public statements to the contrary, as the agreement is signed, we could wake up one day to find that control of GFSA had passed to R (or for that matter someone else) without AAC being in a position to express any views. We therefore welcome and would like to take up your offer formally to inform Anglo American (as a co-shareholder in GFSA) as distinct from Minorco, well in advance if CGF ever intended to approach Rembrandt under the pre-emptive provision of your agreement. Further, we would hope that Rembrandt would confirm in writing to us, which I imagine they would, what Johann said on the telephone and publically [sic] – i.e. that they do not seek control.

b). As I read the agreement if shares are offered to R and they decline to buy, (or they do buy and subsequently decide to sell) they do not have the right to place with a third party. That right remains with CGF. What we are seeking here is an equal say, with Rembrandt, as to where the shares should go. If you could see your way clear to confirm to us that we would have such a say, I think we may be able to square the circle as best we can. Best wishes.

TO: Mr J Ogilvie Thompson
FROM: Rudolph Agnew
29.7.87

Thank you for your message of July 17th. I do not see any difficulty in reaching an understanding to discuss with you any further sales of GFSA at either of the two stages you mentioned. You will, of course, recognise that at the end of the day, we would have to make our decision based on the interests of shareholders as a whole. However we would be happy to try to reconcile this with your thoughts and those of Rembrandt as far as possible.

When you mention the discussions in February, I am sure you will recall that these were in the context of a two-sided understanding, integral to which was Minorco's long-term attitude to its holding in CGF. I believe the above must also be seen in the same light. Since you mentioned that this is also an Anglo matter, I believe that Gavin [Relly, then Anglo chairman], you and I should try to get together as soon as possible so that we can agree our mutual commitments.

I see no particular reason why Johann should not be happy to confirm the statement that he has made to you that he does not seek to be the largest shareholder in GFSA but, of course, that is a matter for him. Best wishes.

And that was the end of the matter: Anglo's desire for a position of influence over GFSA unequivocally expressed, weighed and apparently conceded. Or not, as your fancy dictates. Agnew never quite lost the Machiavellian skill of ambiguity. Had he capitulated to Anglo's demands – or merely offered a sop to them? There is an ironic undertone to the exchanges since they were written in the days of sweetness and light, when Minorco was courting CGF. The days before the gloves came off. The hostile bid was still a year away.

PERHAPS inevitably, the ruling from the Competition Board, when it came, disappointed Gold Fields. The board took the view that, since there was no competition on price – the Reserve Bank sets a standard price for all gold mines based on international norms – Anglo's actions did not constitute anti-competitive action. Gold Fields' argument that the two groups competed fiercely in other ways, for mineral rights and in exploiting them, swayed them not.

But, in a curious way, the ruling finally provoked GFSA into doing something that it had been wanting to do for ages. It fired Peter Gush – the Anglo American director on its board.

The fact that there was an Anglo man there at all had been a source of aggravation down the years. He had no particular legal right to be there. It all began in the 1930s when Anglo, as a founding member of West Wits, acquired the right to appoint two directors. West Wits was an exploration company and it was 'understandable in the circumstances', in GFSA's view, that Anglo should have representation. But everything changed in 1971 when West Wits merged with Gold Fields and Anglo was asked to withdraw its representatives. Reluctantly, it agreed to give up one seat, but insisted on keeping the other. Gold Fields' chairman at the time, Bill Busschau, complained repeatedly that this, in effect, gave Anglo a permanent spy in a competitor's boardroom, but to no avail. The directors tolerated an intolerable situation because they feared that Anglo might be tempted to exercise even more 'restraining control' if they didn't.

In 1983, when complaints were made yet again, chairman Gavin Relly scoffed at any suggestion of 'leaks'. Any confidential information received by Anglo's representative would go to Relly or his deputy, and no further, he stated. Gold Fields was thoroughly irritated by the statement – it knew that confidential information was seeping out. So it decided to put Relly's assurances to the test.

Several times in the next few months it deliberately gave classified information to its own board. 'As a matter of course, this classified information was shown to have become general knowledge within the executive committee of the Anglo/De Beers Group,' said the Gold Fields petition.

An extreme example occurred at the time of the Minorco bid. GFSA board members were given a memo about a possible rights issue. Despite its 'confidential and extremely sensitive nature', a copy of this memo was reproduced in the *Sunday Telegraph* of London as 'proof' that its story of the rights issue was correct. The reproduced memo was distinctively underlined – in precisely the way that Gush would mark his board papers.

Besides, complained Gold Fields, Gush repeatedly got himself involved in conflict-of-interest situations, voting against resolutions that had the support of the rest of the board and generally being obstructive.

When the Competition Board found against GFSA, members of the Gold Fields executive sat down to consider their options. One such option was provided for in the Companies Act. It said that a director could be fired if all other members of the board agreed to it. That did it. Peter Gush got his marching orders at the next board meeting.

'He was actually quite a nice guy,' says a mischievous Bernard van Rooyen, one-time executive director, 'but we had to do something ...'

There remained a couple of loose ends to be tied before GFSA could get down again to the mundane business of everyday mining – the drama, trauma and fleeting triumphs that are a constant accompaniment to one of the world's cruellest and most rewarding occupations; before any of those things ... it had to get back the GFSA shares that were still in Hanson's hands. They knew that Anglo would not rest until those shares were firmly beyond its reach.

Enter, once more, the Silver Fox, aka Van Rooyen.

In London, again, Van Rooyen saw the Hanson acquisition as an opportunity, not a threat:

> Consgold had this 49% interest in us. We'd acquired Remgro and Liberty as shareholders. We had an agreement with them that they would support management. When Michael Edwardes encouraged Hanson to come in, that was it. We knew we were okay because all we were interested in were the residual South African mining interests held by Consgold, mainly Driefontein and Kloof. We now had something to offer Hanson for these assets. So I trotted down to see Hanson and his pal and partner White. We did a deal in, I think, about half an hour. It was about R6-billion worth of assets for the Consgold interests. There were various legal complications and Hanson couldn't be seen to be doing a deal at that stage. So we just shook hands on it.
>
> I called Robin [Plumbridge] and said we've done this, and he said you'd better call Johann Rupert. I think he was already getting a lot of shit from Johann so I called him and said: 'We've done this.'
>
> Rupert said: 'Bernard, what was the value of this deal?' and I said, about six billion. And Rupert said: 'Bernard, how big does it have to be before you ask me instead of telling me?' He was a very autocratic sort of guy.
>
> Frankly, I'm amazed that Anglo was not more ruthless about the

whole affair. They hung around and entered into quadrilles with Agnew. The consequence was, I believe, that Harry Oppenheimer issued an instruction that there would be no more unagreed takeover efforts. Hostile bids were out.

Actually, there was a period after that when Julian [Ogilvie Thompson] wouldn't acknowledge my presence if we met on social occasions. He was about two and a half metres high and he would just look over the top of my head. Then we had a large rights issue – a very big sum for the time, about R1-billion – and Anglo had traditionally participated in the underwriting. So I phoned him and said, would you like 40% of the underwriting? And he said: 'You'd better come down and have tea.' Money always told with Julian.

And so, at last, the ghost of the Minorco bid was laid to rest and the feud with Anglo resolved. But the suspicion and mistrust never quite went away.

CHAPTER EIGHT

WHAT RHODES STARTED

A LIFE-SIZE portrait of a man's head stares regally from a wall in the executive suite of Gold Fields Limited in Sandton, Johannesburg. A few metres away, a bronze bust of the same man stares back from a plinth. Their eyes do not quite meet. For those of a fanciful bent, the art works convey two messages.

The first is that Cecil John Rhodes, co-founder of this great enterprise, is today part of the folklore of the company; not necessarily a revered figure but more a talisman to be trotted out on special anniversaries. What does he represent in the minds of today's executives? The truth is: hardly anything. His actual words and deeds are irrelevant. Besides, it would be hard to present Rhodes as a hero in modern South Africa – he was far too much an arch-colonialist for that. But he serves a different purpose. He illustrates how deep the roots of Gold Fields burrow into the history of the country. And when his spirit is thus summoned, he transmogrifies into the embodiment of honest enterprise and dogged resolve that has characterised the company from the beginning.

The second message is rather more ambiguous. Two heads imply two people, two personalities not making any connection. Two faces, if you like. The 'other' face of Rhodes is not endearing. It goes well with clay feet.

It is one of the curiosities of history that not Rhodes but his partner, Charles Durrell Rudd, is the one who should be on the wall and on the plinth. Rudd was the one who raised the capital for the venture in London and nurtured the company in its precarious early years. Rhodes preferred to involve himself with diamonds, and took so little interest in 'his' gold company that he never met a single shareholder. His major contribution was to nearly kill it – twice.

To be fair, the first near-death experience – more than a hundred years ago, before the company had celebrated its fifth birthday – was a joint exercise by the partners. Their shareholders accused them of pursuing the 'risk and reward' philosophy of business too avidly. And in the wrong order: reaping early rewards for the principals while the shareholders were still experiencing only the risk. They weren't far wrong.

Rhodes, in his thirties, and Rudd, in his early forties, had met in Kimberley and decided to team up. Together, they accumulated and then amalgamated enough diamond fields to create a significant company they called De Beers. (Add another historic irony: a century later, it was De Beers, now part of the Oppenheimer empire, that tried to swallow up Consolidated Gold Fields and its South African affiliate. Dog eats dog in the world of big business.)

The lure of gold drew them to the Witwatersrand, where activity was feverish. It seemed like a good second string to add to their bow. They agreed that Rudd would go to London to raise capital while Rhodes fretted in South Africa. In 1887, the year of Queen Victoria's Jubilee, Gold Fields of South Africa Limited was registered as a mining and prospecting company. The partners opened an office in Saratoga Avenue, Doornfontein. Or rather, Rudd did. Rhodes, they agreed, would keep an eye on the diamond business. Before a year was out, the two founders decided the Witwatersrand was a damp squib and they would turn their attention to a concession north of the Limpopo, in a country that would come to be called Southern Rhodesia.

From their perspective, the timing was impeccable. Gold mining had hit a major snag on the Rand. An unexpected layer of pyritic ore meant that old techniques for extracting the precious metal did not work. 'The mining community took fright,' wrote Gold Fields historian Roy MacNab. 'People were saying the Witwatersrand, after all, was only an old river bed. The market collapsed. There was deep gloom at the Rand Club and *The Star* reported that no fewer than 169 members had failed to pay their subscriptions.' Some feared that Johannesburg would turn into another disappointing Barberton. Author Percy Fitzpatrick predicted gloomily that grass would grow in the streets.

By 1891, Gold Fields' prospects looked grim. Shareholders were anxious about the motley companies it owned; the puny dividends; the money Rhodes and Rudd were diverting to the north; the contract that allowed the founders to take a disproportionate amount of the diminishing profits. The anger was palpable at the next AGM. No business can survive that degree of disillusionment for long. Something needed to be done.

Not for the last time, luck turned for them. A pioneer at the Simmer and Jack mine devised a new technology that overcame the extraction problem and, suddenly, confidence returned. Experts determined that, whatever the expense, there was still a huge potential in mining on the Witwatersrand, albeit at deep levels. Now all they had to do was restore confidence in their own business.

It took a few years, a special meeting of shareholders, a blow-up with the founders and a new company with a new name to achieve that. The new company was called Consolidated Gold Fields of South Africa, and was an amalgamation of several mining companies. Still resolutely at the head of this brave new endeavour were Rhodes and Rudd, survivors both.

NIMBLE footwork saved them. In the next crisis, which wasn't far away, it looked as though nothing could. The crisis was created by Rhodes alone. He decided to put Gold Fields at the centre of the Jameson Raid. It was a decision of such recklessness that, by rights, it should have destroyed the company then and there. What drove him to do it?

Rhodes was a man of many parts: entrepreneur, visionary, explorer, pioneer. He is the only man in history to have two countries named after him in his own life time: Southern Rhodesia and Northern Rhodesia. He made fortunes out of the diamond fields of Kimberley and the gold fields of the Witwatersrand. He was what was known then as a patriot – a fervent British patriot – in the days before it became fashionable to see patriotism as the last refuge of a scoundrel. He dreamt of extending the British Empire from Cape to Cairo

His imperialistic ambitions earned him the undying enmity of President Kruger in the Transvaal, who was already having problems with the *uitlanders* – the foreigners – in his domain. Today we would call Rhodes a colonialist and a jingo. But his achievements would still command respect.

He was the Prime Minister of the Cape Colony in 1895 when the raid was planned. Leaders of the mining industry on the Witwatersrand were growing restless about what they saw as a corrupt and inefficient Boer administration. Rhodes and Jameson met Gold Fields consulting engineer John Hays Drummond in Rhodesia and decided that an armed revolt could bring Kruger down. Jameson would lead a force of British South Africa policemen on the pretext that British lives were in danger. It should be a brisk battle and a great victory.

Rhodes thought the obvious command centre should be the Gold Fields offices and appointed his brother, Colonel Frank Rhodes, as managing director – an odd title for a man whose primary task it was to organise a revolution. Soon the plotters were meeting regularly in the Gold Fields building; guns and ammunition were being smuggled in as mining machinery; and other mining companies were being recruited. Rudd later protested that he knew nothing about the plans and added: 'They could only have been arranged by a madman.'

Starr Jameson proved no more sensible. Tired of waiting for orders in the hot sun in Bechuanaland (now Botswana), he decided to march anyway. He thought it might be nice to celebrate the New Year of 1896 with a victory parade in the streets of Johannesburg. The Reform Committee, planning the coup and every bit as muddled as Jameson's Keystone Cops, decided to allay Kruger's fears of a British invasion by swearing allegiance to a Transvaal flag and then flying it upside-down from the roof of the Gold Fields building. At dawn on 2 January, an advance bugler arrived at the Gold Fields building to report that Jameson was only hours away. He never got there. The Boers stopped the column at Doornkop, near Krugersdorp, and took them all prisoner after a mild skirmish. When the citizenry of Johannesburg heard the news they gathered outside the Gold Fields building and threatened to blow up the building and the Reform Committee.

When Rhodes heard the news he said: 'Twenty years we have been friends and now he goes in and ruins me.'

When Rudd heard, he said: 'The news that our company was playing a prominent part ... came upon me like a thunder clap.'

When Gold Fields, London, heard, the board issued a statement: 'Employees of the company have acted without authority.' And invited Rhodes to London 'for a chat'.

A British parliamentary committee considered the matter and concluded:

> Mr Rhodes occupied a great position in South Africa; he was Prime Minister of Cape Colony and beyond all other persons, should have been careful to abstain from such a course as that which he adopted. As managing director of the BSA Company, as director of De Beers Consolidated and Gold Fields of South Africa Mr Rhodes controlled a great combination of interests; he used his position and those interests to promote and assist his policy.

After that less-than-stinging rebuke, Gold Fields determined that survival depended on reforming the company.

By this time, Rhodes's brother Frank and Gold Fields consulting engineer John Hays Drummond had been sentenced to death with two others for their role in the uprising – a sentence later commuted to a fine. Jameson had been tried in London and sentenced to a term in Wormwood Scrubs.

But something curious was happening – fate was once again preparing to come to the rescue. In the eyes of the British public the villains of the Jameson Raid were morphing into heroes almost overnight. Jameson came out of prison, was awarded a baronetcy and returned to South Africa, later to inherit the job of Prime Minister of the Cape Colony. Harrison was ordered to 'carry on the mining operations of the company with the staff he doubtless dominates'. And Rhodes and Rudd? Well ...

They had felt bound to resign as joint managing directors. Now they had to face the wrath of the shareholders at a special meeting in March 1896. They were told how much damage they had done by associating Gold Fields with the raid; that their generous contracts were a thing of the past; that they would no longer receive two-fifteenths of the profit of the company. They must have felt that the roof was caving in on them.

But then the meeting agreed that they should stay on as directors, and that each was entitled to a share of the company's capital. Between them, they got shares worth £1 200 000, a fortune indeed in those times.

It is possible that knowledge of Rhodes's massive error of judgment has been a comfort to subsequent leaders of Gold Fields. They know that, whatever mistakes they might make, they are unlikely ever to take a decision as crass as its co-founder took more than a hundred years ago. However, they are unlikely to receive such a windfall either.

PROPHETS of gloom and other ill-wishers have predicted the imminent death, dismantling or destruction of the oldest gold mining company in the country from time to time since then. They have always been proved wrong. Gold Fields has not only survived its setbacks; it has often used them to grow stronger.

Its history reveals a repeated pattern of crisis and resolution, crisis and resolution throughout the years. It has had its fair share of luck and good fortune too, but it has never relied on that. Flair, skill and dogged determination always seemed a more reliable combination. With a dash of stubbornness, of course.

It experienced its first strike in 1906. About 300 miners at Knight's Deep downed tools when they were told that they would have to supervise three rock drills and not two as before. Inexplicably, they marched to Pretoria though no one quite knew what they thought Pretoria could do about it. Before long, the strike had spread to 6 400 men. If they had struck over working conditions underground, they might have gained more sympathy. Of the 17-strong committee that had organised the Knight's strike, 12 were dead of phthisis within six years.

In 1911 Gold Fields had a serious discussion with itself, not for the first or last time. Its share price had fallen by half – from £6 to £3 – and the market seemed to doubt its future. The chairman, Lord Harris, concluded that shareholders wanted 'interminable' investments but their company 'habitually invests in properties that have terminable lives'. Since there seemed to be no simple answer to that dismal conundrum, they decided to carry on as before. One hundred years later the industry was still trying to solve the riddle.

Back then, GFSA found something else to occupy its attention. In 1913, a small flare started a big blaze. The manager at New Kleinfontein fired three underground workers who objected to a change of working hours, a 'paltry mistake' that, so the legend would have it, led to a national general strike. Before it was over, British troops had to be called out, shops were looted, fighting broke out in Market Square, bodies lay on the streets and 99 policemen were injured. Eventually, Prime Minister Louis Botha and Minister of Mines Jan Smuts, representing the government, had to capitulate to the strikers' demands.

No sooner had the dust settled than the First World War started. And, when *that* was over, mining was on its knees. Gold Fields changed its name and articles of association to enable it to diversify. Now it was called New Consolidated Gold Fields. It brought no immediate relief. The company experienced its worst year ever in 1921, making a loss for the first time. The gold price was falling, costs were rising, no dividend was paid and shareholders were angry.

Chairman Harris reported: 'Circumstances have defeated us.'

Worse was to follow. Before a year was out the infamous miners' strike of 1922 began – and looked set to destroy not just a mining house or two but the entire industry. For 67 tense and violence-ridden days it seemed the country might explode.

Coming events cast their shadow ... the root cause of the strike was discrimination. The colour bar underground had been relaxed during the war because of manpower shortages. After the war white miners demanded that it be reinstated. The Chamber of Mines said no, and held firm for two months. Some 22 000 miners were idle. In their midst were a strange mixture of extreme Afrikaner nationalists and radical Bolsheviks. Defying union leaders, they decided to do battle with the troops that the government had called up under martial law. They were armed with everything from bicycle chains and crowbars to sophisticated guns. In the clashes that followed, Fordsburg was bombed by military aircraft, mines and police stations were attacked and the government's forces lost 230 men. History does not record how many strikers died in what became a revolution put down by force by General Smuts. But four of them were hanged for treason.

One of the strikers was Colonel Spencer Fleischer, a decorated veteran of the First Word War. He had been dragooned into helping the rebels because of his military experience. 'Nominally I was a striker though my sympathies were not with them,' he recorded afterwards. Which perhaps explains how he came to be the first South African to be appointed resident director of Gold Fields in Johannesburg. He also served as President of the Chamber of Mines – not bad for a reluctant striker.

The 1922 uprising was a watershed. It led indirectly to the election of South Africa's first Afrikaner Nationalist Prime Minister, General Hertzog, in 1924. But, for the mining industry, the impact was even more profound. As historian Roy MacNab records: 'From then on the personalities of the gold mining houses would be a power behind the scenes but would never again dictate the political or economic direction of South Africa.'

CRISIS and resolution, crisis and ...

When the Great Depression came along it looked as if a malignant fate had finally abandoned the mining industry and the country. Somehow Gold Fields had managed to struggle through the lean years of the late Twenties and early Thirties. Survival meant going ever deeper. Robinson Deep was mining nearly a kilometre under the surface; deeper than any mine had yet gone. It was so hot at the working face that men could not have carried on without the blocks of ice that came down the shaft to cool the air. Surely it was not possible to go any deeper? There had to be a limit; a time when the gold ran out or became hopelessly beyond reach. Extraordinarily, that day didn't come for another 30 years.

But, at that time, the only gleam of real hope was coming from a mine called Sub Nigel. In time it would become the richest gold mine in the world. But not yet. Alas, not yet.

And then Wall Street crashed in 1929 and economic calamity struck the globe. The new chairman of the company, Lord Brabourne, reported the melancholy news: 'We have tried to minimise risk by geographical distribution of our investments, but that has failed us.' South Africa's government mining engineer reported that 'the end of the gold mining industry is over the horizon'.

Just when all hope seemed dead, two scientists helped solve an old mystery – and unlocked a vast new fortune.

The mystery was this: what happened to the Main Reef when it disappeared from sight after Randfontein? Like several others, young Canadian mining engineer Guy Carleton Jones and geologist Dr Leopold Reinecke couldn't believe that it just vanished. It had to go somewhere. They introduced a German doctor of mining engineering called Rudolf Krahmann to Gold Fields, and Gold Fields commissioned him to find the gold, using his new-fangled device, a kind of sophisticated magnet. And find it, he did. Or rather, he located the iron-rich magnetic shales that, he believed, would point geologically to where the gold-bearing reef could be. It proved to be an inspired assumption, and it opened the way to the fabulously rich West Wits line.

But in the beginning, no one could be sure of that. Assuming the existence of gold is not the same as recovering it. Gold Fields was a conservative company, but it decided to risk the gamble. It created a new company, West Witwatersrand Areas Limited, to manage the hoped-for bonanza. This company would become known on stock exchanges world-wide as West Wits. It took over all the mining rights that its parent had accumulated secretly and painstakingly over a vast area. But Gold Fields faced potentially vast development expenses too. It needed help. Some mining houses were not interested in the gamble. Anglo American saw the potential and invested £50 000. Later it was to invest even more. So began what Roy MacNab described as a see-saw relationship, an uneasy association between two mining giants that would bring pain and smiles, bitterness and benefit, for decades to come.

And then a kindly fate intervened again. Six weeks after West Wits was floated, South Africa went off the gold standard and the gold price soared. Ore reserves doubled in value overnight. A year later, the United States increased the official gold price from $20 to $35. The company's shares rose from ten shillings to £10. They were declared to be 'the most spectacular shares in the 60 years since gold was discovered'. A year later, just when it seemed that Fortune could offer no more, a random borehole at what would become Driefontein revealed another treasure trove: a new reef below the Carbon Leader. And a year after that, another hitherto unknown reef called the Venterspost Contact Reef. And then another, and another.

Crisis? What crisis?

Nevertheless, those after a quick buck were disappointed. Something happened to upset all the optimistic calculations. The Second World War broke out. A bitterly divided South Africa answered the call. Reliable supplies of gold were essential to the Allied war effort – but war brings austerity, manpower shortages, equipment difficulties. setbacks of many kinds. Mining development programmes were cancelled or postponed. Skilled men were recruited for more pressing war-time jobs. Nearly fifty mine workshops were turned over to making munitions. Mining uranium for atom bombs became a new priority. Curiously, production of gold actually increased, but long-term development slowed.

It took 14 years before West Wits paid its first dividend, proving once again that there are no quick bucks in mining. Only patience and hope. And an absence of war, if that is not asking too much.

FORTUNE'S SEE-SAW continued to rock when world peace seemed to be on the horizon. For Gold Fields, it meant a renewal of another kind of war – the low-intensity battle for dominance that had characterised its relationship with Anglo American for decades. Having common and conflicting interests led to a love-hate affair, though both words are too strong by far to describe the scrupulous surface politeness that disguised their suspicious minds.

Anglo coveted the riches of the West Wits line that GFSA had pioneered. Not that it had been completely excluded. The sheer cost of development meant that competing mining houses were often encouraged to share the burdens and benefits of bringing new mines to production. Indeed, Anglo had a director on the board of West Wits Ltd, but it wanted more. Its competitors called it 'greediness' but, in fact, most mining groups aspired to be the biggest in the field too. It made them feel more secure. In time to come, when Union Corporation appeared to be up for grabs, Gold Fields lunged at it in the hope that a merger could make the combined company bigger than Anglo. There was no call for a holier-than-thou attitude. But that didn't mean passive surrender.

Some believed Sir Ernest Oppenheimer was 'hovering around', ready to pounce on West Witwatersrand Limited after Gold Fields had done all the spadework of discovery and development. In reality, he was quietly buying up land and options and mining rights so he could start his own mine, Western Deep Levels, in the same area. Either way, it seemed a breach of faith. But before the situation could get ugly, Sir Ernest made peace by telling Gold Fields he would still like to participate in the West Wits company 'to cement further the happy relations which now exist'. And there the matter rested – until the next time.

It left Gold Field feeling at a disadvantage because Anglo, as a South African company, could choose its own investments while GFSA had to defer to its British parent. It hastened the day when GFSA would cut itself loose and become a South African company. In the meantime, it continued to be the biggest money-spinner for CGF, providing 80% of its revenue in 1958 – and another good reason for wanting to go it alone.

Besides, its sheer profitability made Gold Fields almost a permanent takeover target in the Fifties. Conditioned by its history, its nervous eyes were focused on Anglo American and Sir Ernest Oppenheimer. Which is why it didn't see a threat from another direction until it was almost too late.

The rise of Afrikaner nationalism in the Fifties brought with it a rise of Afrikaner economic ambitions. At the heart of South Africa's economic power was the gold mining industry. What Afrikanerdom needed was a stronger mining house of its own. Consolidated Gold Fields seemed the best bet for a takeover, but Federale Mynbou suddenly lost interest. Subsequently CGF and Central Mining considered a merger that would have catapulted the new company into top place on the mining house ladder. But the devil was in the detail, and negotiations failed. So this left Gold Fields where it was before – rich and powerful, but not quite rich and powerful enough to remove the takeover spectre created by bigger, stronger Anglo. So it settled on a different strategy. 'In order to secure Gold Fields from the predator,' said CGF chairman Sir George Harvie-Watt, 'it was necessary that we should enlarge our interests by friendly take-overs where possible.' This necessitated dividing the company in two – one portion labelled 'Southern Africa' and the other 'Rest of the World'. It was a decision that brought closer the inevitable independence of the

South African company, although it would take another decade to achieve it. And, of course, it did not dislodge the takeover spectre.

As before, the changes were complicated. The chosen vehicle for the South African interests was African Land and Investment, a property company that had developed the Johannesburg suburbs of Illovo and Dunkeld. (Ever wondered how suburban streets like Bompas, Fricker, Chaplin and Melville got their names? They were named after Gold Fields luminaries.) This brand-new company needed a new name; after all, African Land and Investment was an odd name for a mining company. Resident director Busschau suggested, and London approved, Gold Fields of South Africa, the name that Rhodes and Rudd had chosen in 1887 and which had not been used since 1892. In its 125 years the name mutated four times – from the original to Consolidated Gold Fields of South Africa to New Consolidated Gold Fields Limited to Gold Fields of South Africa to its current Gold Fields Limited.

No wonder some dispute the right of the current company to claim linear descent from the original. Do they have a case? Well, perhaps as much or as little so as those who have managed to trace their family tree back to William the Conqueror, or Henry VIII, or even Simon van der Stel. But that is a side-issue.

In June 1971, ten years and one month after South Africa declared itself to be a republic, Gold Fields of South Africa became a fully fledged South African company unfettered by foreign control. It seemed a sensible move.

Apartheid and international opinion were ensuring that close business links with South Africa were a political and economic embarrassment. Back home it had become equally embarrassing to be subservient to an old colonial master; to send money abroad; to appear to have mixed loyalties. The restructuring, and the introduction of other investors, diluted Anglo's holding, reducing its board representation to a single seat. Profits no longer had to be repatriated. Besides, business was booming and the price of gold was starting to rise steeply: $40, $50, $66, some optimists were suggesting it might even go to $80 ...

As before the mechanics were less than simple. This time the vehicle chosen to absorb all the South African assets was West Witwatersrand Limited. But there were a couple of conditions. The first was that

Consolidated Gold Fields could not hold more than 49% of the shares. And the second was that West Wits would have to change its name to ... Gold Fields of South Africa Limited.

THE GOLDEN DAYS were back again. In 1974 Gold Fields' profits rose by 145% to R35.6-million. An attempt to demonetise the precious metal failed, paving the way for undreamt-of price increases. But another reality made its presence felt too: inflation. Deeper mines, more massive investments brought sharply rising costs. R100-million was budgeted to develop Deelkraal, another mine on the West Wits Line. The figure rose to R140-million and more; what Roy MacNab called 'the elephantine pregnancy' of a modern gold mine. The *Mining Survey* wrote in wonderment: 'The idea of a lumbering earthmoving machine and 10-ton dumper trucks moving along underground, below sea level, on the Witwatersrand is difficult to imagine.'

Other realities imposed themselves. Even when great care is taken, mining is a dangerous business. It can bring disaster and tragedy in a moment. Floods, fires, rockfalls and seismic movements strike without warning. Sinkholes appear, swallowing people and homes.

Above ground, market shifts and wildly volatile gold price movements produce turbulence. Huge gambles need to be taken, involving hundreds of millions of rands. Is terminable gold the focus, or diversification? If so, into what? 'Our first priority,' declared Robin Plumbridge when he was appointed chairman in 1981, 'is to find new projects as a result of our own exploration and metallurgical research efforts. Ten percent of profit goes to this goal.' Old political pressures are replaced by new ones. All the while, industry predators watch and wait for signs of weakness, of vulnerability.

And so the pattern of crisis and resolution is perpetuated. It is the one constant in a very uncertain world. It's what makes mining one of the last great adventures on earth. For gamblers with cautious souls.

CHAPTER NINE

ENTER THE HEAVY HANDS

ONE PROFOUND consequence of the demise of Consgold in 1989 was that Gold Fields of South Africa fell under the influence of two major South African shareholders. Neither pretended to any background in mining, but both had strong feelings about what they expected of their investment. Being forceful people, they had no hesitation in expressing their views.

The two significant shareholders were Anton and Johann Rupert's Rembrandt Corporation and Donald Gordon's Liberty Life. Trying to establish precisely what influence they exercised is difficult. Both companies are bland to the point of evasive about the issue. That is understandable. Big business operates in a rarified world: sharing secrets, setting up deals, discussing possible projects they have no wish to communicate to the public at large until they have to.

Yet it is possible to draw some conclusions about the extent of their influence simply because of what is known about the people at the head of the two companies.

Anthony Edward (Anton) Rupert was the founder of the Rembrandt empire. Born in 1916 in Graaff-Reinet in the Karoo, he needed to make a living during the Great Depression of the Thirties. He tried his hand at dry-cleaning then decided to take his meagre capital of £10 and make cigarettes in his garage that he could peddle from door to door in Karoo dorps. That was the humble beginning of what was to become a diversified giant worth billions, with tentacles in 36 countries on six continents. It would also lead him to a place on the Forbes list of the world's 500 wealthiest people.

Throughout his 60-year career he was the very epitome of an Afrikaner gentleman, but no one ever made the mistake twice of thinking that he was a pushover. There was an iron fist in his velvet glove. He knew what he wanted and how to get it.

He invested in Gold Fields not because he wanted to take it over, but because he thought it was a good company that was well run; and because he, too, believed in gold. He tended to be a hands-off investor. In part that may have been because Gold Fields turned out to be a singularly good investment in those days. There was no need to interfere.

In 1991 Anton was succeeded by eldest son Johann Peter. Like father, like son – in some ways, anyway. Johann inherited a talent for business and grew the empire into a conglomerate of awesome proportions. Unlike his father, he maintained the iron fist but used the velvet glove sparingly, if at all. Born on 1 June 1950, he completed his education and then began working as a banker in New York. In 1984 he was lured back to the family business, becoming vice-chairman of Remgro in 1989 and stepping into his father's shoes two years later. Along the way he developed a reputation for being an unusually outspoken critic. He doesn't believe much in euphemisms. Victims say a dressing-down from a displeased Rupert is one of the less desirable experiences in life.

Back in 1989, Robin Plumbridge was asked to give his assessment of the Ruperts while meeting with a British Department of Trade and Industries' team. The team was investigating possible anti-competitive actions by Anglo American in attempting to acquire more Consolidated Gold Fields' shares. At the time Remgro had a 20% interest in GFSA and a pre-emptive right to take that up to 40%. Anglo objected. DTI inspector Richard Lewis asked: 'How did Johann Rupert react to that?' Plumbridge replied that Johann was 'a very complex young man' who had been surprised, upset and disappointed at Anglo's attitude. There had been 'naughtiness' in the Press to the effect that Rembrandt had stolen GFSA from Anglo. Other mining houses had joked: 'Mr Plumbridge will now have to smoke Rembrandt cigarettes.'

Later, Lewis asked: 'How do you see Johann Rupert?' and Plumbridge replied: 'I wish I could answer you.' And then proceeded to approach the question obliquely.

'Anton Rupert is a remarkable man,' he said. He was a gentleman whose word could be implicitly trusted and he was very much respected by his staff and the business community; a businessman in the founder-patriarch mould. It was very difficult for a son to follow a father of this type into his business. Johann had been very reluctant to join the family business and had had to be persuaded by Dr Anton. 'He is still trying to establish himself. He's a different generation and he's rougher and more boisterous. It is difficult for him …'

ALAN WRIGHT, Plumbridge's successor as CEO, remembers a few occasions when he thought Rupert was going to fire him. On one occasion he was summoned to Rembrandt headquarters in Stellenbosch. He didn't think too much of it because he was in the habit of going there once a month to update Rupert on progress. But this time, he thought, it was going to be a bit tricky. Gold Fields South Africa (GFSA) needed to raise still more money, another rights issue, for the voracious Northam platinum mine. He knew Rupert would not be well pleased. That turned out to be an understatement. Rupert was apoplectic, and he didn't mince his words: 'I thought he was ready to fire me and Robin Plumbridge.'

Eventually, when he had simmered down, Rupert said: 'All right, you'll get your money, but that's it! Make it work or sell it.'

A second tense moment was also related to Northam. In the mid-90s Gold Fields received an offer from Anglo to buy the mine at R4.50 a share. It seemed a puny offer. Wright discussed it with a Rembrandt director, Emil Buhrmann, and both agreed: they would tell Anglo to 'take a jump'. It gave the Gold Fields CEO considerable satisfaction. Unfortunately the bid had been copied to Rupert, who did not share Wright's satisfaction in rejecting it. He sent his private plane to Durban to fetch Wright.

Rupert had had enough of Northam; to turn down a buyer, any buyer, was criminally stupid. It took some hard talking from Wright to half-persuade him that the mine was worth more than that. Much later, Wright was vindicated. Within a couple of years Gold Fields sold Northam to Tokyo Sexwale's Mvelaphanda Resources for R6.50 a share and Anglo paid considerably more than that to get a 22.5% chunk of it. Lacking that foreknowledge, Rupert's anger was unrestrained. And vocal.

The third confrontation was perhaps the roughest. It happened when Rupert was chairman of Gold Fields. Brian Gilbertson came to a meeting and said that Tarkwa [a gold mine in Ghana] was 'the worst investment Gold Fields had ever made'.

'You'll never make any money,' said Gilbertson, 'you'd do better to get rid of it.'

Wright defended the project – and got a roasting for his trouble: 'Rupert can be a very aggressive person when he reckons you have made a mistake. I told him that the main reason Tarkwa wasn't going anywhere was the wage agreement. They were paying their staff in US dollars in an African country. But it wasn't because they were stupid. Ghana mine staff has always been paid in dollars. The union negotiates dollars.'

Gold Fields kept Tarkwa. It became a very cheering source of profits.

Robin Plumbridge became the target for Rupert's ire on another occasion. It was the time of the notorious Boipatong massacre of June 1992. More than 40 residents of the Vaal Triangle township were slaughtered in an orgy of violence. The attackers were Zulus, members of the Inkatha Freedom Party, who arrived after dark in vans with guns, knives and clubs. They began to kill everybody they could find on the street. It was a time of high political tension. The massacre nearly derailed progress towards a peaceful transition to majority rule. The ANC pulled out of the Codesa talks because it was convinced that the massacre was part of the covert war being waged on behalf of the National Party through the police and the defence force. So did half the country. The IFP and the government were seen to be far too cosy.

The next day the media identified an accomplice, albeit an unwitting one. At the request of the SADF, Gold Fields had offered unoccupied mine accommodation to trackers displaced from the Angolan border. They were known to be loyal to the SADF; to be skilled at following almost invisible clues in the shrub and semi-desert of Angola and Namibia; to have led South African soldiers to the enemy's hideouts, where they could be killed. Who more likely to have staged the massacre at the instigation of the defence force? Someone had a vested interest in planting the idea.

At that time of ignorance and alarm and wild conspiracy theories, it made brief sense. So Gold Fields got undeserved blame for housing 'the wrong kind of people'. Rupert was mortified; it meant that Remgro was associated with unpleasant publicity.

Wright recalls: 'He didn't like being on the receiving end of criticisms that came after accidents. He was conscious of his public image. Even less did he like the suggestion that the group had housed killers. Robin Plumbridge got the roasting on that one.'

Later the Goldstone Commission concluded that there was no police or army involvement. By that time, the damage was done. To this day some groups remain convinced that there was a cover-up.

IN A PROFILE, the *Financial Times* of London described Rupert as 'reclusive' and reported that he 'rarely gives interviews and shuns public events'. It is not a profile that his golfing acquaintances would easily recognise. To them, he was a genial host at Leopard Creek, the magnificent private golf course he owns on the boundary of the Kruger National Park. They tell with awe of the story of Leopard Creek's 18th green, newly constructed and pristine. Rupert thought it had been badly sited. He instructed the greens staff to move it to a better place.

'But,' protested the greenkeeper, 'it'll cost R5-million.'

'I didn't ask you what it would cost,' said Rupert. 'I said: move it.' It was the end of the conversation.

The mining industry was a shock for Johann Rupert. Ever the staunch Afrikaner, he thought the whole industry was like a fancy building dominated by an English culture. On the top floor were the Oxbridge lot, all trying to be more British than the British. On the second floor were the English speakers, working at head offices or in cushy positions on mines. On the third floor were the Afrikaners doing the hard work underground. And way down in the basement were the blacks.

He told his father: 'Gold Fields is another world.' He thought the entire Rembrandt headquarters could fit into the atrium of the large and fancy Gold Fields offices at 75 Fox Street. He was told that the staffing formula was one head office employee for every 100 mine employees. He did a quick calculation: 78 000 working on mines, 783 in head office. 'At Rembrandt, if you were not selling you were part of the overheads.'

'People who have been in an industry for a long time often don't question things,' he says, 'but I've never been scared to ask questions.' So he asked what they all did; what in fact HO contributed. The answers did not set his mind at rest. He thought that the GFSA business model had run out of time. Besides, the way it worked would amount to insider trading in today's definition: the company found the ore body, raised the capital to develop it, created a separate company, retained the management contract and then sold shares in the separate company, keeping a substantial portion for itself. Gold Fields could thus be deemed to have inside knowledge that was denied to other shareholders. But in those days the rules were less strict.

He is well aware that practices become entrenched in large companies that are highly regimented. Staff are steeped in company traditions, promotions tend to come from within and structures are inflexible. He had seen the consequences in his own organisation.

Soon after he joined Rembrandt a sales rep said to him: 'I'm entitled to a company car, a Honda Ballade, but it's company policy that the air-conditioning must be removed.'

'Why?' asked Rupert.

'Oh, it's a rule your father established. I think it was because he believed that reps would not get out of their cars and make their calls in hot areas.'

Rupert Jnr found that hard to believe. He asked his father about it. Rupert Snr said: 'Yes, it was a rule once. But that was in 1957 when aircon cost as much as the car itself.' It had been conscientiously observed ever since – because no one had thought to question it.

A similar situation prevailed when Rembrandt took over Rothmans in the late Eighties. Factories in Berlin sent regular reports – measured by the foot – to head office in Bremen and to the marketing office in Hamburg. The marketing office didn't even read them.

Rupert noticed the large air-conditioned room at head office which housed the company computer. In those days computers were the size of double-decker buses. He asked if Bremen was on line with Berlin and was told no. Head office preferred hard copy; the used paper was donated to schools. He ordered that the reports to Head Office be stopped and asked to be informed when someone noticed their absence. It took two-and-a-half months. 'The point is that no one cared, but the system was entrenched.'

He thought the personality conflicts between GFSA and Anglo American – especially between Plumbridge and Ogilvie Thompson – were unfortunate. Yes, he had experienced Anglo interference himself. It happened when Rembrandt bought a 10% interest from Consgold and a pre-emptive right to the remaining 28% if Consgold wanted to sell. Soon afterwards he got a call from Anglo to say he was not allowed to do the deal. That was odd. Anglo had representatives on the Consgold board that approved it. He decided to ignore the call.

As for the perception that Anglo would do anything to get its hands on Gold Fields, Rupert advocated a different response. 'Make so much profit that it becomes too expensive for them to buy you.'

In general, he believed in lifting barriers between companies, mining ore bodies according to the geology of the land, not according to who held the rights. In any case he had a high regard for Anglo's top brass, men like former chairman Gavin Relly, one-time chairman of Anglo American Industrial Corporation Leslie Boyd, executive director Graham Boustred – 'people who built things'.

Relly had told him bluntly at a braai in Hermanus that he didn't understand mining. Rupert had been listening to a little lecture from Bernard van Rooyen on the risks of mining; the odds against success. Relly had piped up: 'It's like rolling dice on a craps table, but over the years it has been very profitable.' Rupert agreed: he didn't understand mining. Rembrandt's expertise was in the fields of branding and marketing. So why was he invested in GFSA? Because his father 'believed in gold' and Rupert Jnr believed it was a good currency hedge and that GFSA was a good company. He liked and respected Plumbridge, but perhaps he had stayed too long. 'Ten years is probably the limit. He was tired. External problems make this a tough job.'

As for a mooted merger between Gold Fields and Genmin, Brian Gilbertson of Gencor had talked to him about it and he had told him what his father used to say: 'If you mix chicken shit with ice cream it still tastes like chicken shit.' Gilbertson had gone away and told his people to get rid of the chicken shit. Nevertheless, 'everyone makes mistakes. GFSA should have been built up. Derek Keys should have stayed. It needed someone to break the mould and I was busy building Richemont. It's very sad that South Africa does not have a mining champion any more. GFSA didn't benefit from the commodity boom. No one anticipated the insatiable appetite for base metals from China and others. It should have brought in a Brian Gilbertson.'

SIR DONALD GORDON is a smallish, slightly plumpish man with a cherubic face. But don't let that fool you. He has a genius for business and getting his own way. He founded two great commercial empires on two continents – the Liberty Life group in South Africa and Liberty International PLC, a massive property company and shopping mall developer in Britain. Today he is honorary life president of both and is widely recognised as a brilliant businessman, a patron of the arts and a philanthropist. He earned his British knighthood for services to the arts and business; and back home he was at various stages Businessman of the Year (*Sunday Times*) and Achiever of the Century in SA Financial Services (*Financial Mail*). He has honorary doctorates from Wits and Pretoria universities.

He matriculated from King Edward VII High School in Johannesburg with three distinctions, but his family couldn't afford to send him to university to do the chemical engineering degree he had set his heart on. So he became an articled clerk instead and qualified as a chartered accountant. At the age of 27, with a meagre R100 000 he had scraped together as capital, he launched his own insurance company. At first, established competitors jeered at him, but not for long. Liberty Life was destined to become the third-largest insurance company in the country.

As his official biography, *Larger than Life* (by Ken Romain, published by Jonathan Ball) makes clear, Gordon is a man blessed by a supreme confidence in his own ability and a dogged determination to achieve his goals. It makes him a formidable adversary. When he was trying to raise his initial capital he walked the streets of Johannesburg, Cape Town and Durban for months on end – knocking on doors, seeking investors, never losing heart at the discouraging number of rejections he was getting.

He describes himself as 'a gregarious person', but it shouldn't be taken to mean that being sociable equates to being amenable and easygoing. He knows when to be tough. Since his investment in Gold Fields represented a considerable sum of money, it wouldn't be far-fetched to assume that he would keep a beady eye on its progress, and be frank if he thought the progress was unsatisfactory.

But the man known as Donny to his friends was not just about making money. By 1971, still only 41, he had been successful enough to launch the Donald Gordon Foundation, South Africa's largest private philanthropic foundation. It gave hugely generous donations to, among many others, the Donald Gordon Medical Centre, the Gordon Institute of Business at Wits University and his old school King Edward's. It is no accident that his name features so large in many of the foundation's endowments. By nature he is a doer. In business, as in his other interests, he liked to play a pivotal role. And, of course, no one creates success in a highly competitive sector without a streak of toughness at the core.

According to Roy McAlpine, one of Gordon's most trusted lieutenants, there was a 'grand strategy' behind Liberty Life taking a 20% stake in Gold Fields Holdings. There were two other significant shareholders: Asteroid, a company created by Gold Fields itself (40%), and Rembrandt (40%). Effectively, this triumvirate created a buffer that would be able to block any future attempt to take over Gold Fields.

Johann Rupert saw his participation with Asteroid as 'a big mistake'. He came to believe that its structure meant that the destiny of the company was in the hands of management, not shareholders.

But Asteroid's purpose was very much secondary in Liberty's mind. More important was the fact that an alliance between GFSA, Rembrandt, Liberty and Standard Bank, which had a holding in GFSA, would attract a huge amount of related business for all its members. Besides, Liberty's philosophy was to invest efficiently for the benefit of policy-holders. In South Africa that meant investing in natural resources, so gold had a place in its vision.

Was it a good investment? McAlpine is equivocal. 'At the price Liberty paid, it turned out to be a pretty average investment. To what extent this can be attributed to poor management and to what extent it can be put down to the gold price is difficult to say.'

Nevertheless, Liberty was not exactly delighted with its investment even though McAlpine believes it would have been happy to invest in the new Gold Fields Limited if it had been asked. With its minority 20% in an unlisted Holdings company, it sometimes felt like a poor relation and was heard to complain that, with only one seat on the Holdings board, it virtually had no say in the mining business. But that is not to say it kept its mouth shut when aggrieved. That would have been alien to Gordon's nature.

Says McAlpine: 'Plumbridge, Rupert and Gordon formed an uneasy alliance. All three wanted to rule. Rupert and Donald eventually fell out. There was an age difference but I don't really know why.'

Perhaps the seeds of division were planted right at the beginning. Rupert had a Scotch with Gordon one day and the two reached an agreement to invest in Gold Fields. Gordon then went to see Anton Rupert and said that his investment company didn't want him to do the deal. Rupert Snr didn't pull his punches. 'If that happened to me, I would either fire the investment team – or resign.' Gordon did the deal.

Certainly, things got off on the wrong foot with Gold Fields when Northam was launched. Gordon got to hear that certain people – Gold Fields staff members, brokers and the like – were being offered shares at below the market price. No offer had been made to Liberty. He complained angrily that the principle was wrong; such a manoeuvre could be construed as insider trading. Dru Gnodde pacified him, but the incident left a slightly bitter after-taste.

Subsequent problems at Northam didn't improve matters. Liberty protested at what it saw as inordinate delays. It didn't hesitate to express its view that the project was being poorly managed. It was not a happy partner. Neither, for that matter, was Remgro.

CHAPTER TEN

WHEN EUPHORIA FADES ...

Perhaps it is true that coming events cast their shadow before them. How else to explain the brooding sense of uneasiness that seemed to underlie the mostly encouraging news that emerged in the handful of years immediately following the centenary?

On the face of it, Gold Fields of South Africa had cause to celebrate during and after its 100th birthday in February 1987. In that financial year it was able to record that earnings (more than R300 million) and net assets (well over R7 000 million) had achieved record highs thanks to a gold price that had performed well in both rand and dollar terms. Its shares were listed not only in Johannesburg but on stock exchanges in London, Paris, Zurich, Basle and Geneva. The highlight of the year, it told shareholders, was undoubtedly the centenary celebration. It had been quite a party – ten nights of banquets at the Johannesburger Hotel, which had the largest ballroom in town. A banquet at head office. A cabaret for the staff called *A Century in Song*, filmed by SABC TV. Even the printed invitations were fancy enough to win an art award in New York.

But all too soon, the last toast had been proposed, the last guest had gone and it was back to mundane business again. In the real world, there is no moratorium for turning 100.

At the end of financial year 1988, aspects of the picture were even brighter. The South African economy had gathered momentum. Earnings and dividends were again higher. But there was a disturbing little cloud: the gold price was indeed going up in rand terms – but operating costs were going up even faster. Inflation was tightening its grip. Of course, this might also have had something to do with the international stock exchange crisis. 'Black Monday' had arrived without warning on

19 October 1987, bringing with it the largest one-day drop in stock market history. The Dow Jones index fell by almost 22%. Many analysts attributed the crash to panic – a panic that spread from Wall Street to the rest of the world with the speed of a tsunami.

As chairman Plumbridge told Gold Fields shareholders:

> While some people are inclined to blame the setback on market technicalities, there is no doubt that the euphoric conditions that preceded the setback were not justified by the fundamentals. A significant correction was therefore inevitable and it is noteworthy that although confidence has re-emerged in most markets there is a distinct absence of euphoria.

Nevertheless, by the end of the financial year 1989, the highlights in the annual report, at least superficially, still looked almost as bullish: The world economy had grown strongly, thanks to the reduced interest rates that came after Black Monday. 'The modest improvement in the Group's earnings and dividends reflects the first significant benefit to be derived from the policy of diversifying into a broader range of mineral and metal products,' said the chairman.

But, if you listened very carefully, it was possible to detect a haunting refrain in the background – a refrain muted but insistent. It drummed out an almost subliminal message: the world may have recognised the warning signs emanating from Black Monday's shock market collapse but South Africa needed to heed its own internal warning signs too. It needed to acknowledge – and do something about – the fundamental structural imbalances that existed in its own economy.

The message was timely. But it is also true that the country, by and large, was not yet ready to hear it.

ONE MESSAGE was so explicit it couldn't be ignored: potential labour problems lay ahead. All the signals were already there. Tensions between employers and employees had been slowly building over years. A single event provided a trigger.

In May 1979 a government-appointed commission investigating

labour relations after the 1976 uprising in Soweto, produced a bombshell report. As Johan Liebenberg, then labour relations adviser to the Chamber of Mines, put it: 'The Wiehahn report came out and changed everything the Chamber of Mines had understood about industrial relations to that point. It recommended that blacks be classed as employees!' For old-style apartheid devotees, the recommendation was outrageous. It turned apartheid on its head.

But the Wiehahn Commission was insistent: legal recognition had to be given to black trade unions and migrant workers; statutory job reservation had to be abolished; an industrial court needed to be created to resolve industrial disputes. It heralded a brave new world – or might have done, had government not found a loophole to continue stifling black aspirations. Their unions had to be registered with the state, a different but effective form of control. Result – more labour tension. Nevertheless, a door had been opened, never to be closed again.

Cyril Ramaphosa, general secretary to the newly formed National Union of Mineworkers, approached the Chamber to negotiate recognition. 'The discussions were a bit Mickey Mouse to begin with,' says Liebenberg, 'It was like a marriage – one has to talk to the parents and go through various rituals.' Out of it emerged an unusual agreement, one that was regarded as a triumph by the young union.

At the time, NUM had only about 14 000 members out of a workforce of 600 000. If the usual yardstick had been used, NUM would have needed more than 300 000 members (or half the work force) before it was recognised. Recognising that the established formula would blow NUM out of the water, the new agreement stipulated instead that the union would be recognised by a mine if it achieved 'significant recognition' of employees in specific categories. 'Significant recognition' might be as little as 30% or less. By this device NUM gained a foothold on 14 mines in a number of categories.

Now came the really clever part. The presence of NUM enabled the Chamber of Mines to negotiate with the union not just for the 14 mines but for the entire industry in the job categories where NUM had achieved recognition. The fledgling union had gained some mighty muscle. Within a few years it would increase its membership to 360 000.

But as black workers progressed by centimetres, the country was sinking deeper into political crisis. In 1985 the townships started burning. Two years later NUM announced that it was going to take over the mines. Later it modified its goal: it would take over the mine hostels instead. 'To all intents and purposes it was the same thing,' says Liebenberg.

And that was how, in August 1987, the biggest and longest strike by black workers in the history of the country began. More than 300 000 mineworkers from gold and coal mines came out, and stayed out for three long weeks.

It was at this point that judgments on the strike's success began to diverge. Not surprisingly, the bosses saw things one way, the workers another. Yet some perceptions were common to both.

The strike brought death and brutality. Twenty-one workers were murdered by co-workers and union members. A popular weapon was a straightened coat hanger, used to strangle an opponent.

Liebenberg has his own memories of what transpired:

> The strike organisers decided to take control of the hostels. Management was expected to carry on supplying the food, but the strikers would distribute it. Now food distribution worked when there was controlled access and normal working conditions, but access was not secure and neither was distribution. Some employees went home but most stayed in the belief they would keep their jobs.
>
> By the end of the second week it was clear that food distribution and access systems were beginning to work against NUM. Management began to use the PA systems to spread propaganda: 'Strikers will lose their jobs ... strikers will lose their jobs.' And, by the third week: 'You have now lost two weeks' pay.' A squabble developed over who controlled the broadcast system. Management eventually won the battle and the propaganda continued. More and more hostel residents were saying this was bullshit, we're losing. NUM was losing control.

Finally, on Sunday 31 August, Chamber of Mines (COM) and NUM negotiators met. COM took a hard line: 'We made an offer back in July. We'll make the same offer now, not a cent more.' NUM accepted and the strike was ended.

There was at least one consequence that none had anticipated. Large-scale firings reduced the number of jobs in the mining industry from 600 000 to 300 000, and the latter figure was never again exceeded. 'You could say,' says Johan Liebenberg, 'that Cyril Ramaphosa lost the jobs of 300 000 people with 3-million dependents – and all for nothing.'

And yet, and yet ...

NUM DID NOT share this bleak view. And neither did some observers.

Certainly, there was no disputing one thing. Management could no longer doubt the depth of discontent among workers or the steely determination of a new generation of union officials. The latter staged a tougher and more militant protest than employers had ever had to deal with before.

It began on the night of 7 August, precipitated by what workers saw as an act of bad faith by the Chamber of Mines. In negotiations with the white Council of Mining Unions, the COM had agreed a general increase of 15%. But in separate talks with the black National Union of Mineworkers the parties were further apart. Black employees believed they had been short-changed down the years; they were entitled to a larger increase. Reluctantly, in negotiations, NUM reduced its demand to 24%. The Chamber, aghast, said that was not possible and decided unilaterally to grant 17%. It believed that workers would accept meekly, even gratefully. After all, none could afford to sacrifice their meagre wages. Could they? Economics, if nothing else, would bring them to heel. It was an error of judgment.

The workers did not capitulate. The strike did not fizzle out in mere days. Instead, it spread – and spread again, until it affected something like 60 gold and coal mines. It lasted for three full weeks. Exultantly, the workers called it 'the 21 days that shook the Chamber'.

Nevertheless, some vestige of the old perception of a toothless union survived in the GFSA chairman Plumbridge's report. It was not surprising. The report was dated 4 September, a mere four days after the strike had ended – far too early to assess its real import:

> Relationships with the National Union of Mineworkers continue to

be less than satisfactory. The high political profile which has been taken by certain elements within the union continues to cause concern. The relationship is further complicated by the idealistic objectives which the union has set for itself. As a result, the Union does not give proper weight to the primary consideration of most employees in the industry, which is job preservation. While the industry is committed to improving the overall position of its employees, it is compelled to take into account the fundamental economic facts.

Super tranche increases in employees' remuneration, which will lead to the closure of mining areas and/or the elimination of job opportunities, cannot be in the interests of employees who have relatively few alternative employment opportunities.

It is to be hoped that the union will learn from the recent strike and that they will be better able to judge the climate for improving conditions for their members in the future. The creation of unrealistic aspirations is in nobody's interests, least of all the unions.

There, in a somewhat paternalistic nutshell, was the Gold Fields philosophy on wages – a philosophy that caused it to be labelled reactionary and conservative by critics. Gold Fields had gained a reputation for being opposed to granting wage increases simply because union representatives demanded them. It thought increases should be linked to gains in work skills and productivity. Arbitrary increases without greater productivity would inevitably result in fewer jobs because businesses had budgets to meet. Besides, Plumbridge was on record as saying that, for the truly poor of South Africa, any job was better than no job at all.

Gold Fields' particular protagonist in the Chamber of Mines was Anglo American, which was notably more willing to consider general wage increases, perhaps partly because the liberal culture at the top made it more susceptible.

Nevertheless, it was an argument that had more than one correct answer, and it raised an interesting philosophical point: which indeed was the reactionary attitude and which the concerned one? Was it more honourable to protect jobs, as Gold Fields claimed to be doing, or to put them at risk by raising the cost of creating them, as Anglo seemed to propose?

AS IT HAPPENED, the dispute paled into insignificance against a more immediate message which both employer factions now had to face. It was this: benevolent feudalism in the mining industry was dead.

After the 1987 strike, an era ended. Never again would things be the same in the mining industry. Black workers had demonstrated their power. They had also accepted the consequences of fighting for their rights and had decided they were willing to pay the price for it – a price that meant, among other things, sacrificing precious wages. And sometimes jobs too.

In fact, the message was neither new nor surprising, merely more forcefully conveyed. Management had been long aware that a major point of grievance was entrenched discrimination underground. All miners were expected to share the dangers but not the opportunities. By law, more advanced jobs with better pay were reserved for whites. Even in the bowels of the earth, job reservation applied.

Gold Fields' shareholders were told: 'The most important and far-reaching development on the industrial relations front has been the passing of the amendments to the Mines and Works Act which will result in the elimination of racial discrimination in the mining industry. It is to be hoped that the amendments will be implemented speedily.'

It was a vain hope. Reporting back the following year, Plumbridge lamented: 'The process of removing racial discrimination ... is proceeding at a snail's pace. Although the amendments to the Mines and Works Act were passed over a year ago, the regulations have only recently been published. Regrettably, [they] incorporate a wide range of provisions which could be used to hamper the advancement of black employees.'

In the characteristically deceptive political language of the time, a law that purported to introduce progress was actually serving to block it. It was not unusual. Laws like the Extension of University Education Act did the same thing. 'Extending education' meant reducing university opportunities for blacks.

Plumbridge also had a message for apartheid die-hards, a not unfamiliar species in the industry: 'The shortage of qualified people is seriously hampering efforts to improve productivity. The shortage is such that no responsible white employee should feel any threat to his employment.'

WHEN the Great Miners' Strike of 1987 ended, employers could claim a victory of sorts. Recognising, after two weeks, that NUM's resolve would not be easily broken, they used a quirk in the law to fire 50 000 ringleaders despite the fact that the strike itself was legal. It helped to break the deadlock. On the last day of August 1987, the workers could hold out no longer and returned to work without achieving their demands. By rights they ought to have felt chastened and abject.

Curiously enough, they did not. They knew they had won a battle of a different kind. They had shown that they could organise and sustain a major protest. They had defied the might of the Chamber of Mines. In the process, they had won the grudging respect of the industry – and a new respect for their own abilities too. And their adversaries had acknowledged it.

A mining trade publication reported: 'The union has shown itself to be much better organised, its strike call well supported. The Chamber appears to have expected the NUM action to last only a few days as in earlier years and was somewhat surprised at the duration and solidity of the union's action and by its organisational capabilities, determination and skill.'

And the well-respected *Mining Journal* concluded: 'NUM has gained considerable stature ... Its influence is now widespread throughout the mining industry and unionisation of black miners is likely to increase.'

One other significant message emerged from the strike. It was left to a little known but fiery young NUM leader to proclaim it.

Cyril Matamela Ramaphosa was the son of a Soweto policeman who qualified as a lawyer and became a union activist. One day he would come to be recognised by the industry as perhaps the most effective negotiator it had ever dealt with; a man both reasoned and reasonable and yet strong enough to stand his ground. And when he changed direction and turned from being an ardent unionist, he became one of the most successful businessmen the country had seen.

Today Ramaphosa serves on numerous boards and has been awarded honorary doctorates by five Southern African universities and the University of Massachusetts in the United States. He is a member of the National Executive Committee of the African National Congress and served as a Member of Parliament for several years.

But back in the time of the strike, he was a unionist, an 'agitator'. And he was confident he had identified the strike's real significance. It was far more than just a bunch of workers showing their dissatisfaction. It was, he proclaimed, a dress rehearsal for throwing off the yoke of apartheid; a dummy run for political freedom.

'Nineteen eighty-seven,' he said, 'is the year that black mineworkers take control ...' Later he elaborated: 'The struggle we are involved in on the mines is a training ground for our people, for the ultimate goal which is liberation.'

Today very few observers challenge the notion that the 1987 strike was as much about black national aspirations as it was about winning a better workplace deal. In that sense, the mining houses were dragged willy-nilly into a more profound battle not of their choosing.

At the time, the country was a political tinderbox, In 1983 – four years previously – President PW Botha had seen fit to stage a whites-only referendum on a new (and hopelessly flawed) constitution and a new tricameral parliament to give Coloureds and Indians an illusion of power-sharing. It was as much a tacit declaration of failure as it was a feeble attempt to pull South Africa back from the brink. But it had one fatal flaw: it excluded Africans. The best that could be said by apologists for the Botha plan was that it was 'a step in the right direction'. And that, indeed, was why most white businessmen chose, forlornly, to endorse it.

Botha's equally infamous Rubicon speech of August 1985 reinforced the message of black exclusion. It fanned the flames of anger that would lead to ungovernable townships, vicious necklacing and political assassinations. Because key political movements were banned, surrogate organisations bobbed up to lead the fight; organisations like the United Democratic Front, later the Mass Democratic Movement and the Soweto Committee of Ten. Every protest, every demonstration, whatever its ostensible cause, became part of an ever-widening political uprising.

For more than five years, the country endured successive states of emergency, each more draconian than the last. Tens of thousands of people were detained without trial and the media was prevented from naming them. Only a few months before the miners' strike the Security Police blew up Cosatu headquarters in the centre of Johannesburg. On the eve of the strike some white conscripts announced that they would refuse to serve in the army because of its role in the townships.

The South African Defence Force, heavily involved in security duties, argued privately but persuasively that the country was not just in the midst of revolution but had lost it too. 'When the tip of the revolution iceberg emerges above the surface, the battle is lost,' said the SADF. In private.

Government declined to admit it, but international sanctions were biting and the country was slipping towards bankruptcy. Hardly a month went by without a new country severing economic ties. International sport was a thing of the past. All in all, it was not an environment calculated to develop business confidence or encourage enterprise. The wonder was not that companies by and large survived but that some, among them Gold Fields, actually managed to grow and even prosper.

OF COURSE, Plumbridge did not deliberately allow his company to become embroiled in political upheaval. He was far too shrewd for that; government did not take kindly to businessmen being 'political'. He was careful to describe himself as 'apoliticial' and in successive annual reports maintained a coolly dispassionate tone. Yet his assessments of the shoals ahead, many of them rooted in politics, were prescient. In financial 1987 he noted that, despite mildly stimulatory measures, 'there are a number of structural problems which are inhibiting growth'. New investment in wealth-creating assets was too low. Higher tax for the corporate sector had been mooted. Such talk had 'seriously impeded the development of new investment opportunities'. Higher company taxes would be sheer folly. South Africa couldn't afford the low growth which had prevailed since 1980. Unless 'existing constraints' were eliminated attempts to correct social inequities would fail.

Not a word of political rabble-rousing anywhere. But very few of his readers would have had difficulty in deciphering the political import of the code words he chose. South Africa had to change, or else.

The following year Plumbridge returned to the theme: 'There is no doubt that the unavailability of foreign finance is a major constraint.' This time the central message was less guarded:

It is quite clear that there will have to be a series of major policy shifts which will be unpalatable to various groups. Economically, South Africa cannot afford the existing and proposed political structures with their overlapping bureaucracies. A simpler and more efficient model is a necessity. In the social field, there is an understandable desire to correct the social problems of the past as quickly as possible. Unfortunately it is economically impossible to achieve many of the current objectives. In simple terms, both the political and social elements in the economic equation are absorbing an increasingly disproportionate amount of the country's human and financial resources.

In other words, stop tinkering with separate development and discredited attempts to pretend the policy could be made to work. Apartheid was killing the country. Then he softened the blow by having a dig at his own peers and, by implication, the unions: 'It is astonishing that in a developing country such as South Africa, so many industrial enterprises operate a 40-hour week, which is only 25% of the time available.' Competitors in south-east Asia aimed to utilise plants for at least 85% of the available time. If the country followed that example, the impact on productivity would be dramatic.

By the time that Financial 1989 had arrived, Plumbridge was increasingly dispensing with the niceties:

> For South Africa, developments in the world economy have provided mixed blessings and on the whole have aggravated developments in the local economy. Given its complex political background, it is essential that certain economic realities are recognised. Nobody would deny that South Africans would like to see low interest rates and a strong currency. Sadly, a precondition for such a scenario is low inflation and political reconciliation. During the past year neither condition has been met.

With hindsight, two other aspects seem noteworthy. Of the problems identified by Plumbridge, few, if any, related to Gold Fields alone. Most were common to the mining industry, and indeed to industry as a whole.

So they avoided the charge of being self-serving. And the second point was this: despite his forthright analysis, he avoided any suggestion that he or his company had been brought to despair by the obstacles and were ready to throw in the towel. Rather, he seemed to have identified them only as a prelude to fixing them, much as a prudent ship's captain might note the presence of shoals before changing course.

It is not possible to say whether this overall approach offered some protection from government disapproval; or even whether that's what he wanted to achieve. In both cases, probably not. Government took scant notice of business, even big business, until the dying days of the PW Botha regime. But change came anyway, forced by events beyond the control of any of them.

CHAPTER ELEVEN

BAPTISM OF FIRE ...

It was going to be the dawn of a new age in mining, shedding old techniques, old race prejudices and the old South Africa. There, in the arid wilderness of the Bushveld, several hundred kilometres north-west of Johannesburg, an oasis was being created, a potentially very rich oasis indeed. The excitement was palpable when the first sod was turned on 8 July 1986.

Northam Platinum Mine was the biggest project Gold Fields had ever committed itself to in one of the most inhospitable places in the country. At the start there was no water, no power, no amenities. Much of the land surface consisted of heaving clay that would have to be replaced by rock and stone before the ground became stable enough for infrastructure.

The plan was to bring the mine to production in four years. To do so, the company estimated it would have to invest more than half a billion rands, an unimaginable sum in those days. It turned out to cost a lot more.

It was going to be the hottest, deepest platinum mine in the world. It would pioneer methods never fully tested before in challenging conditions above and below the earth. Summers are well-nigh intolerable in the bushveld, where rain is rare. But that was nothing compared to the temperatures that would be encountered when they hit the 2 000-metre mark underground. The broken rock there was at a temperature of 65 degrees Celsius; hot to the touch, far too hot for men to work in comfort for even a few minutes, let alone a full shift.

But, as difficult as it would be to dig out the precious metal, it might be even more difficult to dig out something else: the engrained racial attitudes that had been fostered by an apartheid society. For decades, the law had enforced strict discrimination in mines. No black man was allowed to qualify for a blasting certificate that could open the door to promotion. Now, at long last, Government had relented and was about to repeal the scheduled persons clause in the Mines and Works Act. It was the fulfilment of a dream for Gold Fields and, in particular, for its chairman and CEO, Plumbridge. This was what he had been working for over many years.

For the first time in modern memory, blacks and whites would enjoy equality, earning equal pay for equal work, living eventually in equal accommodation according to their seniority and not the colour of their skin; men of different races working together, united by the single goal of ensuring a successful mine and a successful community. And all this was going to happen within twenty or so kilometres of Thabazimbi, a notorious fortress of right-wing ideology. It was an unlikely area for an experiment in race relations. Still, it was a comfort to know that Northam's life was estimated at well over a century. It would certainly outlast the diehard attitudes of yesteryear.

IT SEEMED like a coup when Gold Fields acquired mining rights to 11 068 hectares adjoining Johannesburg Consolidated Investment Company Ltd (JCI)'s Rustenburg Platinum Mine in 1981. News of the impending birth of a new mine – expected to be the highest grade and lowest cost platinum mine in South Africa – caused a stir in investment circles. The rights issue that launched it was the second largest in the history of the Johannesburg Stock Exchange. It was over-subscribed. Initial forecasts were for production of 250 000 ounces a year. But the reserves were so large that this could be quickly quadrupled.

On top of that, the timing seemed impeccable. The world had discovered global warming and the compelling need for cleaner-running cars. A few years before the rights were awarded to Gold Fields, the United States had made it compulsory for all production models to be fitted with catalytic convertors. Soon, all car manufacturers around the world would regard convertors as essential. Better still, platinum, or its allied metals, had been found to be by far the most suitable for these new-fangled devices to reduce exhaust pollution (first produced on a commercial scale only in 1973).

Demand seemed limitless; sources of supply delightfully limited. South Africa had the world's largest known reserves of this scarce metal. What could possibly go wrong?

Well, in a word – lots. Some predictable, some not.

The first and most important problem was that Northam was ahead of its time – a state-of-the-art project pioneering techniques and equipment no other mine was using on the same scale. It would be deeper than any other platinum mine. And it would have to have the ultimate in sophisticated air cooling to enable miners to work at all. Two solutions presented themselves: back-filling and hydropower.

Back-filling was simple but time-consuming. It involved re-filling the excavated areas with sludge as each segment was mined out. This achieved two goals. It provided regional underground support, reducing seismic risk. More importantly, it reduced the area that had to be kept cool and heat-flow into the mine. Obviously, it slowed production.

The second solution was altogether more daring. It had been tried on an experimental basis at Kloof's No 3 shaft, and had worked effectively. But it had also been the cause of the calamity of 1993 when a section of its massive steel pipes collapsed. Hydropower was an ingenious idea. It entailed chilling water to five degrees Centigrade in giant surface refrigerators and then allowing it to gravitate underground in high-pressure pipes, developing intense pressure. The chilled, compressed water served two purposes. It provided efficient cooling and power to drive rock drills and other equipment. Drills driven by water power were considerably more efficient than the old ones driven by compressed air. Underground signs offered a warning: 'DANGER – EXTREME PRESSURE'. There was no need to add that the water jets that helped to clear the rock were so powerful that they could cut a miner in half in an instant.

Brian Moore, subsequently a senior consulting engineer, headed the feasibility study for Northam. He had seen what hydropower could do when he was at Kloof, where it had initially been used for cooling and only later for powering equipment. He knew it had tremendous potential so he allowed for its use in his planning. But he was well aware of its experimental nature too.

He recalls:

> I built the new technologies into the feasibility study because I knew that Northam would take at least five years to come to production. That gave time to iron out problems. And if the technology didn't work, we could always go back to standard methods. When production began costs were very high and there were lots of teething problems. The technologies were revolutionary and Northam was the only mine world-wide using them at that stage.

In mining, water can be either a friend or an implacable enemy. At Northam, it was both. They discovered the enemy first: unsuspected underground reservoirs. The first was encountered while the initial shaft was being sunk. When the compartments were inadvertently penetrated a jet of superheated steam shot out with the force of a cannon.

Unfortunately, no one had realised how numerous the compartments were. They added a new hazard and ensured an immediate setback to the timing schedule.

'You drilled 150 holes at Northam,' complained major shareholder Johann Rupert, 'but you didn't bother to drill any holes at all before siting the shaft. No wonder you didn't find out about the geological problems.'

'Yes,' admitted Bernard van Rooyen. 'That was a mistake.'

But current senior vice-president Jimmy Dowsley thinks the criticism unfair. He, together with Ian Watson, built Northam from scratch. He has vivid memories of what it was like when the water genie was released from its underground bottle:

> We intersected high pressure water while sinking the two shafts. It was a surprise, and it shut us down for a couple of months. You have never seen water like this. It was trapped in very thin veins, most of them vertical, so the system of cover drilling designed to detect the presence of water simply wasn't picking them up. Once intercepted, it was under extremely high pressure and very difficult to control. We used some fairly fancy rubber technology, again fairly ground-breaking, to seal it. But we lost the time. Were we guilty of negligence? Absolutely not.

In the Bushveld complex there was no reason to believe we'd be intercepting water in significant quantities at depth. The water was ancient, locked into the system aeons ago when this lot was melting. So super-heated steam was what we were dealing with. High-pressure super-heated steam.

It was frightening.

When the same kind of water was intercepted on the west side of the concession, mine management had to make difficult decisions. How rife was it? No one knew for sure so they put the whole west side on hold until the problem was better understood. This meant Northam could mine only half the area it expected, and that in turn meant a slower, more expensive build-up to full production.

'We were always sure we were going to get there,' says Dowsley. 'Grades were in our favour, higher than those in neighbouring mines. But first we had to face the challenges. It was a technical nightmare.'

FROM the beginning, Gold Fields was not made to feel exactly welcome by its neighbour and competitor, Rustenburg Platinum, an Anglo American enterprise. In the year that Gold Fields acquired the mining rights, Plumbridge received an unwelcome visitor.

The visitor was Gordon Waddell, chairman of JCI, executive director of Anglo American, son-in-law of Harry Oppenheimer and a former Scottish rugby international. He had earned himself a reputation as a tough businessman. He wasn't about to mince words.

'You have no right to mine here,' said Waddell. 'You're in breach of an undertaking made by Consolidated Gold Fields not to enter the platinum business.'

According to him, Consgold had signed the agreement when it sold its minority share in 1977. Plumbridge listened politely and replied equally politely. 'I know of no such agreement,' he said. 'In any event, GFSA couldn't have been party to an agreement without board approval. And this it certainly did not have.'

Was Waddell trying a bluff to stop Northam in its tracks? Who knows? But two consequences are clear. First, Gold Fields heard no more of the alleged agreement. Second, Rustenburg Platinum mine was curiously uncooperative from that moment on. Very often, there is a camaraderie in mining, even among competitors. Mines help each other out in times of need – come to each other's aid in a crisis. But the proprietors of Rustenberg seemed to prefer a different approach.

When Waddell saw Gold Fields MD Colin Fenton at a cocktail party he wished him 'the best of bad luck' with Northam. Rustenberg refused to allow Northam to build an access road across their territory, forcing Gold Fields to buy an adjacent farm. No one bar the Northam manager was permitted to visit their mine or observe its operations. Rustenberg had empty mine houses on its property but declined to rent them to Northam employees. Barry Davison, an Anglo director who was chairman and CEO of Anglo American Platinum, once told Fenton that he had no desire to take over Northam. He would prefer to wait until the mine was tottering and then scoop it up at fire-sale prices.

BEFORE the big problems came to bug Northam, the little niggles began. To save money, Fenton ordered that houses in the mine's village should not have air-conditioning or gutters. Occupants complained that both were essential to comfort in the bushveld. A combination of climate, erratic working conditions and a general sense that the mine was troublesome lowered morale and raised staff turnover.

Mike Eksteen was a happy man when he was manager of Kloof. The mine ran smoothly and head office mostly left him alone. He had had his 15 minutes of fame as the mine spokesman in the dramatic rescue of 150 miners trapped at the bottom of No 3 shaft in 1993. It had been a harrowing time but, in the end, richly rewarding when all were saved. Yes, there was a bit too much red tape and the occasional niggle. But that was Gold Fields for you. Still, Eksteen felt generally appreciated. Then, in 1994, he was appointed manager of Northam and right from the start things seemed to go sour. He didn't get on with his consulting engineer Ian Watson, who had managed Northam in its earliest days. He was also uncomfortable with the culture he found at the mine.

The previous manager, he thought, had been an old-fashioned disciplinarian, making all decisions. There was no culture of delegation and far too much red tape. Initiative was stifled and the general atmosphere probably accounted for some of the problems experienced. One day a senior employee came to him and asked for permission to cut the grass on the verge of a mine road. For heaven's sake, why ask? Eksteen told him he would be fired if he ever asked permission for so trivial a thing again.

Alan Jones remembers his appointment to Northam vividly. He was told by Fenton on a Wednesday that he was to be Northam's consulting engineer, effective the previous Monday. He delayed his retirement by two years to try to get Northam off the ground. He was confronted by one problem after another. He thought the feasibility report had been alarmingly over-optimistic. It allowed for 7km of development work to get the mine into production. When Jones finally left, there were 20km of development, and production was still well short of target. Cost overruns were frequent. The feasibility guys had made an odd prediction: that costs would go down as the mine went deeper and further from the shafts. Any mining man would tell you that distance adds to costs.

Alan Munro was an executive director during the early Northam days and subsequently sat on the Northam board. He remembers the pervasive anxiety that seemed to hang in the air. He wanted to mine surface deposits of platinum in the Dwarsrivier area of the Bushveld when Northam was delayed. He was not allowed to do so.

Gordon Parker joined the board of GFL in 1999. He remembers that Northam was 'in trouble and not working well'. Production was not on target and hydropower was playing up. Later, Gengold chairman Michael McMahon joined the Gold Fields board and brought with him a very blunt opinion indeed: 'Northam destroyed GFSA – the mindset that led to its development.' For all the hyperbole (Gold Fields lives on) it was a view shared by some others.

Bernard van Rooyen – at the time an executive director – believes that Northam was fine technically, but made mistakes. It turned down an additional seismic survey recommended by the geologists because it would have cost R20-million. The result was that 'to this day we are still sweating on costs because we don't know the pothole situation. We also hung on for too long with three prototypes of hydropower. Finally, at the time of going into production, the mine did not have working equipment.

This was a huge cost.'

These concerns filtered through to the Gold Fields boardroom. For almost the first time, Eksteen felt the weight of head-office intervention.

Before long costs began to run away with the project, forcing Gold Fields to ask investors to support rights issues running to well over a billion rands. Delays bedevilled development as technical problems arose and had to be solved. Shareholder Liberty Life grew thoroughly disillusioned, aggravating an old grievance. When Northam listed in 1987 some shares were allocated to staff and others. Liberty was not alone in believing it to be unfair and amounting to insider trading. The row had a brief life in the media.

Deputy Gold Fields chairman Dru Gnodde went to some lengths to persuade Liberty that the criticism was unjustified. It was not only employees who received shares, he insisted, it was also institutions and stockbrokers who got parcels which they, in turn, offered to employees and clients. All dealings were done at the issue price of R10 a share. Had the price not rocketed to R50 and more there would probably not have been such a furore. The price fell back subsequently. Liberty was only partly mollified.

A few years later, when Northam was clearly a huge drain on the Group, Donny Gordon complained to Gnodde about his 'disastrous investment'. Investor confidence ran low, then ran out for some. Analysts and media made the company the butt of jeers and disparaging comments. The Gold Fields share price dropped to a new low of R86.

Even after stoping started in 1991 and smelting of concentrates a year later, the critics still carped. 'Northam is a bottomless pit,' wrote *Business Times* in February 1993. 'It has cost R1.5-billion so far and more is still needed.' Finally, in 1992, limited production began – just at the time when the platinum price had sunk to a new low. To compound head office woes, the price of gold, the company's lifeblood, was undergoing what chairman Plumbridge described as a 'long, savage downturn'. Gold Fields was bleeding and the board could no longer tolerate the drain on the company. Besides, its major outside shareholder, Rupert's Rembrandt, had issued his ultimatum: make money or close the damn thing.

In February 1994 the Gold Fields board issued its own ultimatum to

Northam: turn yourself around within four months – or face closure. At Liberty, disillusion turned to dismay. It thought the company was managing the project badly, and said so. Rupert was fast losing patience with the whole group. In the words of ex-director McMahon: 'Johann had become fed-up with the loss of value in GFSA. He was also fed-up with Robin Plumbridge and Alan Wright.'

The board deadline came and went and Northam struggled on, showing tantalising signs of recovery but remaining cash-hungry. In November 1994 the board of Northam Platinum Limited announced publicly that it needed more money. The announcement sounded plaintive:

> After consideration of a comprehensive technical assessment, the board has decided to refinance the company. The assessment has concluded that a production rate of 150 000 tons per month to the concentrator is not achievable in the near term. A lower operating cost structure is being put in place. The attainment of the revised initial targeted metal production, productivity and operating cost performance levels should result in a break-even cash flow situation. An equity injection of up to R500-million is considered necessary to retire outstanding debt and to see the company to the self-financing stage.
>
> The plan is not without its risks but the conclusions of the technical assessment, taken with the company's substantial platinum metals resource, have motivated the board's decision. All alternatives for expanding the scale of operations and maximising the value of the resource will be investigated. Gold Fields of South Africa Limited, the major shareholder, has indicated that it fully supports the decision.

Put in simpler terms, it was saying: 'We need a lot more money. We hope like hell it will be enough. And that the mine will work.' But willing investors were becoming harder to find. By early 1995 Gold Fields was obliged to increase its own stake from 65% to 83% as minority shareholders declined to take up the rights issue.

Throughout this interminable period of strain and setback, at least some of the men behind the project retained their faith in it. Even at the lowest moments, they remained convinced that their investment would pay off in time. Wright, destined to become CEO after Plumbridge retired, was one of the believers. Not out of blind faith but because he understood only too well that mining was not about making a quick buck; that you sometimes had to wait 10 or even 15 years before getting a return on an investment. As it happened, he was right and – a bonus – he was still in office when the magic moment finally came. But for many years before that, and for many people, that welcome outcome was only a distant light in a dark tunnel. To some of them, the light seemed more like an approaching train.

But Wright prefers a more optimistic picture. This is how he remembers things:

> As with all new projects the costs were underestimated. It was always a good project and it would have made money more quickly if it had been implemented as planned. The engineers dropped us. They had five years to perfect hydropower while the shaft was being sunk but they didn't do it. From the outset drills didn't work. They packed up every few hours. Development had to be done by conventional means which added to costs and increased the heat underground. Finally we had to leave it to the mine itself to sort out hydropower. If the engineers had been able to do in five years what the mine eventually did in two, everything would have been fine.

A little further down the line, head office decided that the manager was the problem. It made sense to offer him retrenchment. The manager had the last laugh. Sensing trouble brewing, he arranged another job for himself before blandly accepting the retrenchment package.

Said Wright: 'At one point Northam was down to its last R5-million in the bank, a drop in the ocean. We had to make money or close. Just then the mine began to make production and the rock drills began to work.' By 1995, nearly ten years after the first sod was turned, Northam Platinum Mine began to generate cash. Three years later Northam was sold to Tokyo Sexwale's empowerment company at a significantly higher price than the R4.50 Anglo had once offered. And 18 months after that Mvelephanda was able to redeem its entire debt to Gold Fields.

BAPTISM OF FIRE ...

EVEN SO, the unknown 'if' in mining came into play. Profitable production came when the price of this precious metal was in a slump. That, of course, is the hidden time-bomb. Today's selling price is not a reliable guide to tomorrow's market. Sometimes it seems that whimsy is the determining factor in influencing selling prices.

Irrationality comes into play. What makes India decide one year that gold is essential to jewellery, and the next year that it is not? And the year after that, that it is again? Why does demand fluctuate? Will China expand its hoard, or suddenly begin to sell it off? The current price of gold is not necessarily related to simple yardsticks like production costs. It is set by people who don't much care what production costs are. Platinum is even more volatile, perhaps the most volatile of all precious metals because it is among the rarest of them.

In mining, you can establish with reasonable certainty the size of the ore body science has enabled you to identify. You can anticipate the likely grades. You can apply a formula to calculate development costs. You can second-guess inflation and the vagaries of the labour market. You can make provision for unexpected delays.

But you cannot say for certain what the world will be willing to pay for your product when, a decade down the line, you actually begin production. If global warming had turned out to be a damp squib, if platinum had not revealed properties ideally suited to catalytic converters, if the world had not become hungrier for cleaner cars – what might have been the fate of platinum then? What if someone had invented a cheaper, better way of processing exhaust gases? Might platinum have remained a rich man's indulgence, suited for exotic jewellery and little else? Questions without answers; gambles without guarantees. In short, the very essence of the mining ethos. That is why mining needs leaders with hardened nerves.

The turning point for Northam came in 1999, 13 years after the first sod was turned. For the first time Johann Rupert – chairman of GFSA – was able to present an optimistic report without qualification: 'This company [Northam Platinum Limited] has had a very profitable year and is starting to produce the results expected of it despite a relatively weak platinum price.' At last the 'problem child' had begun to repay the faith and confidence of its pioneers. But even that outcome contains an irony. All but one of its doughty protagonists would not be able to enjoy its new-found bounty for long. Northam was soon to acquire a new owner.

The solitary exception was Bernard van Rooyen; and that was only because, after retiring from Gold Fields, he became deputy chairman of the 'substantial and successful black empowerment company' that Gold Fields helped to create and which bought Northam from its mentor.

In April 2010 Mvelaphanda Resources sold 12.2% of Northam to the Eurasian Natural Resources Corporation stake for R2.2-billion. The price per share? – R50, a far cry from the Anglo offer of R4.50. Said Van Rooyen, now deputy executive chairman of Mvela: 'The R2.2-billion will substantially reduce Mvela's debt and enable it to proceed with the simplification of its corporate structure.'

With only a hint of mischief, Van Rooyen claims in his updated CV: 'I promoted the rescue and reconstruction of Northam and persuaded Tokyo Sexwale to invest in it.' Alan Wright would beg to differ about the 'rescue and reconstruction' bit. So presumably would Johann Rupert, who hailed Northam's 'very profitable year' in 1997.

Be that as it may. The reality is that the once unloved mine in the bushveld became a fairy-tale success but, alas, not for Gold Fields, which had risked its reputation to grow it.

Plumbridge offers a melancholy conclusion: 'For people with a short-term perspective, Northam was a problem. Once the complex mining issues were resolved, and the metal price moved up the price cycle, the mine blossomed under the management of high-quality people that Gold Fields let go.'

CHAPTER TWELVE

A LITTLE GOLD MINE

AFTER THE travails of Northam, who would have thought that a failing mine in the hinterland of a small central African country would become ... well, a little gold mine for Gold Fields?

You could say that God is everywhere in Ghana today – God and MTN and Vodafone. In that order. Occasional villages straggle along the country roads that lead from the capital, Accra. They are usually no more than a collection of assorted shelters. The lucky ones, on the roadside itself, feature ramshackle market stalls, beauty salons and mini-factories making furniture from the local teak. They revel in such names as 'By God's Grace Hair Salon', 'God is our Light Beauty Care', 'Trust in Jesus Chop Shop' (for casual meals) and – an ultimate destination – 'Hotel Messiah, A Glimpse of Heaven'.

There is no village without a flurry of signs for the cellphone giants too. Every now and then, a tall mast towers over the dense tropical shrub and palm trees. It is somehow appropriate that religion and cellphones should dominate. After all, they share the job of spreading the word.

This small tropical country was optimistically named The Gold Coast in the days when it was a British colony. Even today, independent for more than 50 years, it is still dotted with about 19 or so mines that help it to be ranked the second-largest producer of gold on the continent. In the early Nineties, one of them – a fairly rundown affair about 300 km south-west of Accra – caught the eye of the ubiquitous Van Rooyen and his two-man team of explorers.

At the time Van Rooyen, aka the Silver Fox, was an executive director of Gold Fields responsible for new business and technical services. Part of his job was to oversee major exploration programmes in sub-Saharan Africa and elsewhere in the world. Exploration became increasingly important to Gold Fields as time went by. It would lead it to unlikely sites as far apart as the tropics and the Arctic Circle. The company recognised that gold in South Africa was a depleting asset. Its mines were slowly and inevitably dying from the day mining first started. Survival demanded new sources of wealth. Later it would acquire the rights to what was commonly believed to be the last great gold mine in South Africa, South Deep. In the meantime exploration continued.

It was a job that suited Van Rooyen. It gave him the freedom to roam the world, untrammelled by bosses and established routines. It fed his insatiable curiosity. It pandered to the compulsive wheeler-dealer in him. Because he was street-smart, it also fostered his gift for irritating slower-thinking, more conservative souls. Sometimes it lit his short fuse and his fiery temper got the better of him. But he got things done. With Robin Hope he had pioneered South African involvement in Australia. Now he set out on a voyage of exploration with two GFSA lieutenants, Brian Moore and Maurice Toros. They visited Venezuela and picked up some good green fields territory, then on to Ecuador to look at the possibility of extending old workings.

They also turned their attention to Africa. Somewhere along the way, Moore heard that Ghana was looking to privatise its gold operations. It had taken over the industry soon after independence – partly because low gold prices had discouraged earlier investors. But Jeremiah (Jerry) John Rawlings, a military dictator, had obviously realised that governments are poor substitutes for private enterprise when it comes to running large companies requiring sophisticated skills. Van Rooyen told his colleagues to look into it.

Moore recalls: 'We hired a car and went off to meet an exploration geologist. Along the coast we passed the castles that Christopher Columbus once visited and were later used to house slaves destined for the United States. Once we turned inland, the roads were terrible and we arrived late at night.' After the ordeal of the drive, the mine seemed to be a damp squib in the view of Moore and Toros. What now?

Van Rooyen suggested that Moore meet the Minister of Mines in Accra; find out what else was available. The Minister had worked in

South Africa as a youth and there was a vague fellow-feeling. He offered two mines: Tarkwa and Prestea. Prestea was by far the better bet, he said. Van Rooyen told Moore: 'Well, get on with it then.' Within a week Gold Fields had won a contract to do a due diligence exercise on both mines. Moore worked seven days a week for three months. Technical teams arrived from Johannesburg and returned to write their reports.

The day came when Van Rooyen was ready to make a bid. He hopped on to a plane to Ghana's capital, Accra, a seaside city of almost four million people, most of whom appeared to be milling around on the streets around him, talking cheerfully. He was struck by their good nature, despite the fact that whites from the land of apartheid weren't exactly welcome. He met the Minister of Mines and this led to a meeting with Dictator Rawlings, who happened to be building model aeroplanes when he called. He was given a political lecture – the price of admission, as it were – and allowed to stay. It was either a tribute to his undoubted charm or a concession to a potential buyer. He didn't spend much time wondering which it might have been.

The traditional bright cloths of Ghana, the hawkers and stalls, the bustling streets, made for a colourful scene. There was a friendly feel and smiles were frequent. He thought he could get to like the place. He hired a car and followed the indifferent roads and tracks westward for 300 km into the forests of the southern region until he reached Tarkwa. It looked even more ramshackle than he had imagined.

Much of the effort was concentrated underground with desultory attempts at surface mining. The abundant vegetation in the immediate vicinity had been cleared to ease the task of finding the precious metal. Men, some shirtless, most without hard hats, toiled with old-fashioned shovels and buckets in shallow trenches. There was scant, if any, shelter from the tropical sun. The raw dirt they were excavating was turned into mud by constant watering before being trundled off in wheelbarrows for further processing. The overflow pooled in stagnant brown puddles on the ground, slowly steaming. To an untutored eye it would have looked like a scene from Dante's inferno – without the flames.

'The government had really buggered up these operations after nationalisation,' he says. 'Tarkwa was now a very broken down little mine milling about 30 000 tonnes a month.' Grades were low and the technology very 1930s. Automation didn't exist. But the Silver Fox could see potential – and needed to see more.

He headed for Takoradi, capital of the western region and Ghana's fourth-largest city. There was an air force base there and he had made friends with some of the officers using a sure-fire formula: buying drinks in the bar. He enjoyed drinking with the boys.

> There was no general aviation in Ghana in those days because Jerry Rawlings thought it was a threat to the state. I managed to persuade my new air force buddies to give me a flip over the area in a helicopter. There were 40km of gold-bearing outcrop; you could actually see it from the air. Sure, it was only about one gram a tonne but it was an awful lot of tonnes. I knew I had to move my ass. I prepared a presentation, participated in the public bid and ended up seeing the Minister of Mines again.

He began with an apology. He was going to reject Prestea, the mine the government had recommended. It would be a nightmare to get at the ore reserve. But Tarkwa – now that was something else. It had potential.

The Minister said: 'Lock the door – offer Prestea to the Anglo American Corporation before the news gets out.' (Later, as a gesture of goodwill to the Ghanaian government, Van Rooyen persuaded JCI to take it.)

Then they got down to discussing Tarkwa, a mine that had been rejected by several companies. Van Rooyen proposed to mine both on the surface and underground: 'No one else had proposed that, and they liked the idea. So I signed on the dotted line and bought Tarkwa for US$3-million.' Government retained a 10% interest.

Van Rooyen drives a hard bargain. He promised to undertake a three-phase exploration programme and feasibility study. But the government had to contribute something too. To run the mine efficiently, he would need to fire half the staff. Government would have to bear the cost of severance pay and accept environmental responsibility. Deal done.

Van Rooyen went home to tell his boss what he had done. The response was predictable. Plumbridge pulled him to one side and said sternly: 'You know you need board authority to make a deal like that?'

Van Rooyen said: 'Do you want Tarkwa or don't you?'
Plumbridge said: 'Well, yes ...'
And Van Rooyen replied: 'If I hadn't acted promptly you would have lost it. In any case you can't repudiate an agreement which has been signed by one of your directors. You'd end up being sued.'

That settled, they went together to convince the board. Van Rooyen took a flier: 'I told them we could revive the underground mine and make enough money out of it to fund the exploration of the new surface scene. I said there were 20-million ounces in the ground. I was just bloody lucky with the guesswork because there was 20-million ounces there. And Robin and the board bought it.'

NOT MANY people at Gold Fields had the courage to challenge Plumbridge. Van Rooyen knew he was taking his business life in his hands when he says:

> Look, he didn't take opposition lightly. I think I was probably about the only one who did that. But we'd started at about the same time with the company and, anyway, as a bloody-minded Afrikaner I had been used to fighting for my rights all my life. Then I suppose he had perhaps gotten to trust me to some extent because I had delivered the Consgold scene. So he tended to just let me get on with things.
>
> It was the same with the Black Mountain development. We kicked that bloody thing into production in 20 months in the middle of the desert and we came in on budget. But I broke all the rules. Decisions were supposed to be taken in this compartment and that compartment; but if you were going to do it in 20 months then there wasn't time for that. The original plan was to put in a decline. I had one look at the amount of sand over it and I said, we'll put a shaft in. That was done in half an hour. Robin disliked bending the structure, but I thought we had no choice.
>
> This was a complex ore body – copper, lead, zinc, quite a lot of silver – and it was going to be mined on a bulk basis. We had a lady geo-statistician who designed the system so I said to her: 'Once you've done that you're going to go down and put it into operation.'

That was another thing that wasn't in the book; unheard of. She was much amazed but she went down and laid it out, and it worked.

He proposed to apply the same brand of individualism to Tarkwa – and anything else he chose to dabble in.

Plumbridge offers a wry postscript: 'Anybody who knows Bernard well will chuckle over his takeover of all decisions – relating to Tarkwa, for example. It underplays the role of his executive colleagues and the project team. It also suggests that the CEO, far from not delegating authority, actually abdicated it. Oh well, I suppose there are always three sides to every story.'

BRIAN MOORE, senior consulting engineer, was due to retire in 1991. But the board asked him to stay on to help with exploration. He jumped at the chance. Besides, he thought his new boss, Van Rooyen, was a brilliant fellow so it didn't really matter that his wife, Margaret, had a somewhat different view. She refused to allow Van Rooyen into her house. What precipitated her displeasure was a dinner the Moores gave for a couple of her husband's colleagues. Van Rooyen's capricious temper let him down once more and he spent the evening attacking Richard Robinson and threatening to fire him the next day. Margaret Moore didn't think the clash enhanced the occasion.

In a flash, Moore transformed from a verge-of-retirement pensioner to a participant in a tropical crucible. He found it stimulating. The first task was to fire the existing management, bring in their own people, make changes to procedures. It wasn't plain sailing. Newmont Mining was supposed to participate in the venture and Moore desperately needed geologists. The US company agreed to provide some. The first geologist arrived the week before Christmas 1992, found the weather and the working conditions unacceptable and went home a week later. Newmont paid half of the exploration expenses then suddenly pulled out. Personnel manager Dave Rosenstein sent his 12-year-old daughter to the local school. Most of the pupils had never seen a white child and wanted to touch her. She had to be moved.

Mining began in June 1993. The Gold Fields team felt there was tremendous underground potential, but early drilling revealed nothing. However, surface drilling was more successful and they identified a possible 18-million ozs. Brian Moore was careful to cultivate the unions for the sake of peace. Eighteen months after Gold Fields took over, Van Rooyen paid his first official visit to Tarkwa. Moore laid on a big party, invited the unions, introduced him to the local area labour manager. Van Rooyen said: 'Ah, you're the chap we're going to fuck up.' And Moore sighed and thought: that's 18 months of hard work down the drain.

For the feasibility study they needed to estimate the number of illegal workers operating unofficially at the mine. They thought, 40 to 50. Gold Fields' very efficient security service was called in to deal with the 'garamperos' as they were called. Instead of the handful they expected, they found 900 working illegally underground or in the plant. Every now and then they would come across a body in a tunnel or an incline. To stop the influx, they had to seal the makeshift shafts the intruders had dug.

Illegal mining is a back-breaking way to earn a dishonest buck. The unofficial miners scrambled into the mine within 15 minutes of any blast. There they would load 80kg of freshly broken ore on to their backs and begin the 900m climb to the surface. The scam was very much a community affair; all officials in the area, including the mayor and the chief of police, were involved.

But all was not doom and gloom. The management improvements led to a profit for Gold Fields in the first month of operations. From then on, the mine never looked back. Neighbouring operations were bought up and incorporated. Damang, about 30km away, was bought by Chris Thompson, and began to run as a separate entity. Within five years Gold Fields had recovered its entire investment. Local Ghanaians were developed and taken into the management structure. Staff morale improved and a community spirit began to emerge. Up to 200 people took part in a quarterly 12km race through forest and river. They built, laboriously by hand, a golf course: 18 tees, 11 sand greens and innumerable parrots in the trees. The clubhouse became a centre for social activity, sometimes rivalling the parrot cries in rowdy exuberance.

BY THE TIME that Helgo Kahle was appointed CEO/MD of Gold Fields Ghana he had been with GFSA for about 17 years and had formed a fairly fixed idea of what the company was like.

He thought Robin Plumbridge was brilliant and had insights into the industry lacking in other mining houses. His policy of developing people by throwing them into the deep end in various disciplines was unique and effective. He realised that labour issues were as much about politics as they were about wages. But Kahle – like Van Rooyen – had a streak of the rebel in him, and he thought people in the company were being straitjacketed. Plumbridge did not seem to trust staff or give them real responsibility. 'He didn't appoint rebels at any level and executives had to keep in line,' says Kahle. 'Bernard van Rooyen was the only person who stuck his neck out but even he, ultimately, had to toe the line.'

That was why he welcomed the Ghana appointment when it came in 1996. Mine managers generally were hide-bound by the systems they had to adhere to. But in his new job he would be separated from head office, freed of some red-tape constraints, more able to do his own thing. Not completely, of course – but at least somewhat.

There was an office legend that he recalled fondly because it captured what he meant. Glynn Lewis, first Gold Fields manager at Tarkwa, was running short of explosives and phoned Van Rooyen for help. Van Rooyen promptly charted an aircraft, loaded it up with explosives and told Lewis to organise landing rights, which he did at the military airport, courtesy of Van Rooyen's old air force buddies. Production was not interrupted.

Kahle thought: That's initiative. That's the way things ought to be done.

The new CEO/MD found a mine in sound operating state but with some big problems. Somehow, the number of illegal miners had grown; as fast as one entrance was sealed, another was opened. Kahle guessed there were now 5 000 of them burrowing away. All had to be removed. Later the underground operations had to be closed for good. Somehow he managed to do it without alienating the unions or the workers. About 25 000 locals had to be relocated to enable them to work the outcrop. Anger grew and attacks on the mine became common. Slowly, over time, the tensions were defused. Relations with government had soured over how an agreed allocation of 15% to local citizens should be managed. Finally a solution was found: the shares were sold to the State National Insurance Fund for the benefit of all Ghanaians rather than a chosen few. Kahle now had to restore the lost goodwill. The company found a magic way to do it: it sponsored the national football team, the Black Stars, in a country football-mad and at a time when players were being asked to pay their own fares when gathering for international matches. It was a winning move.

Helgo Kahle took early retirement in November 1999. He was not quite 55. He stayed at Tarkwa just long enough to discover that he was not quite as free from head office as he thought he was. A new era and new bosses had come to Gold Fields.

One of those who enjoyed every moment of his time in Ghana is Peter Tuner, a man with a remarkable track record over 34 years in the mining industry. Having graduated as a mechanical engineer and finding a secure job at Anglo American, he decided that he needed practical experience of mining. So, at the age of 33, he signed on as a learner miner and began on the lowest rung, underground at the working face. He now has a mine manager's certificate.

He was general manager of the Africa region for AngloGold Ashanti when, to his own surprise, he was lured to Gold Fields in 2005 by CEO Ian Cockerill who quite soon after that resigned to return to Anglo. Until mid-2011, Turner was Gold Fields' executive vice-president, West Africa region. He left Ghana with mixed feelings, having won the respect of the local community. Today he is executive vice president responsible for all South African mines. But part of his heart will always be in Ghana.

CHAPTER THIRTEEN

Trapped – Three Kilometres Down

WAY BACK in the mists of time, the Chamber of Mines had a standard format for the press releases it produced for the mining industry in the event of underground accidents. A typical press release would begin: *Two white miners were injured and seven mineworkers killed in an accident at XXX mine yesterday. Production was not affected.*

It conveyed an unintended message of appalling callousness, but it was the way of the world at the time. White lives were more important than black lives to the predominantly white investors and newspaper readers at home and abroad. As for off-shore shareholders, they expected people to die in mines; it was part of the job. The workers should just be grateful that they had a job to die for. They would have preferred the second sentence in the announcement to be placed first so they could be aware of the really important news immediately; whether the mine would make more money or less. After that, they could turn to the page containing the stock exchange prices, where gold mining shares were recorded under the heading of 'Kaffirs'.

Over time, the insensitivity of the announcement struck home and the Chamber mended its ways. Yet it remains true that the South African public seems to be inured to run-of-the-mill mine tragedies just as it is inured to run-of-the-mill road deaths. For the most part, it's a case of 'accidents happen – get on with it!' But, of course, that has never been the case on the mines themselves, where an unexpected paradox occurs.

Traditionally, and until recently, the spirit of apartheid thrived on the surface, as it did in law and in practice in the country itself. White and black miners were housed separately, lived separate lives, travelled underground in separate compartments, whites on top, and were represented by separate unions. The Mine Workers' Union was resolutely white and right wing, providing a spiritual home for, among others, ardent white supremacists. NUM was equally resolutely black and political. A combination of those factors created an explosive formula for tension above and below ground.

Add to that the language problem. To communicate at all, since most black workers were rural and tribal and spoke various Bantu languages, the industry was forced to create a language called 'Fanagalo'. Learning and speaking it at work was compulsory for all recruits. But communication has political nuances too. In the melting pot that is South Africa, all tongues have a variety of words to convey respect without subservience for an elder or a superior. In Fanagalo, the word chosen for blacks to convey their respect for all white miners was 'Baas'.

Herein lies the paradox. A sudden and unexpected alchemy occurs when men go underground. Historical prejudices don't necessarily disappear but they become overlaid by something else: a sense of mutual dependence perhaps; of dangers shared. When accidents happen there is no time to establish a man's colour, nor any desire to. When things go wrong underground – a rockfall, a faulty blast, a slip, a malfunctioning machine – there is no way to know for sure the extent of the problem. Is the danger over, or is worse to come? Two or three kilometres underground, there is no easy way to flee or to seek immediate outside help. There is only one first line of defence: your fellow-workers. And when the specially trained Proto teams arrive on the scene they ask only one question. It is not: what colour are you? It is: who most needs help?

This simple reality leads to extraordinary acts of colour-blind courage. Whites unhesitatingly risk their lives to save blacks – and vice versa. They plunge into situations where the slightest nudge can precipitate a new crisis, or worse. And when it comes to treatment and rescue, priorities are set by need and not by colour. It is part of this tradition that dictates that supervisors, invariably white in the old days, come out last after an accident – unless they require urgent treatment.

The only thing that doesn't happen is that both sides, when they return to the surface, join each other to relive the triumph over a beer. That would be carrying tolerance and compassion too far.

Mining is a dangerous business. Happy endings after an underground event are rare. One death or many, it casts a pall over the entire community in the village that is a mine. But sometimes, just sometimes, a serious accident can lead to a cause for jubilation.

Such an event happened at Kloof Gold Mine, No 3 Subvertical Shaft at exactly 11.45 am on Wednesday, 13 October 1993.

IT WAS a day like any other on a mine; an early spring day under clear skies. There was the usual subdued babble of early-morning voices as about 3 000 men prepared to go underground for the morning shift. Of them, 150 miners, black and white, were scheduled to go to Level 43, the lowest operating level. They would spend their seven-hour working day in a man-made cavern nearly three and a half kilometres beneath the earth's surface in one of the deepest mines in the world. It didn't faze them unduly. They were used to it.

They knew their workplace would be kept tolerably comfortable by chilled water. Before Northam, Kloof was in the forefront of experiments with hydropower. Tons of water driven by gravity through steel pipes under immense pressure powered the tools they used to clear the working face and dislodge the cracked ore. That same water was used to create a tolerable working environment at a depth where rock temperatures could be anything up to 65 degrees Centigrade. A man's blood has been known to boil – literally – when air cooling has failed.

Using water for both power and cooling was a simple, ingenious combination of uses that had yet to come to most mines and was considered experimental. In the safety lectures that were a part of their lives, Kloof employees were warned that, if an uncontrolled burst occurred at a weak point, the resultant spurt of water could cut a man in half. They were protected by a series of valves that would reduce the pressure in such circumstances, but they should be careful anyway. Nobody had ever pretended that mining was the safest occupation.

At 11.45 am, something – a seismic shudder perhaps? – dislodged the steel piping that carried the chilled water down No 3 Sub-vertical Shaft. About 260 metres came loose; 23 tons of deadweight metal smashing everything in its path, tearing and crumpling the steel infrastructure until it lodged somewhere just above 27 level, creating a formidable obstruction. In an instant, services fed from the shaft were cut too. Lights went out, communications died and air-conditioning stopped. Only the glimmer of helmet lights pierced the damp and inky blackness.

The shaft itself was impassable. Save for a single conveyance on the surface, all others had been jammed where they stood. Nothing could move up or down. It was the kind of emergency mining men dread – and it initiated a rescue operation without parallel in South African mining history.

WEDNESDAY AFTERNOONS were golf afternoons for the mine management at Kloof. They had a mashie course on the property and the regular weekly games were introduced by manager Mike Eksteen, who believed they helped to breed team spirit. They had just reached the first tee when the news arrived. There had been a bad accident; no details. Golf forgotten, they raced back to No 3 shaft. Things looked serious. Eksteen immediately set up an operations centre in the mine offices and assigned his senior assistants to specific tasks. From there, proto teams and auxiliary medical staff were assembled and plans laid to get the 3 000 workers out of the mine. But, like the trapped men beneath them, they were working in their own kind of darkness. They had no idea yet what had happened; how bad it was down there. Could it get worse?

'We had to draw on our experience, our knowledge,' remembers Eksteen. 'Decisions had to be taken at speed. There was no time for second thoughts. Only for prayer – and action.'

Chief safety officer Daryn Brown stationed himself at the top of the shaft, ready to record the name of each miner as he returned to the surface. That way they would know who was still trapped. He would not see his home or his bed again until the Thursday evening, and then only for a short time. He remembers the frustration. He wanted to help more but there was nothing that could be done from the surface. The real drama was in another world far beneath their feet.

IT IS part of the ethos of mining in South Africa that, when disaster threatens, human lives are more important than profits, hard as it sometimes is for shareholders to accept that. In the front line, always, are the proto teams – almost legendary heroes of any mine rescue. Specially trained, they go anywhere, do anything, face any risk when fellow-miners are in trouble. Time and again, they achieve almost miraculous rescues.

As ever, other mines, some as far away as the Free State, quickly offered manpower and support. Before long, more than 200 emergency helpers had been assembled. They would go underground as far as they could to create a rescue staging post. They didn't stop to consider the risk. One of the first to be called in was Dr Pete Lowe, chief mine medical officer and a man noted for his courage underground. He was always among the first to go underground after any accident. There was never any time to consider whether it was safe or not. Once he was sent to help a trapped miner and found the man lying under a pile of rocks and stones. He couldn't even begin treatment until he had manhandled the rubble out of the way. On another occasion the call was so urgent that he had no time to change into mining gear and had to go underground in a business suit. He recalls:

> In the old days victims were put on stretchers and taken to hospital, by which time many of them had died. By treating people on the spot in the first hour after an accident, hundreds of lives were saved. Our nurses were taught to do what any junior doctor can do. It was our first line of defence. I think Gold Fields was the first company to promote immediate treatment at the site of the accident.

On this fraught day Dr Lowe's first task was to see whether the trapped men had air and water. Fortunately, the jumble of collapsed piping allowed for air to enter and offered a tiny passageway for water. But it was apparent to him that the 23 tons of steel, precariously balanced, might collapse at any moment.

MOST of the men on the morning shift that day were lucky. They were the ones who had been assigned to work at levels above the obstruction in No 3 Shaft. Alternative routes were available – if only they knew how to find them. Even for experienced miners, much of the long and intricate maze of underground tunnels is alien, unknown. Their escape routes had to be plotted on maps on the surface, and then conveyed to them despite the loss of phones and power in some areas. These routes might be up to 9km long, and would take them through hot, dark, unfamiliar corridors. It would be an exhausting and nerve-wracking experience, trudging through darkness for kilometres, climbing inclines, negotiating broken rock, turning back on themselves in switchback patterns. But at least it would take them, eventually, to the surface and blessed sunlight. If they followed the maps correctly.

For the 150 men caught at levels below the obstruction in No 3 Shaft, there was no such option. Gradually it became clear – to those above and to those below – that their path was hopelessly blocked. It would be a major exercise to clear it, and might take weeks. There didn't seem to be an alternative escape route. At first the trapped men didn't even know whether anyone knew where they were. For 24 long hours there was no contact from outside their tomb; no word of encouragement or hope; no sound of activity. Extraordinarily, there was no panic. 'They kept calm,' says Eksteen. 'They were always convinced they would be rescued.'

But how?

Painfully slowly, the outline of a plan began to emerge. If a rescuer could be lowered through the tangle of steel in the shaft, he could look for a gap, possibly assess whether something smaller than a conventional hoist could be used to bring the trapped men out – a bosun's chair, or even a mountaineer's abseiling equipment. He might even get close enough to reassure the trapped men that they had not been forgotten, that rescue was at hand. Most important, he might pioneer a route to get food, water and medical supplies to the trapped men.

Derek Rautenbach, a proto member, volunteered to be the first to try to make contact. He didn't allow himself to think of the danger. Sitting in a makeshift bosun's chair, he agreed to be lowered with a simple block and tackle into the black void beneath the obstruction in the shaft. Looking up, he could see how precariously the tangled steel was perched, how easily dislodged it might be by a sudden shudder of the earth or even a movement in its own weight. Looking down he could see

... little or nothing. The journey into darkness was 270m, the equivalent in distance to being lowered from the top of the Carlton Centre, with the added dimension that he couldn't be certain of what lay ahead, had no way of knowing whether he could be hauled back to safety if things went wrong and had to proceed by the single light of his helmet torch. A slight shift in the fiddlestick jumble of metal above and around him and the access passage he was pioneering as he dropped could be closed; his route back to safety barred.

Miraculously, he reached the trapped men and was greeted with a cheer. There was a way through; a way to get food and drink and medical supplies down and, perhaps, a way to bring the men to the half-way station; slowly, a single victim at a time. It would take days, maybe weeks, of round-the-clock work – if nothing went wrong. Did they have that kind of time?

Realisation dawned: there was a new threat – and a new urgency. With the mine largely disabled, pumping had stopped. There was nothing to prevent water flooding back into the lower levels. How long would it be before the trapped miners would drown?

On Thursday 14 October the rescue began. It was not as simple as it sounded. The journey up was a scary affair. Some of the trapped men needed coaxing and comforting, their nerves already shattered by the experience. It took an hour to bring the first victim to the half-way station where nurses and paramedics could help prepare him for the 9-km hike through tunnels and inclines to the surface. One hundred and forty nine men to go ...

On Friday someone had a bright idea. The block and tackle was too laborious. What about sky-jacks – those powerful little machines that are used by window cleaners on tall buildings? They were sturdy enough to haul two miners at a time and compact enough to operate in the restricted space available. Soon afterwards, four sky-jacks had been located and brought to the mine.

The miners had been trapped for three days and nights now. Though their confidence in ultimate rescue seemed unshaken, they were feeling the physical effects of entombment. They needed food, water and basic medical supplies.

Could men trapped underground really remain calm in such

circumstances? 'Yes,' says chief safety officer Brown:

> Their supervisors were trained to keep people calm, and they were highly respected. They convinced the trapped miners that they would be saved; they just had to keep their cool. They would not be left totally in the dark. They explained how everyone would turn off their helmet light, leaving only one burning. When that faded, another would be turned on. Darkness would be kept at bay. The important thing to remember was that their plight was known – and that being so, rescue was certain.

Brown was still at his post, recording names, when the last man emerged. He had seen no sign of panic on any of the faces of the rescued. Their implicit faith had been justified.

ON THE third day a two-man cage was created and the rate of rescue doubled. By Sunday, the fourth day since the accident, the rescue rate had trebled – to three an hour. In the darkness, with the single helmet light, time lost its meaning. The trapped men thought it must be Sunday by now. Or even Monday. In strict priority, dictated by need, the men were selected for rescue. As each bedraggled miner was brought to the staging post, he was met by paramedics and first-aid workers and given immediate treatment for shock, dehydration and exhaustion. Only then did they make their 9-km way to the surface.

Many of the rescuers had remained underground for hours on end, day after day, and were near exhaustion themselves. But each new face that appeared out of the void that was No 3 Shaft helped to lift their spirits. Even then, there was uncertainty. Could they rescue everyone? Before the water rose?

In the event, they succeeded. To the joy of those who had been following the drama, and who saw the hours and days tick by relentlessly, every single trapped miner was brought out alive. The last men emerged, blinking into the sunlight, at four o'clock on Tuesday afternoon, 19 October, to be hugged by their anxious wives. For the record, all the women would say, several times: *'Ons is baie bly, so baie bly.'* (We are glad, so very glad.) Their husbands had not seen the sun for six frightening days.

There is an ironic footnote. The entire operation had only one fatality, and that had nothing to do with the accident. One working miner had a heart attack and died underground. His mates said he was suffering from a terrible *babalaas*.

THE RESCUE drama apart, mine manager Eksteen had his private dramas to contend with. As was standing operating procedure in those days, news of the accident was followed immediately and instinctively by a barricade against the media. Until management knew what it was dealing with, it didn't want reporters snooping around.

Eksteen didn't want to make any public statements until he could offer real information. Alan Munro, chairman of the mine, spent hours pondering whether a proposed press statement would describe the missing miners as 'trapped' or 'awaiting rescue'. Awaiting rescue won the day. The media were sharply critical of the slowness of communications. Something bad had happened at Kloof, TV 3 reported, but the mine was covering it up with a blanket of silence. Finally, enough information had been gathered and the media conferences started. It all added to the pressure.

Wright was CEO at the time. He thinks the real heroes were unsung. He says: 'Head office consultants were the main driving force behind the rescue. They used their vast experience to direct operations. It was a world-beating rescue effort.'

It was also a lifetime tribute to the common decency and human concern that could transcend prejudices when the chips were down.

CHAPTER FOURTEEN

SOMETHING GOING WRONG

IT WAS a situation designed to fray the nerves of any CEO, even one as composed and in control as Plumbridge. Slowly, almost imperceptibly, Gold Fields began to crumble at the edges as the turbulent Nineties took hold. Not, of course, that it was in danger of collapse; the Group was far too secure for that. It was just that some things seemed to go awry more times than they used to.

It was easy to identify the external problems: pressures imposed by a stubbornly static gold price, inflation-driven costs, ageing mines and labour turmoil were unrelenting. Add to that a couple of sometimes dissatisfied major shareholders who weren't afraid to express their feelings and you had a formula for extreme stress in a chief executive. Not that Plumbridge showed it to his senior colleagues; he was not a man given to displaying emotion. 'He worked behind a closed door,' says Peter Janisch, a one-time senior executive director. 'Who knows what he was going through in the privacy of his office?' But no, he wasn't aware of any sense of strain in day-to-day business interactions. Except once, when the mask slipped for a moment. Recalls Janisch:

> I went with him on a routine visit to Rembrandt headquarters to brief the Ruperts. As ever, it was a bruising encounter with Johann. Robin was pretty tough-minded himself but those who challenge Rupert usually end up losing. Afterwards, in the car going to the airport, for almost the first time he didn't seem himself. He made it obvious that he hadn't enjoyed the visit. I remember thinking that I hadn't seen him that vulnerable before.

Alan Wright, deputy chairman of the company and an executive director, didn't notice any particular signs of strain. Yes, Plumbridge would come into the office, go up in the express executive lift, sit with the door closed. If he walked down the corridor, he tended to be engrossed in his own thoughts; not greeting anyone. But then he was always like that; no change there. 'In any case, he was away a lot, I didn't see all that much of him,' said Wright. There was the World Gold Council and the overseas directorships and the important contacts.

'If he's talking about the time when I was a reluctant chairman – perhaps,' says Plumbridge. 'But as CEO I had regular contact with Alan.'

Johann Rupert was heard to utter an exasperated cry one day: 'Robin keeps rolling these boulders in my way …' It was a comment that was doubly revealing. On the one hand, it showed that Rupert was losing patience despite his high personal regard for Plumbridge. In an interview in 2008 he explained his feelings: 'I both liked and respected Robin. But ten years is probably the limit in this type of job. Robin was tired. External problems made it a tough job.'

In a more general context, Rupert offered another insight that seemed to be a commentary on Gold Fields itself: 'Structures can become inflexible in large companies which are highly regimented. People are steeped in the company's traditions and ways. Promotions tend to come from within. Systems become entrenched.' It seemed an obvious reference to the 'boulders' he felt he was encountering.

But the second implication in Rupert's quote was perhaps the more significant. It implied that Plumbridge was resisting change – or, at least, the kind of change Rupert wanted. That would not be surprising. Plumbridge was single-mindedly devoted to Gold Fields. It provided him with his first job, and gave him his last. He had been CEO and chairman for years. He had unrivalled experience of every aspect of mining and was widely acknowledged as an authority on gold. He had twice been President of the Chamber of Mines and had pioneered the marketing of pure gold coins, a money-spinner. Generally, his career had been a sparkling success. To the public at large he was Mr Gold Fields.

He had fixed ideas and seldom had occasion to doubt them or himself. As the undisputed mastermind of the company's fortunes his edicts were seldom challenged even by his board, let alone his subordinates.

Alan Munro, former executive director, described it like this: 'In my day the boss was the boss. You expected him to call the shots. That's what he was paid for. There was none of this nonsense about the boss being your buddy or your mate. He gave the orders. I liked it that way.'

It would have been surprising indeed if Plumbridge had meekly accepted advice, let alone instructions, from a man who freely admitted that he knew little about mining and whose field of expertise was in consumer goods and market branding.

So what went wrong?

SOME PRESSURES were common to the industry, the country and sometimes even the world. The global economy was in a mess. For the first five years of the Nineties almost every major industrialised country was struggling to emerge from recession. In 1992, making his chairman's statement, Plumbridge painted a bleak picture of his universe as he saw it:

> It is painfully clear that those countries which have failed to harmonise fiscal and monetary policies are paying a heavy price and it is even more worrying that certain countries are being severely hurt by the policies of a dominant neighbour. Overall, there is deep concern that the economic policies pursued by many countries in recent years have been so mismanaged that the very fabric of the modern world economic order may well be threatened.

The laissez-faire fiscal policies of the Eighties had finally caught up with the United States, he said. Its economy was still bedevilled by fiscal excesses: 'It is difficult to foresee any improvement until the new administration takes the reins.' The Japanese economy had faltered dramatically, and asset deflation on a massive scale threatened the stability of the banking system. Germany had failed to assess the cost of reunification and had probably one of the most distorted economic policies with fiscal laxity being counterbalanced by stringent monetary policy. The commitment of other nations to the European Monetary System meant currencies had been dramatically strengthened against the dollar

irrespective of their own fundamentals. It remained to be seen whether the linkages being created would survive the next year. Britain was 'almost powerless' to reverse the chronic recession pervading the country
As for South Africa, well ...

> The economy clearly has been unable to isolate itself from international economic events. In addition the overlay of an unstable political and social environment has seriously eroded confidence with the result that the country languishes in the depths of its worst recession in living memory. Regrettably, attempts to bring fiscal policy under control have failed dismally.

Inflation remained high and, worse still, the central statistical service was having great difficulty in monitoring what was happening. The official Consumer Price Index and Producer Price Index had deviated by 10% over the last two years. A tendency had emerged where analysts would select the set of facts that best suited their preconceived argument. 'Clearly there is an urgent need for the South African authorities to make a clear-cut judgment on the factors that should be used,' he argued. 'The present policies, which are exacerbating the depth of the depression, cannot continue as the level of unemployment has now reached the stage where social unrest has become endemic.' Those who argued that an interim political settlement would solve the problem were forgetting a fundamental fact: A society with excess unemployment will always be unstable.

It was imperative that political players 'face up to the economic disaster which will occur if they do not set aside their differences to establish a forward-looking economic policy. It is a sad commentary on the state of South Africa's economic policies that the country which once had some of the most far-sighted mining policies is now largely uncompetitive with the emerging nations.'

Sharp words indeed from a man who claimed to be 'apolitical'.

FOR MUCH of the Nineties, Gold Fields came under fire from the media. There was a knee-jerk tendency to refer to the group as 'ailing' even when there was no apparent reason for doing so. It was criticised for its labour policies because it stood fast against union demands for higher wages without the quid pro quo of better productivity. Actually, the company was often much better and certainly no worse than its competitors. Of course, it wasn't perfect and there were things to criticise. But much of the newspaper comment was snide, like this throw-away line from *Business Times*, in the *Sunday Times*: 'A weak third quarter performance compounded by some bungled handling of mine labour disputes confirmed Gold Fields' pre-eminence as the whipping boy of the industry.' Most of the industry had a weak third-quarter, and were experiencing labour problems. How does a CEO handle the insidious effect of low-level disparagement? Denials merely re-emphasise the criticisms. Caution suggests that the victim grins and bears it. But silence is read as assent. It's a lose-lose situation.

In the midst of this, Gold Fields experienced its own version of social instability: murder in the hostels. And was rewarded with still more criticism.

Over three months in the mid-Nineties, on three Gold Fields mines, 48 workers died in ethnic conflicts. A judicial commission of inquiry headed by Judge John Myburgh found that ethnically segregated hostels were a root cause. Evidence was that the killers would demand that potential victims show their clock-cards because these identified their ethnic origins. If they turned out to belong to the wrong group, they were killed. Senior Gold Fields spokesmen seemed surprised that the clock-cards provided this information. Mike Eksteen, then manager of Northam, said he wasn't aware of it – if it was so, he agreed, it ought to be changed. Alan Munro, executive director, promised that he would 'personally oversee' that the system would be reformed. Neither seemed to know why it was there in the first place.

Not long afterwards, Anglo experienced a similar ethnic outbreak. It recorded 65 deaths.

A YEAR LATER, in 1993, Plumbridge's tone remained sombre. 'The prolonged weakness in world economic conditions since the beginning of this decade has had an unusually adverse effect upon nearly all commodity prices, many of which have been depressed to below those prevailing in real terms in the Great Depression of the 1930s.'

In South Africa, the move towards democracy continued to be slow, painful and racked with violence. The economy had now been 'in the depths of depression' for four years. Underlying circumstances had created an extremely difficult environment for the Group and its companies. The new ANC administration, when it achieved power, would have to come to grips with the reality that the country had been living beyond its means for years, which meant that the 'exaggerated expectations of certain sections of the population' could not be fulfilled in the short term. Or at all, unless it allowed the private sector to operate in an open economy.

He concluded with a wan optimism that was, presumably, designed to sugar the pill; a message even more pointed today than it was nearly 20 years ago, when the debate on 'decent work' had not even begun.

It started with a simple SWOTS analysis. South Africa had distinct strengths: a sophisticated infrastructure and professional managers. Its significant weakness was a labour force largely unstructured and unskilled, with a low work ethic and a high wage expectation. However:

> I do not subscribe to the view that the position is hopeless because the peoples of South Africa, despite all the painful experiences of history, have a remarkable desire to succeed. It is the over-riding desire of the great majority of unemployed people to be given the opportunity to obtain employment, albeit at a humble wage which is well below that demanded by the trade union movement.

But even that blunt view was softened by the offer of a quid pro quo. The private sector had a responsibility too. Every employer should seek to develop 'the remarkable capacity' of the potential workforce to respond to training. That would be their greatest contribution to developing the economy.

AS IF TO applaud South Africa's political transformation, 1994 showed signs of economic improvement. After the tense years of negotiation and setback, the mood of the vast majority had been lifted by the first democratic election and the foregone conclusion of the ANC in power. For a few hard-line whites, it was disaster. But for most of the country's former top dogs, the mood had shifted from apprehension and near-panic to acquiescence and even joy. They stopped hoarding cans of food in anticipation of chaos. They discovered that Nelson Mandela was a natural leader with a genuine commitment to non-racial democracy. They thought they could live under black rule. Some felt a lifting of the guilt that they had imposed on themselves over apartheid.

The white community, by and large, emerged blinking into the sunshine of the euphoria that swept South Africa. Archbishop Desmond Tutu, ever the optimist, christened this new political creature 'The Rainbow Nation'. And, for a while, it seemed to be just that.

Plumbridge had still more good news for his shareholders. Global economic conditions had improved. International sanctions were falling away. South Africans could travel the world again. He reported: 'After the pressure that had been placed upon the Group's operations by the prolonged recession, the 23% recovery in earnings underlines the resilience of the Group's primary gold investments.'

The domestic economy had clearly been impacted by the dramatic political events of the last year. Could it last? He thought it could – if the new administration addressed the many complex problems, there was reason to hope the economy could perform strongly. But he wasn't going to be swept away by overblown euphoria:

> Society needs to identify closely with the freedom concepts and distance itself from the strident rhetoric of rights and demands. Violence and crime have been stripped of their political veneer and need to be addressed. It needs to be recognised that the underlying cause of criminal activity is the massive level of unemployment. Above all, it has to be recognised that there is a pre-condition for any substantial amounts of new foreign capital and that is the elimination of the financial rand and exchange controls. There are high risks in taking the steps needed, but it is clear that the decision needs to be taken quickly and decisively.

And a final prescient warning:

If South Africa fails to recognise the importance of eliminating trade and other barriers [in Southern Africa] it will hinder the growth of all economies and accelerate the already uncontrollable influx of people into our country.

ALAS, 1994 was in some ways an Indian summer. The idyll was not going to last. By 1995 there was a new issue to be gloomy about: labour relations. The chairman's opening words in his annual review were: 'The past year has been a particularly difficult one for the mining industry …'

In his final report to shareholders as CEO, Plumbridge painted a picture of an industry in a 'turbulent and unstable state'. The relentless campaigns by unions for higher minimum wages had awakened expectations that could not be met, creating turmoil. Poor labour relations, low productivity and higher costs were threatening the industry's very existence. Many shafts and some mines were in immediate danger. There was a severe risk of significant job losses in an industry which had shed 150 000 jobs in recent years. A new Labour Relations Act was being rushed through Parliament, flaws and all. It was imperative that restrictions which prevented 24-hour operations underground were lifted quickly or it would be too late to save a significant proportion of the mining industry. Counselling HIV-positive workers was getting more and more expensive. Employees were beginning to question the presence of AIDS sufferers underground where an accident might lead to blood contamination.

There was some good news, of course. Northam had been refinanced and was looking forward to an improved financial performance. Base metals had had an excellent year. Industrial fabrication of gold had burgeoned. Tarkwa showed promise of becoming a major open-cast gold mine. But, somehow, the good news seemed to pale in the face of the problems.

THERE WERE a dozen good and obvious reasons why Gold Fields should rail against fate. It was indeed a victim of factors beyond its control in the first half of the Nineties. That fact should not be discounted. But still there seemed to be an additional something that was holding it back; something difficult to define or identify. Outsiders thought they could see it; so did some insiders. Yet there was a curious reluctance to put it into words; perhaps because it was a factor that, if identified, *would* be within its control.

But first, the external factors. Prices of all commodities had sunk to new lows and rampant inflation had bumped up costs almost monthly. Since 1986 the real price of gold had declined by about 50%, accounting for the heartfelt cry from Plumbridge in 1993: 'Gold has undergone a long, savage downturn.' Base metals like copper, zinc and lead fared not much better. So too with platinum, hovering year after year at long-term lows. South Africa – beleaguered by politics and international sanctions and internal unrest – seemed unable to get a grip on inflation. It sat stubbornly in double digits throughout the Eighties and early Nineties, rising to a massive 21% in January 1986 before settling to more manageable single figures 12 years later.

Some of the older gold mines were approaching the end of the road. Doornfontein made more losses than profits in a five-year period. Profit at Deelkraal dropped from R96-million to R46-million in a year. Libanon and Venterspost were incorporated into Kloof to rationalise costs and extend their lives. Black Mountain – a rich source of zinc, lead, copper and silver – veered erratically from loss to profit and back again. Rooiberg Tin hadn't paid a dividend in years. Gold Fields Coal was holding steady, making reasonable profits after dipping into loss in 1991.

Just operating in South Africa brought an extra dimension of risk. Plumbridge said the economy had survived political transition far more robustly than many had predicted. However, 'present economic conditions do not encourage one to believe that essential growth targets can be achieved.' 'The fast-changing environment is presenting an array of challenges ... that would daunt the most nimble of international managers.'

Change drenched the country, bemusing many, beyond the control of businessmen.

WHAT THEN was the mysterious X-factor – if indeed there was one – that seemed to exacerbate the external problems? At the risk of glibness, it could be summarised like this: Gold Fields had become a victim of its own successes. It wasn't doing anything it hadn't done reasonably successfully before, and that was the problem. What had usually worked in the past no longer seemed to work quite so well. There was a sense, for instance, that the massive changes in the country and in the very fabric of society hadn't generated corresponding changes in the company.

In short, Gold Fields was failing to adapt to the times in fundamental ways. It continued to rely too heavily on its old stalwarts, Kloof and Driefontein. And those two mines continued to fulfil their obligations. Even under adverse circumstances, Kloof made a profit of R318-million in 1992; then, with the benefit of amalgamation, pushed this figure up to R481-million in 1993; 748-million in 1994; and R575-million in 1995, Dividends rose accordingly – from 90c a share in 1991 to 190c in 1995. Driefontein Consolidated, the jewel in Gold Fields' crown, pushed profits up from the low R500-million at the start of the decade to R857-million in the middle. So, even under adverse circumstances, gold remained the mainstay of the Group.

Did this situation encourage complacency? Some hostile observers will nod knowingly. Some old hands will reject the thesis with contempt. The truth is that complacency is too harsh a word. It doesn't fit. But it does seem possible that the sturdy performance of the two golden giants, the fact that the Ghana investment was showing promise and the pleasing turn-around in base metals all contributed to a feeling in some quarters that Gold Fields was still on the right track. As it always had been, said the diehards.

THE 1995 ANNUAL report was Plumbridge's last as CEO of Gold Fields. He was stepping down at the age of 60 to become non-executive chairman. Some said he was pushed by Johann Rupert and some said no, he was just tired. All agreed: handing over the reins like that wasn't characteristic.

And indeed his successor as CEO sometimes felt that he hadn't really handed over the reins at all. However, he didn't put it in those words. In an interview much later, the successor said with heartfelt vehemence, *à propos* nothing in particular: 'A CEO becoming a chairman? I wouldn't wish it on anyone.'

TOP: Nelson Mandela creates a stir at the New York Stock Exchange. He was there to ring the bell to mark the New York listing of GFL.

BOTTOM: NYSE Chief Executive Dick Grasso meets Mandela. Three generations of Gold Fields CEOs are in the picture: Nick Holland (*extreme left*); Chris Thompson and Ian Cockerill (*extreme right*).

GFL chairman and CEO Chris Thompson: A Chinese fortune cookie foretold his future – he would go to Africa and take charge of the richest gold mine in the world.

Ian Cockerill. He was in the hot seat at the time of the hostile Harmony takeover bid – 'the toughest time of my business career.' His departure from Gold Fields occasioned speculation.

Nick Holland. Current CEO. He is determined to show his shareholders that the company not only has big dreams, but also the ability to make them come true.

LEFT: Richard Robinson, first managing director of GFL. Within months he would be replaced by Tom Dale (ABOVE).

Alan Wright. One-time CEO of GFSA and subsequently chairman of GFL. He took the fateful steps that would change the face of the company forever.

Dr Mamphela Ramphele. GFL chairperson. She wants to bring a woman's touch to the harsh mining world – and convince the country that sustainable mining has the potential to rescue previously disadvantaged South Africans from poverty.

BELOW: Thompson and Brian Gilbertson (*left*). Gilbertson employed Thompson after asking one question only: 'Why you?'

Protagonists in the Harmony battle: Bernard Swanepoel (*left*). He masterminded the hostile takeover bid. Willie Jacobsz (*top*) and Jimmy Dowsley (*below*) – key figures in the Gold Fields defence team. The battle made world headlines.

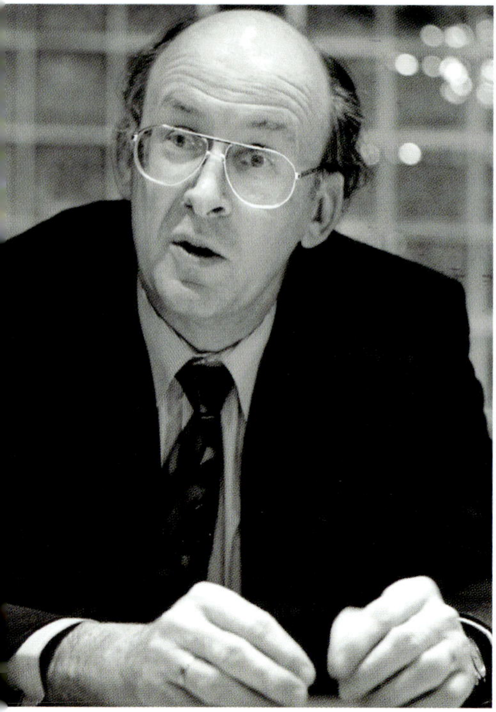

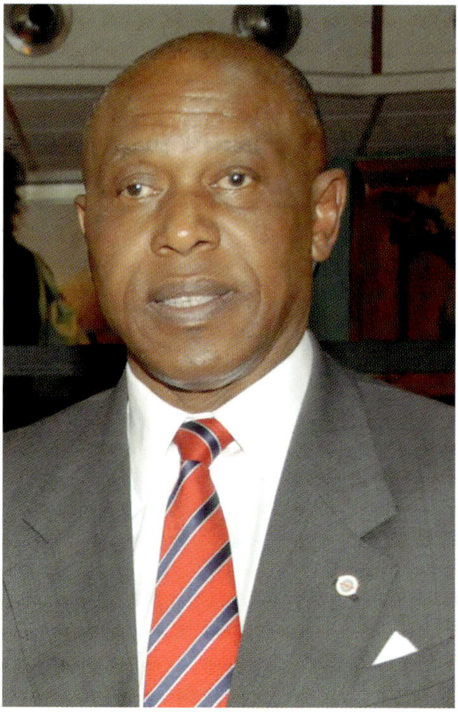

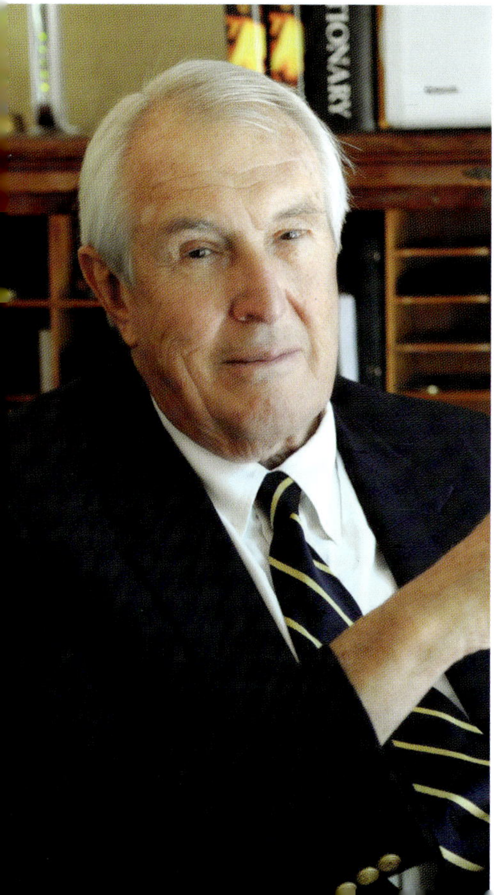
TIONARY

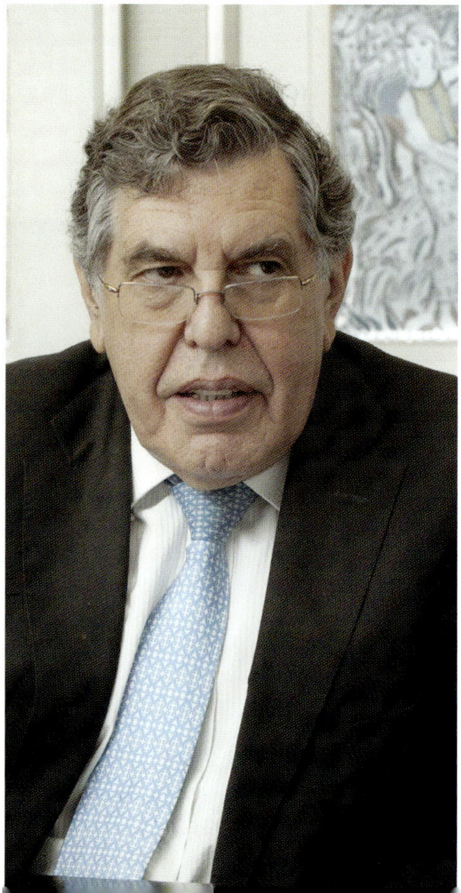

FROM LEFT TO RIGHT, TOP TO BOTTOM: Michael McMahon, director ... 'a plain-speaking kind of chap'; Tokyo Sexwale, Mvelaphanda chairman ... GFL's first BEE partner; Cecil Rhodes, co-founder who nearly destroyed his own company; Anton Rupert, shareholder ... had faith in gold. Gordon Parker, director who found the GFL board invigorating; Michael Katz, GFL counsel who masterminded the Harmony defence; Johann Rupert, shareholder ... he 'took no prisoners'; Robin Plumbridge, GFSA chairman and CEO who pioneered the sale of gold as an investment.

TOP ROW FROM LEFT: Rudolph Agnew, Consolidated Gold Fields chairman who fought off Anglo American attacks; Donald Gordon, GFSA shareholder ... grew disillusioned; Cyril Ramaphosa, union leader turned business magnate who nearly became GFL's BEE partner; Sir Michael Edwardes who launched the Minorco hostile takeover bid.

BOTTOM ROW FROM LEFT: Bernard van Rooyen, GFSA director who helped to thwart Anglo American ambitions; Harry Oppenheimer, mastermind behind the Dawn Raid on Gold Fields; Julian Ogilvie Thompson ... he promised GFSA to Oppenheimer 'for a birthday present'; Michael Young, CGF executive who organised secret talks between the ANC and Afrikaner leaders.

The Shaft at KDC East 2 (Kloof 2) mine towers over the West Rand landscape at sunset.

South Deep is South Africa's only fully mechanised deep-level gold mine. Its iconic Twin Shafts have been extensively upgraded since Gold Fields bought the mine in 2006.

Heavy machinery, such as this dumper truck, are used in the underground operations at South Deep.

LEFT: Gold bars are refined to over 99 percent fineness and stamped at the Rand Refinery in Germiston. Gold Fields is a minority shareholder in the Refinery.

BELOW: Gold pour at KDC West (Driefontein).

OPPOSITE PAGE

TOP: Headgear and plant at KDC West 1 mine.

BOTTOM: Women have only recently started working underground in the South African mining industry. They still make up only a small percentage of the underground workforce.

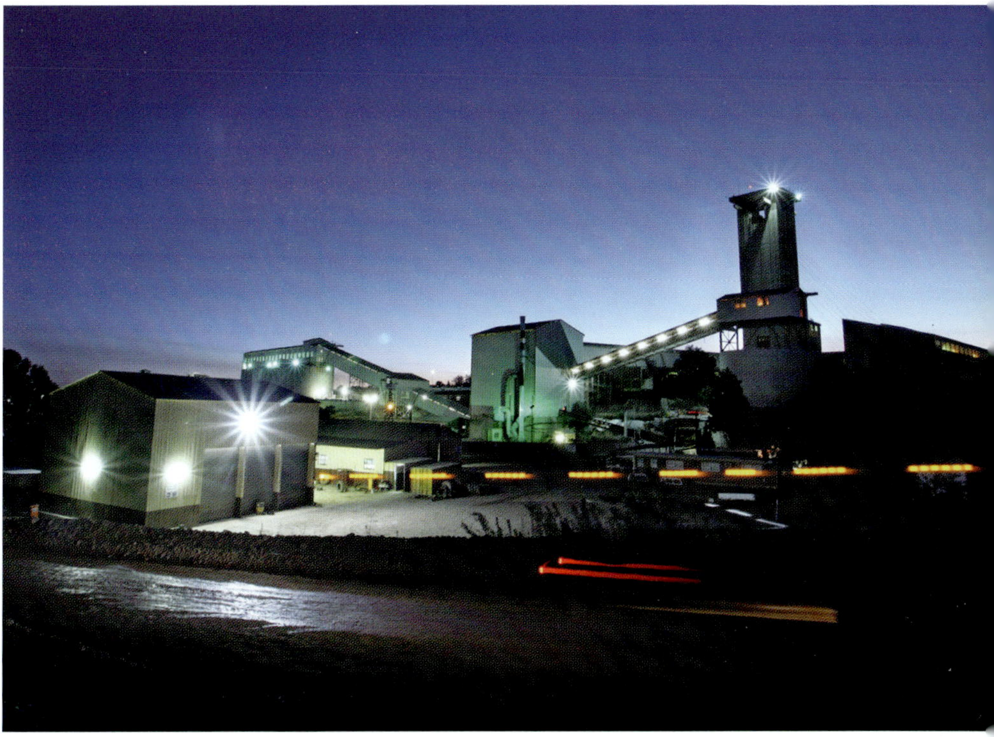

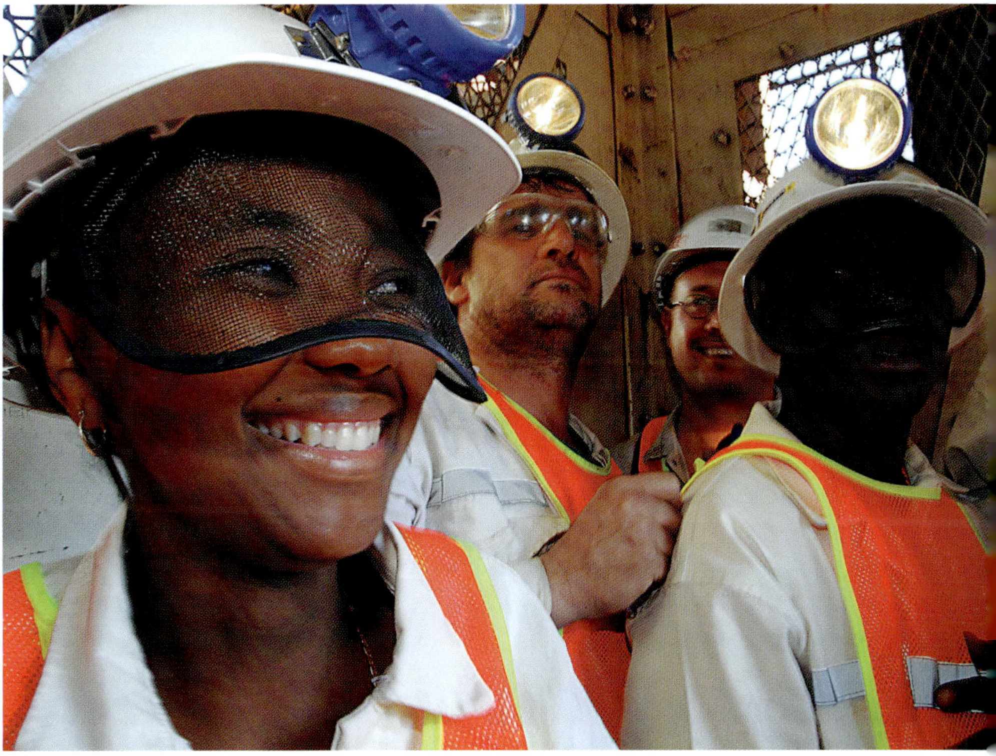

Artisans repairing equipment at underground workshops at the KDC East (Kloof) mine.

A headgear at sunset at KDC West (Driefontein).

The acquisition of the Cerro Corona mine in Peru (pictured here) in 2004 kicked off Gold Fields' extensive activity in South America.

The Lake Lefroy plant at St Ives in Australia. Gold Fields acquired the St Ives and Agnew gold mines in Australia in 2001.

The secondary crusher at the Damang mine in Ghana.

Gold Fields acquired the Tarkwa mine in Ghana in 1993. It has since been transformed into an open pit operation (*above*) and is now West Africa's largest gold mine. Continued exploration drilling activity is taking place at the mine (*below*).

As is often the case with a crucial appointment, some felt the successor was the right choice, some felt he wasn't and some preferred to wait and see. But on one point, at least, there was unanimity. Not in a million years would they have predicted that during his relatively short term of office, the new CEO would institute changes so radical and profound that some would argue later that the old Gold Fields – the real Gold Fields – had been destroyed.

For heaven's sake, the new CEO was not that kind of person. Alan John Wright was a level-headed accountant, not a wild-eyed reformer. Nevertheless, he told shareholders what he had been telling his own staff:

> It's not a matter of returning to the ways that have made Gold Fields great in the past. The ways of the past do not meet the demands of the present or the future. Change is about doing things differently. While GFSA has added R6-billion to its assets base over the last five years, recent operational performance has been poor. Management has expended enormous energy in trying to return the operations to their previous profitable levels. Despite intense efforts, the results have not been satisfactory. It is clear that fundamental transformation is required across the Group.

CHAPTER FIFTEEN

Nightmare Start

IN HIS OWN undemonstrative way, Alan Wright felt good about the world as he drove home from work on the evening of Tuesday, 28 June 1995. Though he was not given to public displays of emotion, he felt a stir of excitement. He was three days away from achieving all he ever hoped to achieve in his working life.

On Friday, 1 July, he would assume the office and the duties of chief executive officer of one of the great companies in the country, Gold Fields of South Africa Limited. The appointment was 'somewhat of a surprise' to him. He thought it might have gone to Alan Munro or Peter Janisch; or perhaps even to an outsider. But it didn't. So the first of July would mark the end of one era, the beginning of another. Wright would be taking over from a man who was almost a legend in some mining circles, the brilliant, aloof Plumbridge.

In his younger days, he had been in awe of the man. He recalls:

> I called him Mr Plumbridge until the day I joined the board. Things were fairly formal anyway in those days. But he never had what you might call an open door policy. His door was always closed. If you wanted to see him you spoke to Pam Steyn, who was his secretary. Maybe you saw him that day, maybe you didn't. But you would start at the door and you would go in and you made sure you were wearing a jacket and tie.

He made a silent resolution for himself as he approached the day when he took over the running of this internationally known conglomerate: his door *would* be open to all. People would know that, if it was closed, it was not because he was unapproachable. It was because he had someone with him.

He felt surprisingly relaxed about becoming deputy chairman and CEO. He was not the kind of person to worry unduly about extra responsibility. Besides, he thought he had a very good idea of what the job entailed. He had been with Gold Fields for 25 years, working closely with Plumbridge for many of them. He had also been the beneficiary of the latter's rather idiosyncratic but effective form of staff development.

Plumbridge believed that mining house executives needed to have wide experience rather than narrow expertise; that they should be adaptable enough to move anywhere at short notice and use their natural intelligence to learn the new job. So, once he had identified staff members who seemed to have promise, his close lieutenants of the future, he made sure it happened. He would summon a favoured one to his office on, say, a Thursday and inform them that, on the Monday, they were moving from their comfort zone in accounts to something outlandishly different in base metals or whatever. Then he would inquire, solicitously, whether that was convenient for the chosen one. Most of the people so favoured quickly assumed that saying no without good reason might be a career-limiting move.

Nearly all of them came to believe that the diversity of experience stood them in good stead.

For Wright, the Plumbridge touch had meant a working lifetime of brisk changes. He started at Gold Fields as an accountant because he had a CA (SA) degree and had trained as an auditor. But that's not the way he ended up. Before long he was being moved from position to position, at first in the field of accountancy but subsequently in more exotic directions. He moved from the financial division to the property division and just as he was settling into that he was promoted to general manager and given responsibility for corporate finance and non-technical services. Two years later he joined Colin Fenton running precious metals operations and found himself on the boards of a number of listed gold mining companies within the group, and chairman of some of them. When he was appointed deputy chairman in 1994, he took over human resources.

So, yes, he was comfortable with change. In fact he quite enjoyed making a mockery of the stereotype of an accountant. He also learnt a little lesson on his own account. As a head office representative, and sometimes a board member, he felt obliged to attend mine social functions from time to time. This is not a duty for sissies: 'As a guest, you did not pour your own drinks. Mining hosts tend to drink brandy – and they have a heavy hand. After a while, I learnt it was safer to ask for a beer instead. To this day, that's all I drink.'

But for tonight he was just a husband and a father hurrying home for dinner with the family – something he made a point of doing if he could. He tried never to take work home if he could avoid it. He wondered idly whether that sort of indulgence would continue to be possible in his new role. Then he put it out of his mind. There were better things to think about.

It was well after 6 pm and wintry dark already. There were no electronic gates at the entrance to his house in Sandton. He turned into the drive and drove directly into the garage. Then he got out and walked to the boot, where he had put his bag. 'You don't travel with your bag in the car in Johannesburg,' he says. 'As I opened the bag I was suddenly surrounded by three men. It was very swift. One of them grabbed my arms and pulled them behind me.' They wore no masks; made no attempt to hide their identity.

'Where's your gun?' demanded one.

'I don't own a gun,' said Wright. That's when he felt the first jarring blow to his head. It was the last thing he remembered until he regained consciousness in intensive care at Sandton Medi-Clinic.

Inside the house, his wife Barbara had decided to start serving dinner because the children were hungry. She heard the Mercedes come in and, a little later, a kind of crunching noise from the garage, as if the plastic chemical containers stacked there had become dislodged. It wasn't obtrusive enough to alarm her. A few minutes later she heard the car go out again. It seemed odd, but not disturbing. 'He's got an early-morning appointment and he's gone to fill the car,' she thought. Then she heard the door from the garage to the kitchen open and, moments later, she and the children looked up from the dining-room table to see a bloodied apparition standing on the threshold.

To this day, neither Alan Wright nor Barbara can explain how he had been able to get to his feet and stagger through the kitchen and to the dining-room door. He doesn't remember doing it. She remembers only that he kept wanting to pass out and that it seemed important to keep him conscious:

'He didn't seem to recognise any of us. He looked as though he was about to collapse at any moment. My second daughter Judy was telling him: "Just hold on, Dad. Don't pass out." I was slapping his face and ringing the panic button. Blood was gushing out of his nose and ear.'

Somehow, they got him down the passage and onto a bed. The paramedics from ADT arrived quickly. They wore blue uniforms. Wright, befuddled, thought that the hijackers had come back again and became uncontrollably angry. He had to be physically restrained. The strength felt abnormal in a man so close to coma.

In the days that followed, the neurologist, a considerate man, kept Barbara informed. Wright's skull had been cracked and his eardrum had burst. The neurologist thought that the burst eardrum was a bit of luck. 'I think it saved his sanity,' he said. It enabled the blood to escape before the pressure damaged the brain.

For several days Wright drifted in and out of consciousness. By the end of the eighth day, on Wednesday, 6 July, it was decided that he could be safely discharged. 'There are a few things you ought to know,' the neurologist told Barbara. 'He's going to get black eyes and bruises, probably in about ten days. And he will become irrationally aggressive. He will probably turn it on you, because he knows you are the one person who will stand by him, whatever happens.' And so it was.

The day after the assault Robin Plumbridge sent personal notes to senior executives to reassure them that Gold Fields would not be left rudderless:

> I have to advise you that Alan Wright was last night attacked at his home by car hijackers. He suffered head injuries and is currently in hospital where his condition is described as stable. In the circumstances I have agreed to stay on as Chief Executive Officer until Alan is fully recovered.

It took two and a half months before Wright was able to take up his new position, and then only after a battery of psychometric and other medical tests to establish his competence. Prudently, Plumbridge delayed signing the formal confirmation of his appointment until he was certain that Wright could still do the job. He also delayed the 'decent' salary increase that went with the promotion until 15 September, when Wright was safely in the CEO's chair. Wright thought that that was the unkindest cut of all.

He didn't know that fate had one more blow in store. A few weeks later Barbara went to visit her mother, and her car was hijacked too. Fortunately, she was not injured but the incident provided an unwelcome reminder. Alan Wright made a conscious decision to put all those experiences behind him. There was enough to worry about anyway.

FOR THE company as a whole, the end of the Plumbridge era brought hard times – and not because Plumbridge had gone. Of course his going left a gap, but it remains true that companies adapt to a change of bosses when they have to. What changed was more than a hierarchy; it was the whole darned world. Nothing was ever going to be the same again. Not the country, not the world of business, not mining, not gold.

The first change preceded Wright's appointment by more than a year, but the ripples it induced would last for far longer than that. The change was the coming of democracy to South Africa. Author Allister Sparks captured the extent of it aptly when he called his book *Tomorrow is another country*. Overnight almost, South Africans were living in a place so different from the one they once knew that they might have been dropped on Mars. The 'South African miracle' of 1994 was a cliché of international and local journalism: transformation without bloody revolution. A cliché that kept demonstrating its own truth.

But the fact that democracy came with relatively little bloodshed did not disguise the enormity of the change, or the paradoxical nature of its consequences. Throughout the country, it ushered in a time of joy and dismay; of rainbow moods and black clouds; of reconciliation and violence.

Of course, there had been ample forewarning. From the time President de Klerk announced in February 1990 that Nelson Mandela would be freed and the ANC unbanned, it was always evident that dramatic change was inevitable. Those likely to be most affected had years to anticipate and plan, so nothing was sprung on them. It was relatively easy to predict that, say, removing the cork of discrimination might release the tensions suppressed by the old South Africa; that labour relations would assume even greater importance and would require even greater skill and sensitivity. Plumbridge excelled at this kind of far-sighted anticipation.

It led him to take a step that surprised many of his peers and shocked some of them. He decided to talk, face to face but in secret, to the leaders of the National Union of Mineworkers. NUM had been an upstart black union in the late Seventies which became the fastest-growing union in the world in the turbulent Eighties. The secret talks, a first for the mining industry, took place in February 1994, two months before South Africa held its first democratic elections. Things moved quickly after that. By May Alan Munro, an executive director of Gold Fields, led the industry in negotiating a new agreement with NUM. It was an agreement that sounded like a handbook for the destruction of apartheid. It provided a reminder, if any were needed, that South Africa had indeed been a very strange society.

As a prelude, the agreement said that NUM would be fully recognised as the representative of black miners. Then it went on to list the other proposed changes. Freedom of speech and association would be entrenched. Employers and workers would negotiate in good faith. Harassment and brutality by mine security forces would stop. So would racial discrimination and victimisation. There would be no more ethnically divided hostels. Constructive programmes of affirmative action would be introduced. There would be no more acclimatisation procedures. Health and safety stewards would be democratically elected — and recognised. It was drastic stuff by South African standards.

Not surprisingly, it wasn't a magic wand. Strikes, stayaways and spasmodic violence continued to plague the industry. NUM accused Gold Fields bosses of devious dealing, and about 4 000 angry members marched on management at West Driefontein. Police had to be called to keep the peace. Munro thought it one of the scariest moments he had had. The crowd had turned into a mob, and angry voices had begun a throbbing refrain from which he could pick out one deep-throated, menacing word: 'Hamba! Hamba! ... Go away! ... Go away!' He would have liked nothing better than to do so.

Mysterious fires began to break out underground. No one could prove arson; few doubted that that was what it was. The sudden flare-ups were just too coincidental. The bosses accused NUM of inciting violence and unrest. In 1995, they persuaded the industrial court to stop the union from intimidating contract workers. Labour relations were at rock bottom. Given the history of mutual suspicion, the tension could not be called 'surprising'.

Something a shade more surprising occurred a few weeks after election day. An unexpected segment of the work force found a grievance that it considered serious enough to justify calling a strike. Traditionally, the white miners of Kloof – and every other mine – had enjoyed the privilege of being hoisted first to the surface at the end of a shift. It was a white man's prerogative. Now they had to take their place in a queue. This was too much for the Kloof contingent. 'Strike!' they cried. Damned democracy was delaying their return to leisure.

For most South Africans, especially the poor, the lifting of the apartheid yoke brought bliss. Big business by and large welcomed it, at least in public. The old system was not only morally indefensible; it was economically crippling. But what was less well understood is that the business establishment nonetheless found the change profoundly unsettling. Their status quo had gone; their world was about to be turned upside down.

President Nelson Mandela had been specific in reassuring business that its role in society was valued, and would be protected. But it was also true that the ANC's Freedom Charter – a document adopted nearly 40 years before and long classified by the Nationalist government as dangerously seditious – was equally specific about the desirability of nationalisation, even though it did not use the word. It said:

> We, the people of South Africa, declare for all our country and the world to know ... the national wealth of our country, the heritage of South Africans, shall be restored to the people. The mineral wealth beneath the soil, the banks and monopoly industries, shall be transferred to the ownership of the people as a whole.

Not much ambiguity there.

Ironically, the Charter had been adopted in June 1955 at a place called Kliptown, atop the reef that had given birth to the original gold rush that had led to the creation of the Gold Fields mining company.

Would the Freedom Charter commitment come back to haunt the mining industry one day? Mandela's bona fides were not the issue; it was what others, present and future, might choose to make of the Charter.

But political change was not the only thing on the minds of business leaders in those stirring days. Gold itself seemed to have lost its lustre. Towards the end of the Seventies, the gold price rose steeply to something like $500 an ounce. But for much of the Eighties it seemed marooned in the $300s while rampant inflation ensured that costs kept soaring. Although many in the industry clung to the belief that the value of gold was mysteriously embedded in the psyche of the human race, and that its price was bound to reflect this alchemy in due course, there was no scientific way to say the price rise would come next month, or even next year, which might be too late anyway.

The truth was that hardly anyone could see a silver lining, let alone a golden one.

Meanwhile, the prophets of doom kept busy. Gold was a finite resource. It didn't recreate itself and the richest vein was destined to run out in time. Besides, as mines burrowed ever deeper into the earth, the cost of recovering gold mounted inexorably. They took the 1993 statement by Plumbridge that 'gold has undergone a long, savage downturn' and embroidered it into a litany of woe for the industry. Four years later, as national gold production dropped to a 40-year low, Tom Main, general manager of the Chamber of Mines, told the world that gold mining was 'in terminal decline'.

That sent shock waves through the industry, partly because the Chamber of Mines was not supposed to even think that way, let alone say it out loud; and partly because it was what some in the industry were thinking anyway. In any event, the statement was literally true. From the moment that the first gold was extracted, the existing store began to deplete. Africa had once had the richest supply in the world but it was a diminishing asset – and it was being plucked from the earth at an ever-increasing rate.

It was widely believed that the last great mine in South Africa had been discovered and its name was South Deep. In those days it belonged to JCI, which the notorious Brett Kebble was just taking over. In time, South Deep would be acquired by Gold Fields.

The paradox of mining was being driven home as seldom before in its more than 100-year history in South Africa. A gold mining company had to be prepared to spend years, decades, to bring a mine to production – all the while knowing that, when at last it bore fruit, it was time to look for another because the original mine had begun its journey to extinction.

In later years, when Wright was chairman of the board, he once teased his fellow board members, some of whom were not too keen on gold mining as a business pursuit. They were debating the future of South Deep, which was chewing money and taking ages to bring into production.

'Colleagues,' he said, 'Is there anybody in this room at this moment who has any regrets that Kloof is producing gold for us?'

No, they agreed, no regrets.

He continued:

> Just bear in mind that I sat in a boardroom like this 20 years ago and we took the decision to sink No 4 shaft at Kloof. Now, 20 years later, we are getting the benefit. We are in a business where a decision you take today only comes to fruition in 15 or 20 years' time. In South Deep's case, we have been playing around with it for 10 or 15 years. Yes I know, we were going to take another six years to come to full production, but that's the nature of the business. I mean I built Northam and it took two-billion rands and seven years and a lot of resistance.
>
> But the bottom line is that you take your decision today on what costs and revenue are going to be in 15 years' time. It's very difficult. It's a culture you grow up in. Nobody comes to it fresh.

Now Northam Mine – that was another problem child of the Eighties. Wright had faith that the hugely expensive venture into platinum would

NIGHTMARE START

pay off for GFSA. So did many of his colleagues. But some board members had doubts.

If Wright had been the quittin' kind, he might have been sorely tempted to do just that. But he wasn't – and he didn't. It didn't prevent him being sorely irritated when he discovered an unexpected, and unintended, legacy from Plumbridge. For a while, he began, wryly, to wonder if perhaps he had become invisible.

Having a powerful and impressive figure at the top of a company has many advantages. Outsiders identify more easily with a human being than they do with a corporate structure. He gives an organisation a human face. The company, in turn, is often viewed through the prism of his virtues; his strengths are assumed to be the strengths of the company too. He provides easy access to the inner workings – a short cut through corporate red tape and bureaucracy. But there is one potential difficulty. For many he *becomes* the company. No other executives exist.

Plumbridge enjoyed that aspect of his job. When he visited clients and contacts overseas, he went alone. Being the first South African chairman of the World Gold Council gave him a higher profile still. Senior staff seldom, if ever, got the opportunity to get to know important contacts in the industry, or in international bodies. When Alan Wright made his first routine swing around international capitals to pick up the threads with colleagues and peers, he found to his consternation that he was a stranger to them; a rookie in their domains. He knew he would have to spend time introducing 'Team Gold Fields' to the outside world so that the company itself would never again lack an image and a presence because a single person had left it.

It was a tiny irritation in the bigger scheme of things. In any event, he hadn't been expecting an easy ride. He didn't want one; a job without challenges was hardly worth having. He never even considered the possibility that, in appointing him CEO, the board had handed him a poisoned chalice.

AT FIRST, it was no more than an uneasy feeling, a sense that something indefinable was not quite right. Of course Alan Wright would have had to be deaf and blind not to know that it was not a great time to become a new CEO. The mining industry was in turmoil. In the new South Africa, there was talk of a mining charter to create opportunities for the previously disadvantaged. No one knew how far it would go. Would it amount to nationalisation in a different guise? Mining companies were scrambling for partners because black economic empowerment was the name of the game.

Were they being asked to give away their businesses? No one was sure. Did private enterprise have a future in the industry? That was the lingering question that seemed to have no certain answer though Government reassurances were plentiful.

Gold Fields had other things to worry about too. Its mines were in decline and the exploration effort seemed to be going nowhere. For instance, Wright had no idea why the Group had bought O'okiep and Tsumeb Corporation Ltd (TCL) in Namibia. It must have been an attempt to grow the base metals operations, he thought, but they were 'lousy assets'. In any event, the TCL mines should have been closed after the 1996 strike, but political considerations came into it: the mines were too important to the Namibian economy. Now *that* strike was something else ...

CHAPTER SIXTEEN

STRIKE TO THE DEATH

TONY DE BEER, general manager of Tsumeb Corporation Ltd for six years in the Nineties, will never forget the frightening TCL strike of 1996 and its aftermath, which eventually brought a mine to its end. Today, he and his wife Bridgid can smile at some of the incidents. But not at the time.

De Beer is tall and rangy – a miner in the mould of those men who live hard and play hard and don't worry too much about the hazards and hardships of the lifestyle. He joined GFSA in 1967, became a shift boss at Kloof, moved to East Driefontein and became a mine captain, and then an underground manager before being transferred to Namibia. He was subsequently appointed General Manager of TCL.

TCL controlled three mines which produced copper, lead, zinc and other metals. The copper price had remained stubbornly low and the company made a loss of R30-million in 1995. The result: no wage increases. De Beer sensed the displeasure of the workers, argued with head office. But it was adamant. He tried to compensate by improving housing and medical services for the workers.

Before the 1996 wage negotiations started, De Beer asked head office to approve a 10% increase. Head office offered 5%, then relented and pushed it up to 7%. The workers demanded 15%, then dropped to 10%. And that's where the haggling stopped – the two parties left glaring at each other across a 3% gap.

So the Mineworkers Union of Namibia (MUN) called a strike to start at 3 pm on Thursday, 22 August 1996, but jumped the gun on its own deadline and began action four hours earlier. Groups of strikers blocked the entrances to all three mines – Tsumeb, Kombat and Otjihase – and began threatening those who were legitimately at work or on their way to work. MUN issued a triumphant statement: 'We have taken control of all mines and brought them to a complete standstill. It will remain like that until the company comes to its senses.'

The 46-day strike was almost an act of self-flagellation: vicious, brutal and prolonged. It began with high drama. Tony de Beer knew that two operations, at least, could not be stopped if the mines were to survive: the pumps that dewatered them had to be kept running, and the copper and lead smelters had to remain operational. If the smelters were allowed to cool without proper control, at best the solidifying metals would destroy them, and there would be no money to replace them. At worst, the slowly-cooling boilers could explode. Having been shut down by people who didn't know how to do it safely, a build-up of high-pressure steam could generate a lethal blast that would blow the entire production plant.

On the first day of the strike, all operations came under threat. The invading strikers, about 2 500 men at the Tsumeb Mine, made it impossible to keep the pumps going. The famous De Wet shaft at Tsumeb – which had produced 1.7-million tons of copper, 2.8-million tons of lead and nearly a million tons of zinc and silver – began slowly but surely to fill with water. At the Kombat Mine, water was pouring in at 700 cubic metres an hour.

In Tsumeb, a mob marched to the production plant, rounded up the essential-services personnel and herded most of them like cattle to the mine offices six or so kilometres away, beating them intermittently. Seventeen men were left behind, hostage to the strikers – 17 men and two ticking time-bombs in the shape of the cooling boilers.

The hours that followed were surreal. De Beer closed the mine offices and established an emergency operational centre in the recreation club. Non-strikers were advised to check in daily 'just so we would know that they were reporting for duty. Then they went home.'

> TONY DE BEER: There were a lot of guys walking around with spears, knobkerries and sjamboks. They virtually commandeered our offices. Staff couldn't get in.
>
> BRIDGID DE BEER: Our house was opposite the recreation club. I was

at the club when I heard that the striking mob had attacked the smelter staff on the forced march. I could hear ululating and shouting. Then a bakkie with security staff sped through the gates and shouted: 'Get out. They're coming. Go! Go! Go!' I had children at home and I fetched them and we ran through the orchard to the mine guest house and then on to the nurses' home. I asked the matron to open up for us. No sooner had we arrived than the power failed. It was getting dark so I took the children to the hospital, where I worked as the registrar. We took refuge there.

TONY DE BEER: A police task force came in to take control of the strikers so that our security force could man the gates again. The task force was maybe twelve guys trying to control six or seven hundred. There was just no way … There was some violence and the task force leader got hit over the head quite badly.

On the night of the first day of the strike, mine management flew 400km from Tsumeb to Windhoek to try for a court order to prevent strikers interfering with legitimate workers and thus putting both mine and town in danger. There was no time to prepare written submissions. De Beer painted a bleak picture to the court of what was happening. At Tsumeb, he said, the De Wet shaft was flooding at the rate of 400 cubic metres an hour. In the giant production plant, 'we tried our best to send in our skilled people to shut the smelter down. But we were not allowed to. Any moment there could be an explosion.'

At Kombat the invaders had shut down the pumps: 'We have four hours left and if nothing is done Kombat Mine will be flooded.' At Otjihase, strikers had switched off the power, stopping the ventilation fans. Carbon monoxide was building up: 'Our people are in that mine. It could be fatal if they are not taken out.'

De Beer told the court that he had sent urgent faxes to a MUN official asking for a meeting to set ground rules. 'He told me that he was not interested in a meeting with me.'

The court order was granted, including an instruction to the police to assist TCL in enforcing it. A police task force was mobilised but the mob – some armed with knobkerries, spears and sjamboks – attacked them until they fled, the battle cries of the strikers ringing in their ears: 'Down with TCL … Down with De Beers.' They usually called their manager 'De Beers' because they thought he must be related to the De Beers of diamond fame.

The mines at Kombat and Otjihase were also under siege. Some strikers were injured in clashes with police. And that, effectively, was the end of real police intervention for the remainder of the strike. And it was also the end of any serious attempt by strikers to comply with the court order.

DAYS BECAME weeks. Tension ebbed and flowed. Government sent a high-level delegation to see the union, telling it to get its members to lay down their arms and refrain from violence. They made it clear that government supported the strike itself. A kind of uneasy truce prevailed. Aspects of the court order were implemented. The union allowed non-striking employees back on the property and company vehicles were returned. De Beer made an effort to reopen negotiations but realised it was fruitless: 10% or nothing, replied the union.

De Beer persuaded MUN to accept mediation, but on Thursday, September 26, the talks failed and a headlong dive into anarchy began. Once again, non-strikers were barred and threatened. Mine property was vandalised and mine vehicles hijacked. TCL security officers were held hostage, locked up and denied food. Strikers intimidated shopkeepers in Tsumeb's main street into closing. Government called for an end to violence but did nothing to make it happen. Neither did the police.

By Sunday MUN admitted that it had lost control of its members. The next day – Monday, 30 September – provided proof that this was so. The strike was in its 40th day.

By this time De Beer and his core management team had been driven out of the rec club and were now holed up in the manager's house, trying to control things from there. The strikers decided that the TCL manager was the cause of their problems. Armed with the usual weapons, two bakkie-loads of strikers forced their way through the locked back gates and encircled the house.

De Beer and his colleagues slipped down the passage to the back door. It looked as though an attack was imminent. Says De Beer:

> I thought to myself, at least we're going to defend ourselves. I had a semi-automatic rifle and I grabbed it.
>
> I opened the back door and just fired over the heads of the mob. That was like the movies too. The strikers jumped into the bakkies and reversed out of the gates as fast as they could go. The police arrived and asked if I had a licence for the guns. I showed them my licences. One policeman said: 'You know, Mr de Beer, you really shouldn't be firing them in public places.'
>
> And I said: 'What would you have done, with two bakkie-loads of guys coming at you with spears and knobkerries?'
>
> He said: 'Look, I understand. But you're not allowed to fire these guns.'
>
> I said: 'But you're also not allowed to walk around with spears and knobkerries all the time.'

WHILE ALL this was going on, Bridgid de Beer was having dramas of her own at the mine hospital. She was in the pharmacy when the matron came running up to report: 'Two bakkies loaded with strikers have just driven into the hospital grounds. They're armed with traditional weapons. You can't see their faces.' The interlopers were dressed in blue overalls, mine helmets and goggles and mutton-cloth masks. Seconds later they were inside the hospital, making for the doctors' rooms. Says Bridged:

> I thought they were coming for me. I always thought I might be vulnerable because they could get at Tony through me or the children. Our home was always surrounded by them. It was like being surrounded by armed guards. Only they weren't there to protect us.
>
> On this day, one of the ladies who worked in the office said: Go into the loo. I went for a few minutes and then I thought: I can't just

sit here. I don't know what's going on. And all the other staff at the hospital, I'm responsible for them. So I came out and went to the strikers and said: 'Can I help you?' They said they had heard that the hospital computers were generating pay packets for non-strikers. They had come to disrupt the process. I didn't know that our financial manager, Jan du Plessis, had instituted the arrangement as a precaution. He was in an office at the hospital at the time but nobody knew he was there. They found out later that he had been hiding under a table.

The invaders just looked at me: expressionless, faceless, almost like aliens. I nearly freaked out. They said to me: *We're going to commandeer the mine vehicles in the hospital parking lot* and I said: *Take them.* But there was one mine bakkie for which they could not find keys. They said: *We want the keys.* I said I would try to locate them.

The police arrived but did nothing. They too just stood there expressionless.

Eventually we identified the owner of the bakkie and I phoned him and said: *I'm coming to collect your keys. Meet me at the stop street outside the hotel.* Then I told the strikers: *See that car over there. It belongs to me. I'm going to drive that car to get the bakkie keys for you. Is that okay?* They said it was okay.

As I got into the car three strikers jumped in with me: one in the front passenger seat; two in the back. I thought to myself: Oh Lord, this is the time ... One of the fellows must have seen my look. *It's all right*, he said, *we're just coming with you to see that you're safe.* I looked back and saw that one of the bakkies full of strikers was following behind us.

ON TUESDAY the Minister of Mines and Energy, Andimba Toivo ya Toivo – a man who had been a prisoner with Nelson Mandela on Robben Island – headed a government delegation to try to bring back law and order. He was accompanied by the Minister of Labour and Human Resources, Moses Garoeb, who had previously told an audience of strikers: 'The government is proud of the way you have conducted yourselves up to now, especially in the light of the extreme provocations you have had to face. The discipline you have shown has done honour to our nation.'

Later, in Windhoek, De Beer and Toivo ya Toivo discussed the wage deadlock and the Minister said: 'If you can't take the decision to go to 10%, then I need a director of Gold Fields here, or the chairman.' Says De Beer:

> I passed the message back to Gold Fields. The chairman of TCL reiterated that 7% was the offer. Mine management was told that, if head office personnel set foot in Namibia, they would be arrested and held until they agreed to raise their wage offer. It was decided that it would be unwise for anyone from Johannesburg to come to Namibia.
>
> It got to the point where everything had sort of fallen apart. How long could we sit it out? Inevitably, some non-striking guys who were reporting dutifully every day and then going home came to me and said: *We're coming up for our leave now. We want to take it.* And whether it was right or wrong, I agreed. The strikers got to hear of it and demanded that they be given leave too.
>
> By now the union had stepped aside and we were negotiating directly with the government. TCL accounted for about 5% of the country's GDP.

De Beer was summoned to meet the Prime Minister, Haike Geingob, in Windhoek. He took HR manager, Malcolm van der Mescht as part of the negotiating team. It was not a friendly encounter. No tea, no good mornings, just a formidable body of strangers staring at them – the full Cabinet and a handful of deputies. The Prime Minister was waving a document dealing with leave issues that had obviously come from De Beer's desk.

Geingob demanded: 'Why are you giving leave to white workers and not to black strikers? Everyone is entitled to leave.'

'It doesn't work like that,' said De Beer. It didn't improve his popularity rating. 'Leave can only be granted to those who are not on strike; it's not a matter of colour or race.'

The Prime Minister suggested that Gold Fields appoint a manager who was not 'such a colonialist'. De Beer made no comment. Then the Prime Minister slammed books down on his desk and said: 'I've had enough. You will give them 10%. You phone your chairman and tell him what I said.'

De Beer left the room and made a call to the chairman of Tsumeb Corporation. He told him: 'I'm sitting here in the Prime Minister's office with the Cabinet. They're angry. They say we must pay a 10% wage increase.' The chairman said he needed board approval; it couldn't be done at short notice. 'Just tell them the 7% stands,' he advised.

'Why don't you come and tell them yourself?' asked De Beer. And his boss replied: 'Because that's your job.'

By this time, De Beer knew what he had to do. He went back into the meeting and said: 'Gentlemen, I am happy to inform you that my board has agreed to the demand for 10%. Shall I go ahead and tell the workers that the strike is over and that they should report for work on Monday?'

'Fine', said the Prime Minister, 'but we'll tell the workers.'

As they were leaving the meeting, Malcolm van der Mescht said to De Beer: 'Now you've done it. You might as well just pack your bags and leave.' Back in Tsumeb, at 5 pm that afternoon, the De Beer telephone rang. It was Gold Fields Head Office. The board had agreed to a 10% increase.

THE STRIKERS were told to report to the mine offices on Monday, 7 October, so that they could be re-engaged. It was one of those blazing days that Namibians know well. The sun beat down on the men waiting in the open outside the offices. Sullenness turned to anger. A murmur began: 'Look what they are doing to us. They're treating us like cattle.' To which other voices responded: 'They've already docked six weeks' wages from us and now they make us beg for our jobs back.' The black mood ignited. According to Tony de Beer:

> There was this huge line of people trying to sign on. People were told: Come tomorrow, this is the shift you're meant to go on. This caused resentment and arguments about who was on which shift.

Suddenly the office block was surrounded. The crowd put chains on the doors and locked everything. Management and staff were held hostage.

Five minutes later my phone rang. It was Toivo ya Toivo. He was shouting: *How can you allow black people to stand in the sun while the personnel are all in air-conditioned offices?* And I said: *No, no, it isn't like that.* But the more I tried to explain the more he shouted.

In the meantime, a group of men had armed themselves and gathered at the airport as they prepared to rescue the hostages. De Beer heard about it by chance and said: 'Please don't. We're all right. Let's not start a war.' It proved a wise decision. Long after the strike, MUN told De Beer that if the rescue attempt had been made, another group was waiting in the townships to launch their own attack on the rescuers. It doesn't take much to trigger a mob, just one shot ...

The besieging mob allowed NUM representatives to enter the mine offices. They told De Beer: *You're going to have to talk to everybody.* De Beer said *Okay* and went outside:

> There were thousands of guys standing there with knobkerries, spears and other traditional weapons. They were very hostile. I was unarmed. One of my personnel guys was with me to translate. I said: *I'm sorry that you have had to wait in the sun. But I've got some good news for you. I'm giving you a week's leave, paid. You can all go home and have a week's holiday. Just come back the next Monday. There'll be no signing on or anything. Just come back for your shift.* And then they went away. I phoned the other two mines and told them they must do the same, and that was the end of the strike.

SHORTLY after De Beer was transferred from TCL, Minister of Mines Toiva ya Toivo invited him to his office. He told him: 'You see this piece of paper here? It's your work permit. I'm not granting it. You're a colonialist.'

A year later, on Friday, 17 April 1998, the new manager, JB Ayres, issued a notice to all staff. It said: 'Gold Fields Namibia has put TCL into liquidation. All assets, monies and liabilities of the company are frozen by the courts with immediate effect. The action affects all employees including management.'

About 2 000 jobs were under threat, said MUN smugly, and added: 'Today the Government is expressing their shock. We must point out that we are not shocked. [We believe] TCL/Gold Fields has since 1996 had a perfectly planned hidden agenda for the abandonment of the mines.' Government now had 'a golden opportunity to nationalise these three people's mines'. Meanwhile, the Gold Fields board ought to be locked up for sabotaging Namibia's economy.

The closure had a sequel. The Standard Bank and other creditors launched an action against Gold Fields for 'negligent trading'. A hearing took place in Sandton before Judge Mark Kumleben. Plaintiffs argued that Gold Fields had neglected its TCL property to the point where it was bound to fail. Gold Fields insisted that closure was forced upon it by falling prices, absence of ore, hassles with the smelter and metallurgical problems. And, most of all, recalcitrant unions. The case was settled out of court.

Some time afterwards De Beer was invited to a Namibian Chamber of Mines function and Prime Minister Geingob asked to speak to him. Geingob said: 'We must let bygones be bygones, Tony. We're trying to get TCL up and running again and we want you to come back and run it for us.'

De Beer thought for a moment and, knowing that the Prime Minister was keen on boxing, replied: 'A boxer has two options when he's down on the canvas. He can stay there or he can get up and fight. I'll stay down, thank you, sir!'

Soon afterwards, the BEE Company created to run TCL sold out to a British company for a nominal £1 000 000 and in December 2008 mining was suspended just as the copper price reached and held an all-time high. The suspension continues to this day.

CHAPTER SEVENTEEN

FUTURE SHOCK – NOW

> *'Change is the process by which the future invades our lives, and it is important to look at it closely, not merely from the grand perspective of history, but also from the vantage point of the living, breathing individuals who experience it.'*
>
> – *Future Shock*, Alvin Toffler

DESPITE the problems and setbacks, Gold Fields continued to be regarded by most as a rock in a cauldron of political and economic turmoil – reliable, steady, immovable. It ought to have been a comfort for its executives, but the 'immovable' was the suspect word in that trilogy. Executives were only too aware that their world and their country were changing while Gold Fields appeared to be standing still. It was a disconcerting feeling.

Under the old order everything had been simple. Decision-making was reduced to a formula: Either Robin Plumbridge approved something or it didn't seem to happen. Wright had had four months as an understudy so he had intimate experience of the process. Even after Wright assumed office, nothing much changed for a while.

'When I took over the first thing I did, I tried to lessen the formality.' It was a start – formality was all-pervasive in the hierarchy of most of the mining industry despite Bobby Godsell's valiant and somewhat dishevelled effort to change it at Anglo American. But was it enough change? And what more would Wright be allowed to do? He sometimes got the feeling that he wasn't really a chief executive at all because his old boss was still sitting above him.

'Whatever we wanted to do, well we knew we had to do it through Robin, who was now the chairman,' he said long afterwards. 'Even though I was CEO, if we wanted to spend money I had to go through the board. And I got the feeling that if what we wanted to do was not what Robin anticipated, then we weren't going to get the money.'

Had Wright but known it, Plumbridge felt much the same way himself. He too believed it was not a good idea for a former CEO to stay around to second-guess his successor. He also shared the view that executives should not be in stressful top jobs for more than a decade, at most. Indeed he had told Johann Rupert that he wanted to retire completely after relinquishing the CEO's job. But Rupert had persuaded him to stay on as chairman while other candidates were assessed. Things might have been different if Plumbridge and Wright had been able to communicate their views to each other. But they didn't.

Nevertheless, Wright set out to remove the word 'immovable' from the company's image if he could.

WHAT DOES an old mining hand do if a perky young blonde walks into his office and starts to explain to him where he is going wrong? Yes, you've guessed it: the response is unprintable.

Hiring consultants of any kind is, almost invariably, a controversial step. It becomes even trickier when the consultants operate in the airy-fairy fields of image and reputation. Such appointments are likely to be mocked by competitors and criticised by a company's own executives. Staff reaction is even more predictable. One group, younger and probably smaller, might welcome the intervention of outsiders, believing that a fresh look at old problems can do no harm and might even do good. They are not yet afraid to expose themselves to scrutiny.

The second group, usually larger and older, tends to cynicism. At its extreme are the old hands who believe, quite simply, that consultants are bullshitters. They have been doing their jobs in a particular way for decades, and what's more, the company has been successful. Why change? Clustered in the middle are the sceptics, who expect the worst but may be persuaded to revise their opinion.

The reason why the second group is usually larger is because even the prospect of change – let alone change itself – makes some people, especially older ones, feel vulnerable. Familiar routines are the bedrock on which their job comfort depends. Take the routines away and self-confidence recedes. They fear being 'found out', especially if the perceived enemy, the consultants, employ a quota of cocky youngsters.

To turn to consultants was a clear indication of the depth of anxiety at senior level about the future of Gold Fields after the departure of Plumbridge. It was not so much because of his departure but more to do with his perceived legacy: when a powerful leader goes, he often leaves behind an organisation that has become too accustomed to being dominated by one man; to not making decisions. Wright could see that the company itself had become too set in its ways, too reliant on yesterday's successes. The warning signs were everywhere: in the negative press coverage, the criticism from analysts, the low morale and defection of senior staff, the tense labour relations, even the troublesome new projects. The Group needed a shake-up. The place to start had to be with the staff itself.

But people don't change easily. Change stirs insecurities even while it invites expectations. Employees need to see evidence that the company is changing before they risk changing themselves. If initiative has been drilled out of you, if won't fly back in of its own accord just because a new door seems to be opening. People have to be certain that initiative won't earn reprisals.

Wright's first problem was to signal his own commitment to change. In December 1995 – three months after moving into the CEO's chair – the idea of a change programme was born. It happened when the executive went to Cape Town for a two-day meeting and to hear a presentation by Lowe Bell Africa, a communications company, and an eminent Scottish business school professor named Gordon Hewitt.

Hewitt was an acknowledged world authority who consulted to the top people at such companies as Barclays Bank, IBM, British American Tobacco and British Airways. He was the author of a standard text book called *Economics of the Market*, as well as numerous papers on business strategy. He had clients in major countries round the world. On top of that, he had represented Scotland as an amateur golfer. He was the complete all-rounder. He made a powerful impression.

As the presentation proceeded, the idea began to crystallise. It was all very well talking airily about change – but what, precisely, needed to change? And who should make it happen? To find the answers, a first step had to be an independent audit of external and internal attitudes to the company. That, Wright now believed, would kill three birds with a single stone. It would convince staff that he was serious about transforming the company. It would help to change internal mindsets. And it would surely point the way to what should change – and what should be treasured.

Lowe Bell Africa began work in January 1996 and completed its audit in April. Its conclusions were blunt:

> We asked employees at all levels from the executive to new graduates, at head office and on the mines, what they thought of the company and its business – its image and operations, its policies and values, its strategy and future direction. We listened also to external audiences and their perceptions of the company. The [audit findings] point to an organisation facing a myriad of challenges which reach well beyond the way in which the company communicates. They speak to issues of leadership and strategy, of structure and management style.
>
> The message was clear: Gold Fields will not change its image materially unless it changes the organisation. However, Gold Fields is in a very strong position. Unlike others who attempt a process of change in the face of fierce resistance, the organisation is ready for change and will welcome it.

There's something that doesn't ring quite true about that final sentence; a suggestion of PR hype. It is certainly true that the staff were ready for change, if change meant abandoning the old ways, which had sometimes led to frustration. But being agin' the old doesn't necessarily mean that you support the new, whatever it is.

As the consultants themselves confirmed in their first report: 'If the balance of comment appears predominantly negative, it is because interviews of this kind are always used as an opportunity to air concerns.'

In other words, give discontented staff members a chance to speak freely without any risk of being identified, and out will come the stored grievances of a working lifetime, not all of them valid. Do the negatives add up to a workable formula for a new beginning? True, the audit report insisted that 'the positive features of the Gold Fields organisation were consistently asserted at all levels'. But that could mean anything or nothing.

So what value to attach to the criticisms?

All the comments quoted in the report are anonymous. It is almost impossible to judge whether they are considered views or knee-jerk reactions, vindictive or well-meaning, justified or maliciously distorted. Some are remarkably personal, even offensively so. Plumbridge is criticised for being aloof, distant, dictatorial. Said one interviewee: 'I prepared a proposal for six months and booked a 15-minute meeting with Plumbridge. He gave me one minute and said no.' He didn't say whether that was because Plumbridge thought more quickly than him.

There are a number of spontaneous acknowledgments of his intellectual brilliance but few, if any, references to his successful leadership in the Eighties and early Nineties – a clear sign that staff were more conscious of the here-and-now and less inclined to remember past glories. That is the inevitable fate of anyone who is deemed to have stayed in the job too long.

In one sense, it is unfair to dwell on the criticisms without entering into a debate as to whether they are justified. But such a debate would be fruitless. A mere polemic.

One reality remains: when negative views are as prevalent as they appear to be in this case, a widespread perception exists, warranted or not. And perception, as everyone knows, is reality. It is necessary for this book to convey the perception, the mood, in Gold Fields and outside at the time, because it has a bearing on what is to come in the near future: change so radical as to persuade some observers that it marked the end of Gold Fields as they knew it.

Staff opinions of Wright, the successor, were more cautious. On the revised principle of 'better the devil you *don't* know', a number welcomed the appointment. But a common theme seemed to be that, with Plumbridge as chairman in a next-door office, Wright might not have the weight – or the wish – to do what was necessary. Expectations ranged from the hopeful to the cynical. 'Everyone is looking to Alan Wright with bated breath,' said one enthusiast. And a loyalist hedged his (or her) bet thus: 'Alan Wright is open to suggestions. But not to bad ideas and bad advice.'

Said another: 'Alan has a real opportunity to make fundamental changes – everyone's waiting for something to happen but so far the jury's out.' 'A few superficial things have changed,' said a fourth, 'but it's basically still the same company. He's missed a great opportunity to create a strong first impression.'

It seems a somewhat hasty judgment on someone with only three or so months in the job. But it did emphasise that the new boss was not going to be given a free ride. The staff were ready to stand in judgment on him.

Out of this whirlpool of ideas, suggestions, criticisms and carping was to emerge a company-wide project designed to give effect to the notion that Gold Fields was changing – and to make sure that change happened. It was intended to involve staff at many levels at head office and on the mines in the belief that ordinary employees ought to take ownership of the project. And its task was to ensure that transformation was not mere tokenism, but real.

Not surprisingly, it did not gain universal support within the company. How could it? People are people, after all.

VULINDLELA is a Xhosa word meaning 'open the way'. It seemed a particularly felicitous choice of a name for the new project, leapfrogging the increasingly controversial *fanagalo* to draw from a genuinely indigenous language. Subtly, it sent signals that Gold Fields was really part of the new South Africa, embracing its cultures, ready to participate in the new national sport of transformation.

In April 1997, Wright proclaimed the new direction for all to hear in the *Gold Fields Review*, an occasional prestige publication:

> The last decade has been characterised by change everywhere. South Africa has not escaped. There has been tumultuous political change which has brought economic and sociological change in its wake.

This desire and need for change has reverberated through towns, townships, technikons and trade unions. There have been calls for affirmative action, nationalisation, privatisation, reconciliation. The common denominator in all these demands is for change.

Gold Fields has taken up the challenge. What will certainly not change is our clear line of descent from our founding fathers and upholding all that is good in the company. We are proud of the technical expertise and innovation of our engineers; of the loyal service given unstintingly by thousands of employees; of the excellent work supported by the Gold Fields Foundation. These are our strengths. They are immutable. What we will change is our style of management with the aim of bringing out the very best our employees can offer.

So there it was, then, as clear a statement of intent as anyone could wish for: the old era is over. Gold Fields moves on.

NOW BEGAN a time of flurry and scurry, grumbles and mumbles. The Group had never seen anything like it. Five task teams were created, each reporting to a strategic change team chaired by Wright; the chief executive had to be seen to be involved. The task teams consisted of people of varied disciplines, experience and seniority. For most it was a part-time activity to be added to their daily chores. They were supposed to peer deeply into the very bowels of Gold Fields, identifying what was right and what was wrong. There were no sacred cows, no forbidden subjects. They explored issues like governance and resources, systems and processes, skills and competencies, values and the image of the company.

Complicating everything was the climate of gloom in the South African gold mining industry. Political pressure from the ANC government was rising. Gold production throughout the country had fallen to a 40-year low. The gold price hit a low of $322 in July 1997 amid forecasts that it could drop to $300. Strikes and violence seemed endemic on the mines. Gold Fields' quarterlies looked good but the share price tumbled from R153 in November 1996 to R107 a few months later.

Black economic empowerment was now an urgent necessity, but negotiations with Cyril Ramaphosa's New Africa Investments Limited (NAIL) were interminable and frustrating. *The Economist*, an influential London publication, described the negotiation thus in its issue of 5 June 1997:

> NAIL wants to buy control of the firm Cecil Rhodes started – Gold Fields of South Africa, the country's fourth-biggest mining house (after Anglo American, De Beers and Gencor). A deal is not yet on the table, but there are reasons to believe one will be: one of Mr Ramaphosa's many new white friends is Johann Rupert, whose family company, Rembrandt, controls 40% of Gold Fields' parent company. Together, they want to secure joint control by transferring a further 40%, held by an unlisted company called Asteroid, to Mr Ramaphosa. Asteroid, in a typically Byzantine South African ownership tangle constructed to fend off predators, is partly owned by Gold Fields itself, and partly by one of Gold Fields' operating mines.
>
> But why anyway should Mr Ramaphosa be eager to enter the gold business? The industry in South Africa is in a pitiful state. Last year gold output fell to its lowest for 40 years. The gold price is weak. And since South African gold lies buried far beneath the soil – the deepest mine shafts go down more than four kilometres – it is becoming increasingly expensive and complicated to dig the stuff out.
>
> Nor is Gold Fields itself an obvious buy. It is the oldest South African mining house, with a stuffy, patrician air. Recently it has performed dreadfully. Pre-tax profits fell 30.4% in the first quarter this year, to R254-m. The cost per tonne of mining at Kloof, its worst-performing mine, is over 50% higher than at a comparable neighbouring mine run by Anglo. Overall labour productivity at Gold Fields is about a fifth below that of Anglo gold mines.

Eventually the negotiations with NAIL would fail, and be called off. But *The Economist* paints a cruel picture of what the company was up against when it came to media (and therefore public) perceptions. It confirms, beyond doubt, that the decision to do something was unavoidable. Critics of Vulindlela sometimes failed to remember that.

FOR SOME, Vulindlela was a stimulating exercise; for others, a drudgery and worse. Clive Wolfe-Coote, a general manager of the group and chairman of TCL in Namibia, said openly: 'We are destroying our company by saying how lousy it is. We're also perpetuating the divisions between head office and the mines.' Others were more thoughtful. Executive director Alan Munro told an interviewer: 'I had serious misgivings but I decided that the process needed to be vigorously supported.' Richard Robinson, at one stage being groomed by Plumbridge as a possible successor, thought it 'a huge exercise that should have been cut short and decisions made'. John Hopwood, a one-time Gold Fields executive who joined the board in 1996, said Vulindlela might have worked better if the CEO had driven it through by 'sheer force of personality'.

Company secretary Graham Alvey displayed a delightful ambivalence. Asked to identify the best and worst things that had happened to Gold Fields in 1997, he replied: 'Vulindlela.'

An integral part of the process was the occasional *bosberaad* – that unique Afrikaans word that means, literally, bush deliberation but carries connotations of a momentous, decisive event. There is no English-language equivalent. Senior staff invited to attend these special events at the Cathedral Peak Hotel in the Drakensberg were told that the objective was to be 'well prepared for the challenges that face us'. Lest that sounded too formidable, they were invited to bring their spouses, and promised a leavening of sporting fun and social interaction.

Overall, Vulindlela was designed to last seven weeks and to result in a business plan for a comprehensive change programme.

After a while, when it began to seem that fundamental change was not going to be achieved soon enough, Mike Adan was given Vulindlela as a full-time job. To some he seemed an unlikely choice; as personnel manager he had earned a reputation as a stickler for the rules, a hardliner. Were those really the qualities called for in a change programme? Nevertheless, he had a solid performance record. He had been a Gold Fields bursar in the early Seventies, earning BCom and LLB degrees at the University of the Witwatersrand. He joined the company as a graduate trainee in the legal department, served as manager of the personnel and management services divisions and, in November 1995, Wright plucked him out to be the general manager responsible for making sure Vulindlela worked. He found it tough going.

'Look,' he says with hindsight, 'the executive team had had the stuffing knocked out of them by then. A consultant told me they were like buck caught in headlights. They didn't seem to know where to go or how to make Vulindlela work. Apart from Alan Wright, I didn't get much support from the executive. GFSA was too thinly staffed and the structure was too lean. Most people worked too hard and Vulindlela just added to their load.'

It was an interesting perspective on staffing by a man who had once been the personnel manager of Gold Fields. About a year later, someone would come along and take out more than 80 % of the head office complement, saying that the Group was top heavy. Could they both be right? Adan continues with his impressions:

> Operational staff offered only token support. They were more focused on getting the next ton of ore out of the ground and didn't have time for what one of them called 'scribbling teenagers'. The scribbling teenagers, in actuality, were adult and qualified young men and women, but some old hands persisted in seeing them as Peter Pans who declined to grow up.
>
> Alan Wright was often concerned that Vulindlela was not going ahead as well as he had hoped. He was afraid that it wouldn't revitalise the company quickly enough. But Wright showed no outward sign of concern; quite the opposite.

According to Alan Wright: 'Perhaps the most telling results of all are the improved positive attitudes of the employees. Management has pointed the way and set the example. The men and women of Gold Fields are making it work.'

LOOKING BACK more than 20 years later, Wright remains convinced that the programme bore fruit. It opened people to change, perhaps made them more receptive to the dramatic developments that ultimately came upon them.

He remembers when the Vulindlela proposal was first put to the board somewhere in the third quarter of 1996. Johann Rupert gulped at the anticipated cost – R60-million at that stage – and asked for time to think about it. He might have thought longer and harder if he had known that the ultimate price would be closer to R100-million.

About a fortnight after their first meeting Rupert sent his private plane to Durban to pick up Wright and they had a two-hour meeting in Stellenbosch. They reached agreement on two issues. Rupert agreed the company had to move forward. In an interview years later he insisted: 'Vulindlela was not a waste of time. It was blindingly obvious that there was a huge cultural divide in the company.'

The second issue flowed from the first. Rupert and Wright agreed that not only the structure but the culture of the company needed to be changed.

In October 1997 Plumbridge, an increasingly reluctant chairman, resigned and Rupert himself took over the role to oversee the makeover. Plumbridge was very conscious of a cruel irony. Long before, he had confided to senior executive John Hopwood that he had wanted to retire earlier – but Rupert had urged him not to. Having been persuaded by his major outside shareholder to stay on, the shareholder then proceeded to criticise him for lingering too long. Says Wright of the whole exercise:

> Yes, the audit report did come as a shock to us. I think it made us realise that we had lost too much expertise in the company. The good people had left because they felt restricted. The not-so-good people still had our expertise but, let's be honest, for a manager he must not just have the expertise, he must have the ability to manage people; to see what is going wrong.
>
> Look at my own case. Taking over from Robin I suddenly found we were a company that wasn't known to the rest of the world. Robin was known – not the company. Whenever somebody had to go anywhere, Robin went. He went overseas for us. He went to Cape Town to see the Ministers. He went to Pretoria to see the directors-general. I was like a babe in the woods, meeting all these new people.

Had he ever raised this point with his boss? 'No, because I didn't realise there was a problem until it became my problem.'

In the serenity of retirement, Plumbridge contemplates the criticisms. He has an uneasy feeling that he is being made a scapegoat for the difficulties the executive were facing:

> Nobody's perfect and, yes, Gold Fields had problems, But they can't all be laid at my door. The transition wasn't all that smooth. The new regime still had to earn the confidence of staff and directors. Alan Wright had to recover from the effects of his brutal beating. It didn't help that his first budget presentation to the board had to be delayed because it wasn't ready.
>
> I know it's difficult for a new CEO to find himself reporting to a former CEO. I tried to make it easier. I told Alan: 'You're responsible for the management of the group. If you want my advice I will gladly give it – but only if you ask for it.'

In January 1997 a comprehensive plan emerged from the Vulindlela project and was presented to the board, which approved it in principle. No one realised quite how expensive it would turn out to be. Or, in the end, how comprehensively it would be overtaken by a single unexpected development.

CHAPTER EIGHTEEN

INTO A NEW WORLD

THE NEWS, when it broke, came like a bombshell. For once, the busy gossips of the Johannesburg business community hadn't sussed out what was happening. Only a handful of people knew about it, and they kept their counsel. But the biggest aid to secrecy was the speed with which the whole thing was done.

One day it was just a gleam in the eye of someone. Ten days later it was a reality. That 'very English company', Gold Fields, was going to merge with a 'very Afrikaans company', Gengold – and that was only where the differences began. Talk about oil and water; here were two traditions, two cultures, two styles and only a hunger for gold in common. It was, as one observer described it, 'an unholy mixture' and some people thought it was a marriage arranged in hell. The honeymoon was destined to be tumultuous.

The merger negotiation began with a two-block stroll in downtown Johannesburg. Alan Wright's short walk – to freedom or bondage? – has provoked speculation and rumour ever since, internally and externally. It would end up changing Gold Fields forever.

What it led to has all the elements of office legend; that is to say, the authorised version is not the preferred version; some of the facts will always be murky; and proclaimed truth has not always been allowed to get in the way of a gripping story. And a gripping story it certainly was, with long knives and hatchets, turf wars and bruised egos, upheaval and renewal, all in the name of uniting the disunited and maximising assets.

Did it work? That is what this book sets out to discover. Not surprisingly, there are irreconcilable views.

TO START at the beginning: Long before the idea of a merger arose, Genmin had its eyes on Gold Fields, which had its eyes so fixed on Anglo American that it didn't even notice that it was under observation. One of those aware of the plan for a hostile takeover bid was Nick Holland, then working in Gencor's corporate finance division. He had no idea he would one day end up working for the other side. Recalls Holland:

> The planning took place in late 1995, early 1996, before Gencor had split. We wanted to do this hostile on Gold Fields because our gold mines didn't have critical mass and would benefit from Gold Fields' diversified portfolio. But our plans were blocked because Liberty didn't like it; Roy Andersen didn't support it. It would only work for us if Brian Gilbertson could get hold of all the legs of Asteroid – the somewhat secret, unlisted company with effective control of Gold Fields. But we couldn't, so we dropped it.

However, the seed had been sown. It blossomed again after Billiton was hived off and listed in London, and Genmin was left with platinum interests, which it intended to list, and a few gold mines that didn't seem to have much going for them.

Gilbertson had three simple rules for deciding on the value of an asset. According to Holland he used to say:

> Don't worry about NPV calculations and internal rates of return. It's all a load of nonsense. There are only three questions you have to ask yourself. Are you in the right commodity? Are you correctly positioned on the cost curve? And do you have the critical mass? If you can tick the box on those three issues, you're away, provided of course that the opportunity is in a country with which you can do business.

Holland thought it was a smart formula. Now, with Billiton gone, they were trying to apply it to the remnants of their gold holdings.

'You know,' Gilbertson told his colleagues, 'Driefontein and Kloof are the best gold mines in the world, but they are not well run operationally. If we can combine those mines with ours, and put in our management team, we can create something that will capture the imagination of the market.' Gilbertson thought he might have an informal chat with his old mate Johann Rupert about the matter.

SO DID Rupert instruct Wright to discuss a merger with Gilbertson, as the office grapevine insists? The answer is: maybe. Emil Buhrmann, a director of both Remgro and GFL, says coyly that 'it wasn't necessarily so'; Rupert himself gives the credit to Wright; and Gilbertson has always maintained that the idea belonged to the Gold Fields man. Indeed, Gilbertson said as much in the 1999 annual report: 'The clear vision for this company must be credited to Alan Wright, who was the architect of the new Gold Fields.'

Against that, a contemporary claims: 'Gilbertson would say that, wouldn't he? He wanted Alan to think the idea was his own.' It's not inconceivable: a Machiavellian style in promoting deals was part of the Gilbertson make-up. He was not noted for modesty – his staff would say, when they heard his helicopter arriving on the Gencor roof: 'The ego has landed' – but if it helped to clinch a deal, well, he might make an exception. Former director Peter Flack – no admirer of Gold Fields – remembers that he was once instructed by Rupert to put a stop to the rivalry between Plumbridge and Ogilvie Thompson. He failed because neither party was prepared to initiate the process. Questioned about the merger, he offered this enigmatic response: 'It was first prize for Gencor and it didn't make sense for GFSA. But Johann was running things and he doesn't take prisoners.'

It is also true that some ideas have many fathers and it is not always easy to say precisely where an idea is born and takes root. How many minds have pondered and refined it along the way? Alan Wright would be the last to claim exclusive credit (or accept exclusive blame) for approaching Gencor. He readily agrees that someone might have planted the idea in his mind at some stage or another. He says:

> I believe ideas come from different sources. Often one suggestion provokes another. But I do know that, before I approached my own board I had discussions with Emil Buhrmann, who at the time

worked for Dilly Malherbe, Rembrandt's representative on the Gold Fields board. He and I were always talking about stuff. So what I recall is that the idea arose out of our discussions. But it could be that that was their plan – to lead me down that road. I don't pretend that maybe they didn't steer me down the right road there. Remember, I had already reached the stage where I knew that we didn't have the necessary skills or succession planning in our own company, and that we had to do something. I mean, where was the gold price? You couldn't even see it above the floor.

But of one thing Wright is certain: he was the one who took the positive steps needed to make it happen. First he took the proposal to the Gold Fields board in the dying days of Plumbridge's chairmanship. Then, when he had received board approval, he walked to Gilbertson's office on that August day in 1997 and broached the subject. Tentatively.

To this day, departing chairman Robin Plumbridge insists that the first he heard of the deal was when he was asked to chair the press conference announcing it. Alan Wright says he's mistaken.

'The day I saw Brian he called in Nick Holland, his senior manager, corporate finance,' says Wright. 'We spoke about the idea a bit more and Brian was very non-committal: "Okay thanks, we'll think about it." He didn't say no, he didn't say yes. Brian is good at deals; that is his forte. But, you know, when I left there I felt the idea had been received and listened to – something he would consider.'

FOR TWO people, at least, that day would prove to be momentous. One was Wright; he thought he had made a breakthrough. The other was Holland. Until that moment, Holland was close to despair. He thought he had been discarded and would soon be out of a job. Here's how he remembers it:

> I was working for the Gencor Group before we split Billiton out and took those base metal assets and listed them in London. Everybody wanted to be part of this exciting new group. I'd gone to the Billiton launch only to discover that, after a year of working day and night,

often weekends, there was no position for me. And no one had even bothered to speak to me. It was almost like the morning after the party. I was coming to work every day and wondering when someone was going to tell me my services were no longer required.

So I went to Michael McMahon, who was a Gencor director at the time, and said to him, 'I don't know what's going to happen and I think I'm going to be out of a job ... etc, etc.' Well, he went to Brian and said there were a few people floating around and maybe he should consider getting a finance executive on board for what was left of Gencor – the platinum assets and the gold assets, housed in the wholly-owned subsidiary called Gengold. So Michael had gone and whispered in his ear that I might be interested in helping him out.

Holland seized the opportunity. He made an appointment to see Gilbertson through his secretary, Elsabe. They met and spoke and characteristically the outcome was – silence. Says Holland:

> Brian was the kind of executive that didn't suffer fools for longer than about 30 seconds. And his attention span was 12 seconds. If you didn't get your point across in that time, he had moved on. So of course I was terrified. I blabbed it out: 'You don't have a finance executive in your new group in Gencor ... I've noticed that ... And I'm available if you would like to consider me ...' And then I thought, that didn't come out too well. Brian, being the poker player he was, was fairly impassive. He just nodded and said 'That's interesting ...'
>
> Afterwards, when I didn't hear anything, I thought: well, I'd better start dusting my CV off. I'm going to be moving out of here soon. Weeks later I got a telephone call from Elsabe. She said: 'Mr Gilbertson is having a Gencor executive committee meeting on Tuesday afternoon and you must please attend.' There were about three or four of us, a very small team, and Brian said: 'Right. We need to think about where we're going to take Gencor.' And I thought: I wonder if this means I'm employed. Brian didn't say. I suppose, being the kind of person he was, he was just throwing out a bit of a challenge to see how I would react. So we talked about

splitting the platinum and gold assets because we had different kinds of investors.

The problem with our gold assets was that we didn't have critical mass and enough quality to make this work for us as a standalone entity. But Brian was a tremendous thinker and his vision was: 'Okay, I couldn't do the hostile in 1995 but it still makes sense that we should try to combine the gold assets of Gold Fields and Gencor now.' And of course this created the catalyst for Johann Rupert to move away from his dung and ice cream philosophy and put all these assets together.

SUDDENLY, things began to move. Two days after Wright had planted – or replanted? – the idea of a merger between Gold Fields and Gengold, Gilbertson took his own short walk to Wright's office. 'We've thought about it,' he said, 'and we'd like to move things forward.' Wright recalls:

> We hadn't done any valuations. We were actually just talking a principle: was it feasible to put the two companies together? The next thing was, who's going to pay what? Between us the thought came that maybe we could look at market values. He said he would go back and do the arithmetic. He asked me to go back and see him. I'm talking literally seven days, it was as quick as that.

Holland picks up the story from his perspective. He was in his office at Gencor when Elsabe called again: 'Mr Gilbertson wants to see you now.' Says Holland:

> You drop everything and you run. He doesn't like waiting for people. So I ran upstairs and was breathless and he was with Wright. He said: 'We're talking about putting these assets together.' And then he told Alan: 'I want you to meet Nick Holland. He's going to be leading the team from our side, looking after all the details.'
>
> That was news to me. I was tremendously excited. I had a job! But more than that, when you work in corporate finance, you dream

of something like this – putting together a deal that will redefine the course of history.

Gilbertson believed that speed was essential in closing deals. Markets changed, prices changed, views changed. Close quickly or lose out. A prompt handshake was better than a laboriously written contract. He and Wright had already agreed not to insist on the usual time-consuming routine of getting 'fancy valuations' from merchant banks. They would take a short cut. 'The principal assets were all listed,' says Holland. 'We would take a 30-day average share price, and that was it. We put them together and that was the deal.'

Holland paints a vivid picture of Gilbertson's negotiating style:

> When he wanted to do a deal, he only wanted two people in the room: himself and the other guy. He and the other guy would draw up a MoU [Memorandum of Understanding], sign the deal and then give the MoU to the bankers and lawyers and say: 'There's the deal. Go and implement it.' And of course the bankers and the lawyers would come back and try to redo the deal. I remember Brian saying to me: 'I hate lawyers with a passion because when you bring them in, they screw it up for you every time. Just like the bankers.' That was his style. It was different, it was unusual, but it was effective.

When Wright returned to Gold Fields and told his colleagues what had been agreed, some were outraged. *How can you take market averages? What about updated life-of-mine plans? We haven't even seen the Gengold assets. The investment bankers won't give us fair and reasonable opinions. Etc, etc.*

Holland sums up the outcome:

> I give tremendous credit to Brian and Alan. They stuck to their guns. My instructions were very clear: don't let these guys deviate an inch from what we've agreed. And we managed to fit a square peg into a round hole, as it were. We eventually got all these bankers to sign off. If we hadn't done it this way, we might have been arguing the toss forever.

He adds a self-satisfied footnote:

> We had this technology called Biox which helped to process refractory ores more quickly and easily. And we put a hell of a valuation on it. Even today I look back and chuckle at how on earth we really expected to get it through. But we did. However, the deal was not one-sided. They had the better assets; we had, we thought, the better management. There were benefits for both sides.

BACK AT Gold Fields, it wasn't quite such plain sailing. For the staff, their world was about to be turned upside down for the third time in less than 15 months.

First, there was Vulindlela, formally launched in July 1996, with all its unsettling connotations of change. Then there was the first attempt at a black empowerment deal. It was going to be drastic. Rembrandt, as the major shareholder in Gold Fields, was talking to NAIL about transforming the company radically. Black empowerment would be given real teeth. Speculation was that Cyril Ramaphosa would become the new chairman of Gold Fields. The deal would be valued at R1.8-billion, to be paid for by NAIL shares and 'other instruments'. In the end, negotiations foundered. But for staff it was a time of mounting uncertainty. Would their jobs be safe?

And now, in October 1997, the most traumatic news of all: a proposed R17-billion merger with an alien entity. Or was it a takeover? For the media, the enormity of it all quite overshadowed the topic that had been making the headlines only a few weeks before: the fact that Gold Fields had been forced to write down its investment in Northam Platinum by R456-million.

Says Wright:

> After my third meeting with Gilbertson I can remember going back to my office and calling in the executive directors and saying that this is what has been agreed to, and this is the price. Poor old John Hopwood nearly had an apoplexy. He said: 'You can't do it. The only way you can fix prices is if you get independent people to come

in and evaluate the companies.' And I said, 'John, this is the agreed price and it's a signed deal.' As simple as that. When I look back on it, it was the biggest deal I had ever done and it was the simplest of the lot.

Even so, there was one more hurdle to leap. The evening before the merger was to be announced, Gilbertson phoned 'old Julian' – Julian Ogilvie Thompson, chairman of Anglo American – and told him that he and Wright wanted to see him. Anglo was a shareholder in Gold Fields and a big shareholder in joint enterprises Driefontein and Kloof. It was only courteous to keep the Anglo chairman informed about the plan beforehand. They hoped he would approve. Ogilvie Thompson brought Nicholas Oppenheimer along to the late evening meeting.

'Julian was completely taken aback at the news. He was irate,' says Wright. 'The only thing he said was "my biggest investment in this lot is Driefontein. I don't want my investment diluted." Nicky was more conciliatory. So we left Anglo's part of Driefontein out of it.'

And that is how the merger came into being. The announcement to the media on 11 October 1997 did indeed come as a bombshell to almost everyone and captured the imagination of the market. It was a time of ferment and speculation was rife about a realignment in the entire industry. The new R17-billion company was given a provisional name: Goldco. The final name would be announced later.

Amidst all the buzz, and before the month was out, the Swiss National Bank announced that it was selling off 1 400 tons of gold and the price plummeted to $311 an ounce. It hardly dampened the sense of excitement.

NOW ONLY one more little thing needed to be resolved. Wright had never given the name of the new company a second thought; it would, of course, be called Gold Fields. Any other name would be unthinkable. He was wrong. Another name had been chosen.

He got a phone call from Richard Robinson one afternoon. As he recalls the conversation, it went something like this:

    ROBINSON: I just want to tell you we've been having discussions

	and we've decided on the new name. It's going to be …
WRIGHT:	But I didn't even know you were trying to change the name.
ROBINSON:	Yes well, we've decided. I just wanted you to know.
WRIGHT:	No, it's not going to be called something else. It's going to be called Gold Fields.
ROBINSON:	No, it isn't. We've decided. The market has lost faith in Gold Fields.
WRIGHT:	No it hasn't. But I'll tell you what – you just phone Johann and tell him you want to change the name. See what he says.

Robinson did as suggested. History doesn't record that conversation with Rupert, but it was evidently concise and crystal-clear. Rupert said: 'It *will* be Gold Fields.' And that was that.

Says Wright today:

> Luckily the lord and master understood about the positive value of a name. He was a good marketing man. Gold Fields was a name long connected with the gold business. You don't just give it up. Believe me, if we had dropped it someone else would have been calling themselves Gold Fields the next day.

SO WAS it all a happy band of brothers after the drama? 'Not likely,' said Gold Fields staff. Soon there would be blood and tears in the corridors of the new company. Top-level tensions arose and mass retrenchments were on the way. The executions would be as brutal as they were speedy. Ironically, neither the new chief executive nor the new chief operating officer would survive for long.

Gold Fields Limited, remarkably, quivered and shook and emerged from the battlefield of ambitions to become a stronger and even more vigorous player in the harsh world of gold mining. But that day was still some distance away …

CHAPTER NINETEEN

Shock Treatment

SHORTLY AFTER the merger between Gold Fields and Gengold, Richard Viljoen, a senior geologist, was delivering an induction lecture to new recruits at the Gold Fields training centre. He had just told them: 'When you join Gold Fields, you've got a job for life.' That was when he got the phone call. Alan Wright wanted to see him as soon as possible.

What Wright wanted to tell him was that he was being retrenched with immediate effect. His 15-plus years with the company were at an end.

'I am very sorry to tell you that your application for re-employment has not been successful,' Wright said. 'We will be preparing a retrenchment package for you.' He felt profoundly depressed. He hated having to tell a loyal employee to go. It was like stabbing a friend in the back.

Years later, the memory still haunts him of those painful duties in the early days when GFSA was transforming into Gold Fields Limited:

> It was a very, very stressful time. It's not in my nature to hurt people. The trouble was that so many of them were my friends. I mean, you've worked for the company for 30 years. I spent many a night trying to think what I could do to find employment for these people. We're talking about 600 head office people. But there was no way of avoiding it and, as second best, I tried to put in place the best retrenchment package we could afford.

Wright attended every meeting where staff retrenchments were to be discussed. Each departing staff member was allowed to appoint two people to represent his or her interests. They gathered at the big square table in the AGM room in the Fox Street building because it was the only place big enough to cope with the numbers. He says:

> Oh yes, I went to every one of those meetings. Hated every moment of it, but that was my baby and I wasn't about to fob it off on someone else. At the end of the day I think everyone got a very fair offer and, as proof of that, there was only one person who took us to the CCMA. And the CCMA wouldn't even consider the case.

Did that mean that everyone was happy? No, it didn't – 'but some at least were. There were some who said "well, that's great, I'm retiring." And a lot of them had been working for GFSA for a long time and we had a pretty good pension fund – they got significant multiples of their last year's income. We were moving into an era of engineer shortages and those who wanted to, they were doing consulting work all over the place.'

Nevertheless, the mass retrenchments left a legacy of bitterness that did not dissipate. For many of those who lost their jobs and some who didn't, it tarnished the memory of Gold Fields forever.

Wright had the unpleasant responsibility of handling the 'superfluous' staff members of GFSA, and he had to be prepared to live with the consequences even though he had not expected them to be quite so brutal. If large-scale retrenchment was unavoidable, he could not duck his role in it.

Richard Viljoen, geologist, was one of about 600 head office casualties, most of them arising from the decision to take the gold division into a new gold-only company. The precise figure is hard to establish because old records have been destroyed. The process of retrenchment was simplified for management by a decision that all but four employees of the founding companies would be expected to reapply for their old jobs if they still wanted them. In effect, then, they resigned from the old company and were engaged by the new. This decision had unintended consequences. It bolstered the argument by some staff members, present and former, that the new company was not a direct descendant of the Gold Fields of Rhodes and Rudd, but an imposter that had shanghaied the name.

'If it was still the old Gold Fields, why would we need to apply for jobs we already had?' they asked. It was a beguiling argument, but there are equally compelling counter-arguments, as we shall see.

THE ONLY exceptions to the rule about reapplying were the top four executives of the new Gold Fields Limited. Their jobs were guaranteed; they were appointed to give equal representation to both founding companies. From Gengold, Tom Dale and Nick Holland; from GFSA, Richard Robinson and Clive Wolfe-Coote. Robinson had been with GFSA since 1976. He had done a variety of jobs and had taken over the gold division from Munro. Wolfe-Coote had been his manager in the gold division.

Sitting over them, of course, were Gencor's Gilbertson, chairman, and GFSA's Wright, deputy chairman.

It wasn't an auspicious start. Establishing the management pecking order created the first real clash between the founding parties. Gilbertson wanted Dale to be the chief executive officer, the senior executive job. Wright said: 'No, it must be Robinson.' Holland, still thanking his lucky stars that he had a job at all, remembers what happened:

> I know that Brian wanted Tom to be the new CEO, but Alan insisted: 'No ways, it has to be Richard. If Brian has got the chairmanship then I want the CEO.' It was an absolute sticking point. I know that Brian was bitterly opposed to it. But Alan stuck to his guns, and Richard got the appointment.

Says Dale:

> When Brian confided in me that he couldn't get the CEO job for me, I told him that positions and titles were of no concern to me, I just wanted to get the job done.

Back to Holland:

> Putting these people in a room together, it was clear there was no

chemistry, no understanding of how this was going to work. Richard tried valiantly to put things together but he wasn't really a strong leader. I remember thinking to myself: who is going to be here in six months, in a year? And in two or three years' time, what is this all going to look like?

He got part of the answer sooner than he expected.

MERGERS bring out the best and worst in people. The rivalries go beyond the inherently adversarial situation of 'them' and 'us'. Within the two groups, people break ranks, choose new sides, align themselves with those they think are winners, develop their own defences. The 'them' – just like the 'us' – are seldom as cohesive as they first appear to be. In fact, without the right leader, the situation can quickly deteriorate into a whirlpool of conflicts and ambitions. GFL semed to be headed that way.

Wright was focused on GFSA and a gulf appeared between him and Robinson at GFL but that was nothing compared to the gulf that began to emerge between Dale and Holland – chief operating officer and chief financial officer, respectively.

Dale came from Gengold, Gencor's gold division, and Holland from the umbrella company Gencor. Both were appointed to mould a new company out of the remnants of two old ones. Both knew precisely what Gilbertson expected of them and were happy to undertake the task. It might therefore be assumed that their unity of purpose would be unshakeable. And so it was – to a point. And the sticking point was that they had conflicting ambitions for themselves and no great regard for each other.

TOM DALE, tall and burly, prided himself on talking straight and tough. He was born in a suburb of Manchester, England that, he claimed, made Harlem seem like a picnic site. At the age of 11 he was earning his keep by working 18 hours a day on a farm during harvest time. As a teenager, he was a drummer in a rock band – which didn't help his school work.

His marks were not good enough to earn a place in an agricultural faculty so he signed up for mining engineering instead. He won 'every academic prize for every subject every year'. When he came to South Africa and got a job on the mines, he found himself a lone English-speaker among his Afrikaner fellow miners. 'Now that's what I call a tough baptism,' he says today. 'But I survived it.' And, after a while, learnt to speak a fluent colloquial Afrikaans in an acceptable accent.

From there, Dale worked his way up to the top of a tough industry, step by step. He learnt survival and humility – 'I pride myself on my humility,' he says. Now he was Gilbertson's choice for a key job at the new Gold Fields Limited. Gilbertson didn't need to give him a brief. He knew very well what was expected of him. And the first step was to cut costs and reduce complements.

An optimum structure for a corporate office had been developed by incoming GFSA executives and agreed with the incoming Gencor executives. Gengold had 35 people in head office; GFSA – with its wider interests – had 750. Positions were offered to chosen people in GFSA and Gencor.

The original complement was some 120 but Dale had felt that 100 people in total were sufficient. Naturally, the vast majority of the casualties would come from GFSA. His opinion of old GFSA hands was not kindly. He thought head office was complacent and anachronistic. Dale's relatively brief period at GFL was traumatic for many. His job was to cut costs, which meant cutting people. A stock joke in the office was that so-and-so had been awarded a DCM by Dale. The letters stood for 'Don't come Monday'. Dale responds vigorously to criticisms that he enjoyed that aspect of the job. 'I don't enjoy hurting people and I get absolutely no pleasure out of retrenching anyone. But I'll be honest and say I did enjoy pulling the company right and setting it on a new track.'

Holland, for his part, was under no illusions about his future: if Dale got the top job he, Holland, was a dead duck. He is dispassionate in his assessment:

> What Tom did well is he tackled some of the difficult issues and he did help us to take 10 000 people out of the operations very quickly.

So I think he was very effective in the short run. That was a tough thing to do, and he did it.

It's a funny thing, but the GFSA guys who came into Gold Fields thought that he and I were big cronies. Nothing could be further from the truth. If he had become CEO, he would have replaced me. When Chris Thompson came in as chairman, Dale went to him and said: 'I want to put Brian Abbott in as financial director.' Thompson blocked it. I'll always be grateful to him for saving my bacon.

Dale puts a different complexion on things:

Gilbertson appointed Holland as financial director without reference to me. It was out of character. I had nothing against Holland but he had no managerial experience and wasn't part of the successful Gengold management team. Brian Abbot was the better man. But I never made an issue of it.

AS WAS only prudent, Dale had looked at the pro forma income statement that had been drawn up before the merger happened, just to see how the new company might shape up. It showed a likely loss of about R800-million. He had a very clear idea of what needed to be done:

The merger was part of an essential process to enable parts of a mature industry to survive. In its heyday, mining required substantial financial and technical resources at the centre for expansion and project work. Once the industry began to decline these resources actually detracted from effective operation.

Dale believes the industry rationalisation began when he was appointed head of Gencor's gold division. 'It was here that we created the skills base and started the process. A small, efficient, experienced management unit achieved a turnaround at Gengold and a massive turnaround at GFL, which GFSA management could never have delivered.'

A central element in the GFL turn-around strategy was to return responsibility and authority to mine managers. 'Johannesburg-based executives cannot run mines,' he says.

The other element of the strategy was that staff and production costs needed to be cut and productivity improved. Head office retrenchments were nothing to what was projected for the mines. About 25 000 jobs would have to go, according to an early estimate.

A fundamental production change was imposed. In the old days, Gold Fields tried to ensure that the mills operated at full capacity. It meant milling more of what the industry picturesquely called 'unpay ore'; that is, ore with an uneconomically low gold content. Robinson had already downsized Leeudoorn to 90 000 from 120 000 tonnes a month on taking over the gold portfolio and Gencor had the same approach. It would rather process fewer tonnes with higher grades, even if it left the mills idle from time to time.

A curious inversion of attitudes began to develop in some areas as the new order took over, possibly prompted by the wrenching uncertainty of the time. Some people began to take out their hurt and pain on their old colleagues. The old Gold Fields had let them down; old promises had been broken; job security, family atmosphere, comfortable ways ... all had gone. They felt betrayed. By contrast, some – especially on the mines – began to gain a grudging respect for Dale's bluntness. 'At least you know where you stand,' they said.

According to Dale, Gilbertson offered him the chairman's job when he (Gilbertson) stepped down. Dale declined because 'I wanted to run the mines'. Gilbertson also insisted that 'any new chairman must enjoy my endorsement'. Dale replied: 'At this moment, as long as the company pays my salary I am prepared to work with anyone.' After Gilbertson and Dale had dinner with the first candidate for chairman, and Dale had expressed an opinion, the candidate was rejected. Chris Thompson was the next candidate.

Gilbertson told Dale that he believed the chairman's job required an international outlook. Did he think he could do it? He gave the first answer that popped into his head: 'No.' Later he revised his opinion: 'Of course I can do it, better than Thompson, anyway.' By then it was too late.

Somewhere along the way, the board and fellow executives came to the conclusion that Dale was trying to carve out his own area of authority at Gold Fields. They thought he had become increasingly reluctant to report to anyone. Inevitably, he clashed with the man who did get the chairman's job.

CHIEF Executive Officer Robinson was what might be called a loyal critic of both the old and the new Gold Fields. His supporters said it demonstrated his honesty and his detractors said it showed that he liked to run with the hares and hunt with the hounds.

His assessment: GFSA was a slow-moving corporate business that got bogged down in attempts to minimise risks. Those who wanted to move faster got blocked. Entrepreneurial spirit was stifled. Bringing in the Gengold people with their clarity of purpose and speed of decision-making was mind-boggling. Against that, there was an uneasy feeling that things were being missed in the rush.

There was a mild disagreement over mine retrenchments. Mike Adan, formerly manager of the Vulindlela project and subsequently GFL head of human resources, had embraced the new culture of getting things done, pronto. He came to Robinson to say: 'We need to cut 22 000 jobs on the mines, not 16 000.' But Robinson said: 'Let's just leave it at 16 000. Aids and attrition will make up the rest.'

Wolfe-Coote, on the other hand, wanted more staff for new business and was refused. Robinson thought he was behaving just as he had done in GFSA, not moving things along. So he had reservations about his old GFSA colleague while having a high regard for his ability, insights and experience. As it happened, his opinion didn't matter much for long. Robinson became history before he had had time to even get his feet tucked properly under his new desk.

Gilbertson gave this explanation to shareholders:

> As the first chief executive, Richard Robinson had the difficult task of consummating the merger, and of launching the group on its future course. I thank him for successfully carrying out this task with great determination. He subsequently stood down on 1 June 1998 to facilitate the appointment of a chairman with wide international experience.

He politely failed to mention that it was an unusually short tenure – less than five months.

By the end of the year, Wolfe-Coote was history too. It was like an Agatha Christie thriller: four little miners determined not to flee, one lost his footing and then there were three. And then two. And then …?

There are several versions of what happened to Robinson. Some say that Gilbertson was appalled to discover that he had no real plans for developing Tarkwa, the company's Ghanaian gold mine, and decided then and there that he needed a new CEO. However the formal feasibility study completed under Robinson well before the merger spelt out a three-phase development plan which was being implemented. (It went on to be a success.)

When Robinson and Gilbertson were flying to Tarkwa for the first gold pour at the new mine Robinson seized the opportunity to discuss his future.

'Brian, I believe you're under some pressure to give up the chairmanship earlier than October to concentrate on Billiton. I just want you to know I don't want the chairman's job,' said Robinson. Gilbertson was non-committal, as was his wont. But three weeks later he phoned Robinson and said: 'We see the chairmanship as an executive position, so there is no need for a chief executive officer. We have someone in mind with international deal-making experience, so there won't really be a position for you at all. You'll have to go.'

They agreed that the problem lay in having an executive making major decisions without long-term responsibility.

Robinson said: 'Fine. How soon?'

And Gilbertson said: 'Probably sooner rather than later. Come back when you have thought about it.'

At Robinson's next executive meeting the longer-term decision-making issue quickly arose and he went back to Gilbertson to say he was ready to go. Robinson felt relieved. He'd been with Gold Fields for 22 years and he was tired. He believed that he had had no support from Wright in the governance of GFL and no board support either. He'd seen his father regret staying in the same organisation all his working life and he didn't want that for himself. Besides, gold mining in South Africa was a declining industry. His old sidekick Clive Wolfe-Coote

offers a different perspective: 'Richard always seemed to want the top job but when he got it at GFL, it was clear he didn't want it.'
Robinson duly departed on 1 June 1998.

STILL SURVIVING, still surprising himself by doing so, Holland recalls the early days of GFL:

> I was in this very unfortunate situation, I had strained relationships on both sides of the GFSA/Genmin divide. It was the most unsettling months of my working life, trying to put these diverse sets of cultures together. And it was all happening in the midst of infighting and a lack of leadership. Tom sort of framed my thinking about ex-GFSA staff. He convinced me that they were dispensable. I must say it was probably the biggest misconception I ever had, but it was years before I discovered that. Back in those days, I was convinced he was right.
>
> Sometimes I despaired: how do we create a Gold Fields Limited culture? How do we get to a steady state?

There were no simple answers.

CHAPTER TWENTY

AN IMPOSTER?

BY RIGHTS, the tensions and stresses of the early days should have blown Gold Fields Limited out of the water. In reality, they acted as a forge to unite the new company and give it identity, profit and soul. But not before it made a headline loss of R121-million in its first quarter.

Despite this sobering figure there was a distinctly bullish note to the new company's first annual report for the year ended 30 June 1998. The report opened with a picture gallery of the leadership in ladder formation, as if to establish the pecking order once and for all. The overall impression was of a cheery but serious-minded group of men bent on serving their shareholders.

On the top rung, headlined 'LEADERSHIP' was Brian Gilbertson, chairman, with an enigmatic half smile on his lips. One rung down was Alan Wright, deputy chairman, smiling as if he hadn't a care in the world. And immediately under them, labelled 'EXECUTIVE', was Tom Dale, managing director, clean-shaven, hair neatly trimmed and wearing a grin. A further rung down were Clive Wolfe-Coote, executive director: new business, his face framed by a kempt black beard; and Nick Holland, executive director: finance, eyes smiling, mouth hidden by a bushy moustache which counterbalanced the sparse hair on his head. On the lowest rung, the general managers: Mike Adan, human resources; Peter Robinson, operations; and Brian Abbott, finance.

Abbott's picture was directly under the picture of Nick Holland. If Dale had had his way, Abbott would have been above Holland. Statistically, Gencor had five of the top eight jobs; GFSA three.

Gilbertson had agreed to act as chairman for a limited time; his first priority had to be Billiton. His first – and last – annual report was a model of measured optimism. The merger must surely rank among the most important developments in South African gold mining; a transaction of world significance. GFL could boast three of the world's finest gold mines – Kloof, Driefontein and the complex around Beatrix in the Free State. The company was the world's fourth-largest gold producer (3-million ounces a year) with the second largest reserves (82-million ounces). Operating efficiencies would ensure that unit costs moved from 'fairly competitive' internationally to 'very competitive'. The merger had triggered a major industry rationalisation. Corporations were being simplified, cross-holdings eliminated and pyramids collapsed.

Gilbertson conceded:

> Where Gold Fields currently lags some of its international competitors is in the market rating accorded to its assets. Much upside exists for shareholders if this valuation gap can be diminished. To this end I have asked Gold Fields' leadership to focus on two core tasks: The first and highest priority is to achieve excellence at the South African mines; the second (and lower) priority is to internationalise the group.

The failure of investors to recognise the intrinsic value of the company's assets was to become a familiar lament in the years ahead. The hard truth was that assets in South Africa carried a political discount anyway. Later, rumbles about nationalisation from the politically callow made things worse.

Gilbertson didn't dwell long on this aspect. He had more cheering news: 'The achievement of operating excellence has a number of facets. One is to trim the company down to its core assets.' To achieve this, Fairview Mines had been sold to Avgold and Evander to Harmony. The future of St Helena and the Libanon and Leeudoorn sections of Kloof would be decided before year's end. Best of all, the long stand-off with Anglo American over the ownership and management of Driefontein had been resolved; a stand-off that had 'seriously impaired the performance of that mining complex'. It was now to be a joint venture in which GFL would have a 60% stake.

Knowing investors understood what that portended. Anglo American would not for long be satisfied with being a junior partner. Sure enough, Anglo sold its 40% share to GFL within a year.

Reinforcing the message of optimism, Dale – now with the title of managing director – noted that headline earnings had risen to R47-million in the second quarter after the ugly headline loss of R121-million in the first. Operating costs on the core mines had been reduced by more than 10%. The next year would be even better. Alas, the share price had fallen by 23% in the first five months but, 'given the significant turnaround achieved in the second quarter, and the outlook for further improvements in the September quarter, it seems unlikely that the relative share price weakness can endure.'

Hope springs eternal ...

IN MAY 1998, some new faces bobbed up on the GFL board. They included W Emil Buhrmann, an executive director of Rembrandt Group Ltd; Gordon Parker, a one-time president, chairman and CEO of Newmont Mining; Patrick J Ryan, a mining consultant with a PhD in geology; oh yes, and the irrepressible Bernard R van Rooyen, jack of all trades and director of many.

One of the new faces around the boardroom table, in particular, was to have a profound influence on the future of the company. He was a South African with Canadian citizenship, living in the United States and with a master's degree in management studies from an English university. His name was Christopher MT Thompson, Chris to his friends.

Some months previously he had had a Chinese dinner at the Imperial Restaurant in Denver, Colorado. During the meal he had cracked open a fortune cookie. The message that fell out had said: 'You will go to Africa and take over the greatest gold mine there.' Intrigued, he taped the message to his home telephone until it began to wilt; then he framed it and set it upon a ledge in his study. It is still there today.

When Gilbertson phoned him, out of the blue, to ask him if he would be interested in a job at GFL, he thought: 'That's uncanny.' Driefontein was the greatest gold mine in the world. He was being considered for the top job at Gold Fields, which owned it. But who believed in fortune cookies?

Chris Thompson flew down to Caracas, capital of Venezuela, for his job interview with Gilbertson. They met at one o'clock in the morning. It had been scheduled for earlier, but Gilbertson had phoned to say he would be late. Lateness aside, the candidate was not at his peak. He had fallen asleep at the pool during the day and had ended up with bad sunburn. The job interview lasted less than ten minutes. Gilbertson had only one question: 'Why you?'

Thompson outlined his experience and qualifications. He had been involved in the mining and natural resources sector for many years, starting at Anglo American. He had held numerous directorships and had founded and run Castle Group Inc, which managed private equity partnerships focused on the gold mining industry. Currently he was looking around for a new interest. As ever, Gilbertson was noncommittal. A few months later he phoned again. Thompson was in line for the job of chairman. He better get to know the directors and the company. Would he join the board?

Yes, he would – and in May 1998 he did. Five months later he assumed the top positions.

Gilbertson explained the changes thus:

> I made it clear upon my appointment as first chairman of Gold Fields that my tenure would be of limited duration. Accordingly, Gold Fields initiated an international search for a new chairman. An important criterion was the belief that our future strategy would be best served if an individual with significant international exposure in the gold industry could be appointed. I am pleased to report that the search has been successfully concluded. I intend, at the annual general meeting on 7 October 1998, to resign from the board and the directors have agreed that Mr Chris Thompson of Denver, Colorado, who will relocate to South Africa for this purpose, will become the new chairman.
>
> Mr Thompson's 15 years of experience in managing venture investments in the development of new gold mines in different parts of the world, coupled with his early career experience in the South African gold industry and then the Canadian investment community, makes him eminently suited to this role.

AN IMPOSTER?

ALMOST from the beginning, there was tension between Thompson and Dale. 'The relationship was strained,' says Holland. 'We could all sense it. We watched from the sidelines and wondered when the inevitable would happen.' Minor differences began to loom larger. Little things rankled. Even today, years later, the animosities linger.

Dale's opinion of some of his fellow directors was not noticeably higher. He remembers going on an international road show with Thompson to tell the world about GFL. At one stop a little old lady got up and said: 'I don't mind you two, but is this just another ploy for incompetent GFSA directors to keep their jobs?' Dale thought: You know, she's got a point.

The last straw for the relationship came over an informal hunting – or culling – expedition. West Driefontein boasted one of the most picturesque golf courses in the country. Among its enticing attractions were clusters of wild deer that roamed the rough and fairways, grazing contentedly and without fear of the golfers passing by. Not even the most avid player ever objected to waiting while the buck exercised their right of way. Every now and then the idyllic life led to over-indulgent breeding and the herds had to be reduced. Normal practice was to sell the surplus animals to a game farm.

Dale says he was invited by the mine managers to do the culling himself 'as a gesture of respect because they knew I was a hunter'. According to folk lore in the company, he shot half a dozen of the creatures. He is said to have repeated the exercise the following week.

The second excursion prompted a small group of West Driefontein wives to storm on to the course in an attempt to stop him. Their outrage echoed through the mine property and out to the distant corridors of head office in Johannesburg. 'That's too much,' thought Thompson, though he never formally discussed the incident with the board.

But Dale puts a very different construction on it:

> I love hunting. Hunting and singing. I once wanted to earn a living as a singer. I used to perform in my own band.
> Of course it wasn't really hunting at West Drie, more culling. I've done it on a number of golf courses. People love the idea of game on the golf course but then some bright spark says, we can't

have all these animals shitting on the greens. The bottom line is that you have to cull them. So it wasn't a matter of me shooting tame animals; it was a matter of me having a fully-equipped butchery on my farm and I sell very good venison, and I had a market for it. The managers continued to invite me to cull after I left but I discontinued culling to avoid people losing their jobs if found out by narrow-minded fools.

And the outcry from the good wives? 'Look, have you ever worked in a mining village, how incestuous it is, the level of *skinnering* ...?'

Richard Robinson was the first Little Miner to depart. Tom Dale was the second. That left only two of the founding four: Holland and Wolfe-Coote. One of them would not be there for long.

Dale left with the benevolent words of Thompson ringing in his ears. Wrote the chairman in the annual report three days before Dale's departure:

> Late in June 1999 Tom Dale, our managing director, advised me that he felt the major part of his contribution to the group had been made. Once a suitable replacement had been found, he would like to move on. Accordingly, with Ian Cockerill accepting the position of managing director, Tom resigned with effect from September 10. Tom has made a major contribution in the launch of the new Gold Fields. He inherited a difficult situation with 80 000 people in two diverse mining cultures from Gencor and GFSA. The principal GFSA mines were losing money at the rate of R160-million a quarter and the gold price was continuing to decline.
>
> By quick action to reduce complements, reduce unpay mining and restructure management, the operations were restored to profitability. To him must be given the credit for laying the foundations of the operating philosophy in the new Gold Fields. The board and I wish him well in his new endeavours.

It was not a false tribute, nor even an insincere one. It is perfectly true that someone had to do the job that Dale did, and that some people would baulk at it. Without his willingness to be labelled the bad guy, and to do the dirty work, that quarterly loss of R160-million could have destroyed Gold Fields in short order.

BEFORE this story goes any further, it is necessary to deal with a curved ball from the disaffected staff, a source of endless argument. The new Gold Fields, they say, is an imposter. It bears no relation to the original Gold Fields founded by Cecil John Rhodes and Charles Durrell Rudd 125 years ago. It is laying false claim to a history that does not belong to it.

Superficially, their case is inviting. From its birth in 1998, the executive spoke constantly of the 'new' Gold Fields. So does this book. There is little or no continuity from the past in its management, its staff or its practices. In the last quarter century its chief executives have been drawn from outsiders as often as they have come through the ranks. Inevitably, new cultures and new ideas have replaced old values and practices.

More compelling, the old Gold Fields merged with – or was swallowed by – a relatively modern upstart, Genmin. In the beginning, there was no doubt which was the dominant partner. It wasn't Gold Fields. The scorecard told it all: in the initial retrenchment clean-out, GFSA was the biggest loser. Its head office staff was shrunk drastically. Genmin lost hardly anyone and, for a while at least, its people were kings of the roost. The new alliance even wanted to give itself another name until Johann Rupert intervened.

So how could it *not* be an imposter?

A clue lies in Rupert's intervention. As a skilled marketing man he was aware of the value of a long-standing brand. Yes, Gold Fields as a company had had its ups and downs, and the market might have felt a little disillusioned, but in the bigger scheme of things it had a proud history. It stood for real values: resilience, tradition, pride. It was rooted in South Africa. No one doubted its fighting spirit nor its role in developing South Africa. Such intangibles are not lightly thrown away.

All successful companies reinvent themselves in one way or another over the years. Those that don't often go out of business.

Take a simple example: The Anglo American Corporation, long-time rival to Gold Fields. The company today bears little or no resemblance to the original. It is not even mining gold any more, once part of its *raison d'être*. It is no longer the personal fiefdom of the Oppenheimer family and its hand-picked, blue-blooded lieutenants. It even has, for heaven's sake, an American woman as its chief executive officer. And her publicly stated objective is to sweep away the cobwebs of the past. 'ANGLO REINVENTED,' proclaimed a *Sunday Times* headline in 2010. 'Boss Cynthia Carroll takes group into a brave new world.'

This new world features an overhauled management, ruthless retrenchments, a brand-new board and a quite different mix of assets. Top executives were summoned back from their plush office suites in London to do a hands-on job of controlling their South African business units. The only direct link with the past is Nicholas Oppenheimer, grandson of the founder Sir Ernest, and he is a non-executive director. Carroll says, with a rare flash of sentimentality: 'He brings a link to the group's traditions.' So it could be argued that Anglo has undergone change as radical as that of Gold Fields, and perhaps even more so.

Yet, in the minds of the public and probably most of its employees, it is still the Anglo American Corporation, a mining giant created by Sir Ernest Oppenheimer. There is no great clamour for it to disown old ties or sever itself from its antecedents.

Gold Fields, on the other hand, is now doing what it did at its founding in 1887. It has stopped being a mining 'house', selling services, and has gone back to being what it was – a gold mining company. If its ways have changed, that's because the way of the world has changed too. If, in the eyes of the disaffected, it has married unsuitably, well, that's the way it is. It doesn't require it to cut itself free of its history. Today it has a chief executive who came from Gencor originally, but there is no question of split loyalties. He considers himself to be a Gold Fields man now, through and through. In the foyer of the executive suite stands a bust of Cecil Rhodes; hanging on the wall is an oil painting of the man.

And that, perhaps, says it all. Whether or not this company is an imposter can't be answered by simply marshalling the facts. There are facts aplenty to support both sides of the argument. No, the answer lies in something more amorphous: a state of mind. If enough people believe it to be so, then perhaps it is so. And the former chairman, the current chief executive, most of the senior staff – they all believe it is so.

Chairman Rupert's last words on the subject appeared in the final annual report of Gold Fields of South Africa for the year ended June 2000 – just before GFSA slid into voluntary liquidation on its way to extinction:

> This annual report could well be the final such report to shareholders and it is thus appropriate to make two brief observations. The company had its origins in the consolidation of Cecil John Rhodes' interests in the Witwatersrand goldfields in 1887. The creation of GFL now marks a return to the original core business of this company and therefore the legacy of one of the world's great gold mining companies will continue.

Perhaps that's why the spirit of Cecil John Rhodes still seems to inhabit the rather utilitarian Sandton offices of Gold Fields Limited. If some of the current executives have their way, it is not going to go away.

Chapter Twenty-one

Going International

Chris Thompson's twin brief from Brian Gilbertson when he took over as chairman and CEO of GFL in October 1998 was simple: streamline the South African operations and give the new company an international dimension. There was no question where his leanings lay. At least one director thought he was a little too 'fixated' on internationalising the company. But he left no doubt in anybody's mind that that was going to be his priority.

He quickly agreed that managing director Tom Dale would concentrate on improving performance on the South African mines while he set about spreading the company interests. It might have been a sensible division of labour – instead it led to an early clash. Dale thought that Thompson was interfering too much in what was supposed to be his domain; Thompson didn't agree. He was chairman and CEO, after all.

Somewhere in the back of his mind Thompson saw Tarkwa – the company's gold mine in Ghana – as a first step into the outside world for Gold Fields. For good measure, he would soon begin to negotiate to buy two other mines, Teberebie and Damang, situated about 30km away on the same ore-body. There seemed to be some synergy there.

But within GFL, Tarkwa had become a mild bone of contention. Some didn't think much of surface mining anyway, and regarded it as a non-core investment. But when Thompson flew to Ghana to inspect it for the first time, he quickly realised two things.

The first was that the mine was a major deposit that had the potential to deliver far more than the 14-million ounces then anticipated. And the second was that the potential had not been fully exploited because it lacked a team experienced in heap-leach mining. Under Thompson Gold

Fields spent hundreds of millions to put in 'Rolls Royce facilities' to extend the mine's life, removed some of the inexperienced South African operators and hired Dick Graeme and other Americans to exploit it.

The result was that Tarkwa went from being 'an important developing asset', as described in the annual report preceding Thompson's appointment, to being a fully-fledged multi-pronged operation by the time Thompson resigned as CEO in June 2002. Between Tarkwa and Damang the mines were bringing in net earnings of nearly R420-million for the year.

Not a bad return on an initial US$3-million purchase price plus subsequent development costs.

Today Tarkwa and Damang look like modern mines in an ancient setting, as neat and tidy as excavated holes in the ground can look. Between them they produced more than 900 000 ounces of gold in the last financial year. The target is at least one million ounces by 2015. Nature is kind to these mines. No sooner is the detritus from blasting and crushing bundled into huge heaps of waste than tropical rain and fecund earth combine to cover them with lush greenery. It's near-instant environmental recovery. Ghanaians are slowly moving into senior jobs once reserved for expatriates. White South African miners work comfortably under black bosses. Neat mine houses overlook green fairways. The communal clubhouse is an oasis. Unlikely as it may seem, this tropical jungle seems more like a haven than a hell-hole.

SLOWLY, sometimes painfully slowly, the long-standing dream of internationalisation came to pass. Tarkwa was a stepping stone but moving into Africa was hardly the same thing as moving into the larger world. The company needed to send a stronger signal of its global intentions.

The opportunity came from halfway across the world. In September 2001 Gold Fields announced that it had acquired the gold operations at Agnew and St Ives in Western Australia from WMC Resources for more than R2-billion. It marked, said chairman and outgoing chief executive Thompson, 'the beginning of our internationalisation strategy bearing fruit, and the vindication of our sustained policy of not hedging gold'.

The purchase brought instant benefits. In the next seven months alone it contributed R557 million to net earnings. *Business Report* reported (with the right degree of exultation): 'Gold Fields is now the world's most profitable gold firm.'

Australia had enjoyed its own gold rush in the late 1880s, about the same time as Johannesburg began to boom and overshadow it in the minds of many. The central difference between the two countries was that the South African potential sources seemed richly clustered in a relatively small area, the so-called Golden Arc. (The later discovery that the arc extended to the Free State was destined to surprise many.) It made it easier and quicker to exploit in the frenzy that followed the first gold rush.

In Australia, on the other hand, it was soon realised that the gold was dispersed in pockets over a vast and inhospitable territory. It brought a motley collection of fortune seekers who quickly earned an international reputation for brawling and boozing and gave to the nation the nickname of 'Digger'. Even today in Kalgoorlie, the town that became the rest and recreation centre for the prospectors, barmen are forbidden from serving double tots of any spirit and must add a mixer to the puny singles they are allowed to offer.

The country still has more than 1 000 gold mines and most of them are dotted around the inhospitable segment of WA known as the goldfields – an area larger than most European countries. Modern websites still tell would-be prospectors how to use metal detectors to identify new gold patches. Some of the mines are hardly worthy of the name and lie forgotten next to ghost towns. But others continue to reward exploration more than a hundred years after they were discovered.

South Africa's Highveld may have seemed a dreary expanse of veld to early prospectors. But it paled when compared to the vastness and sheer emptiness of the great Australian Outback.

From the air, the landscape of most of Western Australia resembles the face of an unshaven giant – patches of scrubby green whiskers upon a choleric complexion with acne by courtesy of granite outcrops. But back on the ground, the characteristic dull red soil is redeemed by tufts of dusty green vegetation and, in spring, a proliferation of wild flowers. It makes for a stark and haunting scene. Those who find peace in the endless spaces of the Karoo will discover a similar feeling here. But it will be counterbalanced by a brooding undercurrent. Make no mistake, this is hostile territory to modern man though it provides haven enough for numerous scurrying beasties, kangaroos, birds and a thin scattering of its original human inhabitants.

In summer it can be fiendishly hot and, summer or winter, fiendishly dusty. Even a mild breeze stirs the red sand, distributing it over plants and scrubby bushes and propelling it into eyes and noses. Outsiders cannot thrive there without air-conditioning. Even the rare rainstorm harbours a threat as Indian Ocean cyclones can bring flash floods to the dry river beds.

By luck or good judgment – probably both – Gold Fields Limited owns two of the better mines. Agnew Gold Mine is nearly 1 000 kilometres east and north of the state capital Perth, more than an hour's flying time from Kalgoorlie, the original gold rush town, and seemingly millions of miles from anywhere else.

It got its name almost by happenstance. The Postmaster-General wanted a name for the mushrooming mining village because he was going to establish a post office there. Residents chose several names, all of which were rejected on the grounds that they were too similar to existing hamlets. The post office replied with a suggestion of its own, which found no favour. So the PM-G, exercising the final authority of the bureaucrat, named it Agnew – after John Alexander Agnew, a man who had been manager of a local mine and ended up as vice-president of the Chamber of Mines in Kalgoorlie. Later he went to London as a mining consultant and became a director of Consolidated Goldfields of South Africa in 1922. His son, Sir Rudolph, became chairman and chief executive officer of the company and nursed it into prosperity and then, finally, into oblivion.

At some stage in the 1950s, for quite different reasons, Agnew town died too; killed by the fluctuating fortunes of the mine it was named after. But for many years thereafter, the Agnew Hotel stubbornly refused to die and attracted tourists who found dismal pleasure in its ghost town situation. As a relatively modern frontier ballad tells it:

Yes, the Agnew pub's still standing and the boys still breast the bar

> *Tell modern tales of mining and bush camps near and far*
> *Their dusty throats are dampened as their elbows smartly bend*
> *The Agnew pub's not finished mate – one more before we end.*

The closest settlement now to Agnew is Leinster, a 20-minute drive from the mine. Like most Outback towns, its most inviting feature is its tavern, though it has a primary school, supermarket and post office too. It began life as a dormitory for the nickel mine adjoining Agnew and now owned by BHP Billiton. At the last census it boasted 732 inhabitants, mostly mine employees who chose to make a life there. But the majority of the workers still operate on the old mining camp system and commute from cities. But this is not your everyday commute.

The mining camp system offers a tough but financially rewarding lifestyle. It used to involve lengthy stays of up to three months in rudimentary camps of hostel-style accommodation – followed by generous spells of 'home leave' where husbands return to wives and children in distant cities.

Today it is not quite so demanding. The mine operates 24 hours a day, seven days a week. Employees work for eight days on the trot, ten to twelve-hour shifts, then return home for seven days. On the mine, they live in air-conditioned single rooms with en-suite bathrooms. They have the use of a mine canteen that serves breakfasts, lunches and dinners throughout the day so they can choose the meal they prefer before and after their shifts. They are encouraged to exercise and stay fit, and there's a pub which controls drinking by limiting opening hours. Excess drinking is the one unforgivable sin and breathalysers are employed for each new shift: fail and you're fired. Visitors get the same treatment. A letter informs them: *'Please also note that Agnew has a zero tolerance to drugs and alcohol so you will be breathalysed at the gatehouse when you arrive.'*

While the workers are predominantly men, women are encouraged in some jobs because of their tempering effect on a tight-knit community.

There is a fierce, almost obsessive concern for safety and elaborate protocols for measuring it. Rules are strictly enforced. Visitors are not permitted to enter working areas without safety boots and reflective shirts. The mine itself seems extraordinarily neat and tidy if open-cast mining can be said to be neat. Rehabilitation of the deep mining scars is slow – everything has to fight for survival in the Outback. It will take years, but already you can see it happening. The fervour for sustainable mining is evident. So the inevitable question seems more like a challenge.

'Nick Holland's slogan – "if we cannot mine safely we will not mine"– is it realistic or just a pious sop?'

Until this moment, general manager Tim Gilbert has been an amiable guide. Now he pauses for emphasis and to signal that he is serious. 'It is very realistic and we are applying it. We know it is a totally achievable goal. We are going to get there.'

Agnew mine was originally the Cinderella of the Australian purchase. Now, a decade after acquisition, it continues to provide pleasant surprises. It succeeded in its stated aim of achieving five years of mineral reserves. Near-mine exploration projects offer the prospect of increasing the life of the mine by between five and ten years. There is a sense that Agnew is on the brink of further discoveries and a buoyancy in the attitude of its senior staff that belies any suggestion that they are sitting on a dead mine. Thompson says: 'It grew beyond even our best expectations.'

IF AGNEW is stark and haunting, St Ives – more than 400km south – is positively eerie. The road to its entrance follows the shoreline of a giant shimmering lake. In the sunlight it looks cool and inviting, but its beauty is deceptive. Silver Lake is malevolent. It does not hold the water of life nor is it a friend to any living creature. It is a salt pan, seemingly stretching to the horizon. Its contents are undrinkable and its corrosive evaporation shortens the life of cars and all other metal objects in the vicinity. It is also the guardian of gold beneath the surface, which is why long man-made piers jut out from the shore in the hope that treasures can soon be wrested from it.

St Ives itself is in fact a series of mined-out and open pits in the pitiless red earth. It spirals down to the opening of two tunnels that lead to underground workings. From a lookout point on the surface the scene is awesome. More than 170 metres down, trucks drive into one tunnel and return loaded with broken rock. They look like Dinky toys, but they are massive and carry up to five tons a journey.

The mine seeks to be a place to live as well as to work, leading to friendly rivalry with Agnew over which system encourages greater productivity and a more contented work force. Both believe their system is best.

Of the two mines, St Ives seems to offer the greater potential. According to Gold Fields' report for 2010 it was moving into a position where it was actually increasing its mineral reserves rather than merely replacing them. Two projects only 5km from the central mill have the potential to add up to five million ounces of gold to the mine's mineral reserves, increasing its anticipated life from six years to more than ten. And exploration continues apace. There is optimism that, perhaps, they have merely scratched the surface.

As is the case with all prospectors – large or small – optimism is what keeps them going.

THE ACQUISITION BUG bit again the next year. In November 2003 GFL acquired a gold project called Cerro Corona – high in the Andes of Peru, 4km above sea level. For GFL it meant mastering mining techniques in vastly different environments with vastly different challenges. It gave GFL an even greater international presence and reduced its dependence on its original source of wealth – the gold mines of South Africa.

In the beginning, Cerro Corona was a pain in the butt for Gold Fields. The mine was plagued by all manner of teething problems – difficulties with the local population, who had seen what harm thoughtless mining could do; labour problems; government problems; red-tape problems. It took nearly six years for production to begin.

When members of the board visited the mine for the first time in 2007 they found a project in apparent disarray and far from ready to produce anything. It would lead to disillusionment and drama. Today the picture is very different.

Ask Gold Fields which of its mines best meets its own goals for sustainable mining, and the company answers: Cerro Corona. Says current CEO Nick Holland: 'It's a show-case; a model of what we want to achieve everywhere we mine.'

The Andes has been a source for gold for generations. There are ravaged, pock-marked sites to prove it. Until recently, sustainable mining was an oxymoron – a contradiction in terms, like military intelligence. Early pioneers chewed up the mountains, spat out the detritus and departed with their treasure, leaving impoverished local communities to cope with the damage to their environment and their subsistence farms.

As in many other countries, Government felt obliged to intervene. Gold Fields decided not just to conform to the new rules, but to add new dimensions when it began mining operations in 2008. In the words of an independent consulting company, Maplecroft of London, commissioned to provide a candid assessment of how the mine added value to the local, regional and national economies:

> Gold Fields is increasingly incorporating the concept of sustainability into all aspects of its business.
>
> Alignment to these standards is not only driven by a moral imperative. It is also explicitly recognised as a means of managing its risks, protecting its reputation, maintaining its social licence to operate and securing its long-term shareholder value.

More specifically, Gold Fields was determined to leave behind local villages with measurable benefits when the gold ran out. So far it has generated more than 500 jobs, almost all of them held by Peruvian nationals and more than a third drawn from this remote, impoverished area. The skills acquired will stand them in good stead when the mine dies – a living legacy. Its preference for local suppliers has seen it contribute more than US$100-million to community-based companies.

Most of all, it communicated with local communities, heard what they needed. It voluntarily spent millions on improving their lifestyles. It improved roads and access; taught them how to farm more effectively; how to get more milk from their cows; improved the quality and quantity of water available; and embarked on a US$24.4-million programme to improve health, education and reforestation. It contributed millions to the national coffers of Peru.

It demonstrated, by its emphasis on safety, that mining didn't have to be a hazardous occupation and came first in a national mine-safety competition.

And it was able to do all this because it fulfilled its first duty: make a handsome profit for shareholders. That, says CEO Nick Holland, is what sustainable mining is all about.

The only problem about Cerro Corona is getting there. It is like going to the mountains of the moon. It involves an hour's flight from Lima to the city of Cajamarka across valleys of jagged and tortured rock where rare and isolated settlements huddle under formidable battlements, as if forgotten by the world. Seen from the security of an aircraft window, the mind races: surely there can't be an airfield anywhere in these hostile mountains. But one suddenly emerges, and you are in Cajamarka, a fertile valley that was once a home to the Inca empire and now is a cross between a city and a jumble of shacks with a population of more than 200 000 people. Here is where Inca emperor Atahualpa was captured and held. The emperor offered a room full of gold and two rooms of silver as a ransom for his life. The Spanish Conquistadores took the money – and his life too. Vestiges of a room reputed to be the one where the gold was stored is now a tourist attraction.

From there it is a two-hour drive to the mine, more than a kilometre higher at between 3 600 and 4 000 metres above sea level; one of the highest gold mines in the world. A team of doctors examines visitors before allowing them to proceed to a lookout point where the air is thin and altitude sickness a problem for some. A vehicle carrying oxygen trails the visiting cavalcade as a precaution. For the locals, of course, there is no problem at all. Most of them were born here – and have the barrel-chests to prove it.

The mine itself is purposeful, disciplined, neat. Everyone wears hard hats, heavy mining boot and reflective jackets. Drinking on site is strictly banned. Even a special occasion or ceremony doesn't loosen the taps.

CHAPTER TWENTY-TWO

LIFE AND DEATH

FOR THE new company to live, the old one had to die. Since Gold Fields Limited had taken over the gold assets of Gold Fields of South Africa there seemed little need to keep GFSA going. Controversially, its other base metal and coal assets were deemed not to be viable on their own, though some staff members strongly disagreed.

There was an element of the macabre about the process. In one corner of Johannesburg, a group of 16 souls was going through the ritual of putting the old company to death – a ritual that would end their employment. In another corner of the city, a larger group was trying to breathe life and vitality into the offspring of GFSA – and beginning to succeed quite dramatically after a shaky start.

The 16-strong group, all people who had been retrenched from GFSA, had been offered a temporary lifeline. Their job was to help GFSA shed its leftover assets and collect the proceeds for ultimate redistribution to shareholders. It was a prolonged process. Curiously, it included out-of-town *bosberade*, as if to demonstrate that liquidating a company required every bit as much teamwork as rescuing it. Odder still, some of the mineral rights on offer had no commercial value. One 'acquisition' lay under a Germiston suburb; a second was beneath the playing fields of the Wanderers Club in Johannesburg; a third under a runway at the country's main airport.

This airport was originally named after Jan Smuts, a former Prime Minister; renamed Johannesburg Airport when the ANC came to power in 1994 and decided it wasn't a good idea to name public amenities after politicians; and finally renamed after former ANC leader Oliver Tambo in 2006, when the ANC decided that it may not be such a bad idea after all to name airports after politicians.

Leading the break-up team was Mike Tagg, a man who had joined GFSA as a trainee programmer back in 1969 and risen through the ranks, including managing the property and investment divisions and spells in finance and gold. Having been retrenched with most of the other staff in September 1998, he stayed on to wind up the company, knowing that a successful completion would mark the end of the road for him. GFSA was finally liquidated in September 2001. Says Tagg:

> The general view was that it would take five to seven years to liquidate the company. It actually took 26 months. We made a R4-billion tax saving in the process. I think we saved GFSA a huge amount of money on some of the projects. For instance, the rehabilitation of Glenover and Zwartkloof. The Department of Minerals and Energy wanted to charge us R40-million to do it. We used the DME's formula and spent only R1-million.

After more than 30 years with the company, was it a wrench to leave? 'Not really,' he says. 'I expected it. The old company was living in the past. Robin Plumbridge was an old-style chief executive. By the time he left the only option was to shut GFSA down. Vulindlela was a waste. There was no possibility of the company reinventing itself.'

MEANWHILE, back at Gold Fields Limited the path to progress was, unsurprisingly, proving a little rougher than anticipated. Apart from the scary loss in the first quarter, the 'relentless pursuit' (to quote Gilbertson) of cost savings, the mass retrenchments, the removal of chief executive officer Richard Robinson, the general upheaval ... apart from all these unhappy milestones, the new board had to get to know and understand each other, and their executives. Since directors and executives tend to be strong-minded individuals this is not always an easy process.

Gordon R Parker was a South African who took American citizenship and was president, chairman and chief executive of Newmont Mining Corporation in the United States for many years. He had been a director of GFSA and, in May 1998, was appointed to the board of GFL. He took his job seriously. He had been surprised at the formality of the old

GFSA board meetings; that no one seemed to have much to say; that they consisted mostly of the executive directors reporting to a sort of 'jury'; that the meetings could go on for up to six hours; and that the minutes were about as uncommunicative as the meetings themselves.

He found GFL meetings very different. There were directors with international experience. Management didn't lead the board by the nose. Parker himself managed to dispel some of the old formality. Sometimes he even wondered whether members were being supplied with too much information. But the process was good.

Nevertheless, that didn't stop him crossing swords with the chairman. An early clash came over membership of the World Gold Council. Gilbertson thought it was pointless for GFL to belong to it. There should be, he said, 'no more of this nonsense'. Parker disagreed strongly. 'You can't leave the organisation that is promoting your product,' he said. 'If it's not working, fix it, don't leave it.' GFL stayed on as a member.

Later, when Gilbertson revealed that Thompson would succeed him as chairman, Parker wondered out loud how he could make this decision without reference to the board. There was no objection to Thompson himself – just the process; indeed, he had said as much to Thompson when the latter came seeking his support. Parker convinced the board that head-hunters should be asked to come up with a short list. The head-hunters found no better candidate and Thompson was appointed. A similar disagreement came over Dale's future. Dale wanted the CEO's job; Parker found him 'intensely unsuited for it' and suggested he be removed instead. Parker lost. Dale remained as managing director – for a while, anyway.

Of course, all this was happening behind the scenes. To the public at large, and particularly the investing public, GFL continued to present a united and confident face. It was not merely a façade, despite the fact that it hid serious tensions.

A CLEVER manoeuvre ensured that GFL got off to a running start just before the new millennium dawned. At about this time, Gold Fields persuaded Anglo American to sell its 40% share in Driefontein Consolidated Ltd because, says Thompson, the Gilbertson-designed joint venture was not working. And so, in May 1999, it was able to achieve two long-desired goals: it removed the niggling irritation of a joint venture with Anglo, and it provided the opportunity to buy out other minorities. As chairman Thompson recorded: 'A wholly owned Driefontein makes Gold Fields a much stronger and more complete company.'

But why on earth did Anglo want to sell its share of the richest gold-mining complex in the country? Holland says: 'All of us remember saying: Harry O would be turning in his grave if he knew what Anglo was doing.'

By a curious twist of fate, a man who was destined to become CEO of Gold Fields nudged Anglo towards selling to its traditional rivals. He was Ian Cockerill, and he was a senior employee of Anglo American at the time. Says Holland:

> Cockerill actually started things for us when he was at Anglo. He didn't think the future of Driefontein was particularly bright and he convinced Bobby Godsell to get out.
>
> After Anglo agreed to sell to us, we wanted to take out the minorities so that we could delist and get free access to the cash flows and move the money around as we saw fit. You couldn't do that in a listed vehicle in those days because of all the stock exchange governance rules. So everyone knew we were coming and investors were piling into Driefontein, expecting this big premium. Of course the ratio between Gold Fields and Driefontein [shares] started to shift in favour of Driefontein. Everyone could see it coming. And the deal was busy disappearing for us because it was getting too expensive.
>
> That was when the clever manoeuvre came in. Thompson said: 'No, let's do it the other way round. Let Driefontein buy Gold Fields.' So that's what we did; we reversed Gold Fields into Driefontein because it was cheaper. The guys at Old Mutual ... it took them about five years to get over the audacity. It was a very smart deal. And it was the kind of thing that Chris was really good at. He was a deal-maker rather than an operations man.

Unsurprisingly, Anglo voted against the reverse takeover. Years later Bobby Godsell explained why. 'It was a gesture, really,' he said. 'We wanted Gold Fields to know that we were unhappy about their lack of communication with Anglo as an important shareholder. It was also a continuation of an old-established feud.' Basically, Anglo approved the structure but it was not 'their show'.

The fit of pique did nothing to discourage GFL. It was well on the road to recovery, and flushed with success. Thompson began to look to his second and – to his mind – far more important mandate: to give Gold Fields an international presence. The best way to do that, he thought, was not incrementally but through a Big Bang deal with some outside company. Someone in Canada, perhaps? He thought he knew just the company.

Then he put a foot wrong, and his wife got homesick for Denver, Colorado, and it all ended in tears. But by then he was ready to go anyway.

THOMPSON set up his Big Bang deal and the company announced it on 13 June 2000. There was no mistaking the tone of quiet satisfaction. The satisfaction was still there a few months later when Thompson confirmed the deal in the 'chairman's letter' introducing the annual report for the financial year 2000. But, internally, satisfaction was tempered by anxiety. The announcement had been premature. What Chris Thompson didn't say – at the time or in the annual report – was that the timing had been forced on Gold Fields by circumstances; that, in one sense, it was something of a shotgun wedding.

It came about because the Canadian company concerned felt compelled by Canadian law to announce the deal unilaterally before the parties secured consent from the South African government. Gold Fields felt it had no choice but to follow suit, particularly since rumours of a pending deal were doing the rounds of Johannesburg's business community.

As ever, the leaks were a mixture of truth, half-truths and fanciful elaboration. In the world of big business, the business of the world is gossip. Sometimes it is idle, quite often there is an ulterior motive. But the origins are less important than the effects. The effects were to draw public attention to the fact that something was going on. This led to a media feeding frenzy. Something was on the go, but nobody seemed to know quite what. Speculation flourished, prompted by a report in *Business Day* the previous month which suggested that talks were taking place between Gold Fields and the 'cash-rich mining royalty company' of Franco-Nevada in Canada. Clearly it was a big story if correct. Gold Fields was bombarded with inquiries: Was it true? Was it happening? When? There was a limit to the number of times GFL could evade answering.

Thompson was dismayed at Franco's unilateral decision to go public, forcing Gold Fields' hand. He thought it would have the effect of holding a pistol to the head of the South African government just when it was considering whether to approve the deal. He feared Minister of Finance Trevor Manuel would consider it a betrayal and reject the merger altogether. Governments don't react well to being presented with a *fait accompli*.

That is why both parties had gone to some lengths to ensure that leaks didn't occur before government permission had been obtained. In their own words, they worked 'quickly, efficiently and clandestinely' after the idea was broached at a world gold conference in Denver. Before long they had a deal that both were happy with. All that was needed was for the merchant bankers to dot the i's and cross the t's. That's when the rumours began, and the hastily scrambled Franco announcement made.

Too bad, thought Thompson, but the die was cast. He would have to make the best of it. There was nothing ambiguous about Gold Fields' announcement.

It confirmed that GFL had agreed to a merger with the Franco-Nevada Corporation Ltd, a highly successful company with a billion dollars in cash and primary assets that included royalty streams from some of the leading gold mines in the United States, Canada and Australia. Each GFL share would be exchanged for 0.35 of a Franco-Nevada share. South African investors would be able to trade their shares on the Johannesburg Stock Exchange. Foreign shareholders had a choice of stock exchanges in Toronto, New York, Paris, Brussels and Zurich.

The announcement made it clear that there were still two hurdles to cross: a 75% majority of Gold Fields shareholders would have to approve the deal at a special meeting. And, of course, the South African Minister of Finance and the Reserve Bank would have to say 'yes'. The tone suggested that these might well be formalities. After all, Thompson and his new lieutenant Cockerill had taken trouble to pave the way.

Long before the Franco deal arose, they had visited then President Mbeki to tell him of the dilemma facing South African gold mines. The industry was declining and so were grades; there was no long-term future; wages were rising; it was taking longer and longer to reach ever-deeper working areas. There was only one option: to go offshore. Government, they suggested, should adopt a policy to develop minerals in other countries. South Africa had a wealth of mining talent and experience; it could be exploited. GFL would implement such a policy from its base in South Africa.

Mbeki had an associate with him, who seemed to be taken with the idea. Mbeki, however, was less forthcoming. Thompson remembers: 'The discussion seemed to go over his head. He just smiled and then proceeded to lecture us on why AIDS and HIV were not connected.'

THE FRANCO-NEVADA agreement led first to a ludicrous altercation with the Securities Regulation Panel (SRP) of the Johannesburg Stock Exchange. It arose over the inclusion of a 2% 'break fee' in the event of one or other party pulling out of the deal. This fee would amount to R60-million. It led to a two-hour shouting match between GFL's lawyer Michael Katz and SRP representatives. The SRP had never heard of a break fee. Under Rule 19 of the Takeover Code, nothing could be included in a deal that could be construed as 'frustrating action'. The SRP hired legal counsel to interpret Rule 19 for it. Counsel decided that a break fee infringed Rule 19.

Now Katz knew something about the Takeover Code – after all, he had written it. He was confronted by counsel who insisted they knew better than him what he had intended to say.

'But I wrote the code,' said Katz.

'Yes, but we know what you meant to say,' said counsel.

The shouting match continued into the night while the Canadian regulators were pressing for a GFL response and rumours were flying in the South African business community. Eventually a compromise was reached: a break fee of 1% would be acceptable. It was a very curious compromise indeed. After all, the argument was whether the break fee was a 'frustrating action'; not whether it was an *expensive* frustrating action.

Right at the beginning, Thompson disclosed the deal to Finance Minister Manuel, who said he liked it and would revert to him within two weeks. Thompson warned that it might leak, and then GFL would be forced to go public. Four weeks later Thompson had still not heard from Manuel when he learned that the Canadians were going to make their announcement on the following Monday. Thompson made frenzied efforts to contact Manuel, but without success – until the Monday, when Manuel called him.

'I assume Franco-Nevada has gone public,' he said. 'Now we'll see if you ever get your permission.'

WAS FRANCO-NEVADA a good deal? Thompson had no doubts as he and Cockerill responded to the inevitable media barrage after the initial Gold Fields' announcement. 'Think of it as a takeover of Franco,' Thompson told *Business Day*. 'Gold Fields survives and dominates management.' To *SAFM* he insisted: 'The issue is that royalties are cost-free, so gross revenue equals net revenue.' To others who wondered about the insertion of the 'break fee', he explained that this didn't put a pistol to the heads of shareholders. If they voted against the deal, the fee fell away.

Look at the positives, he urged them: Franco-Nevada had a magnificent cash kitty. Gold Fields International would generate $9-billion in revenue each year. Its market capitalisation would be $3-billion. It would produce 4-million ounces of gold a year. It would be in a powerful position to grow internationally.

Cockerill told Alec Hogg on *Classic FM*: 'It means that R14-billion of inward investment comes into the country. Dividends will be paid in South Africa so the 15% Canadian withholding tax won't apply.' At least one analyst said the deal was 'a vote of confidence in the South African mining industry'.

Nevertheless, after three months without an official answer, Thompson's worst fears seemed to be coming true. No news was not good news. Why was the government taking so long to rubber-stamp the deal? It led to a rather puzzling semi-warning appearing in what was otherwise a cheerful chairman's letter in the 2000 annual report:

> The new company, which will be formed through a merger of equals, will be named Gold Fields International. The motivation for the merger is fundamental to the future of Gold Fields Limited. In the absence of such a transaction and for as long as exchange control limitations prevent the exploitation of Gold Fields' cash surpluses in the development of new mines outside the country, the Group will face a future limited largely to exploiting its South African assets, accompanied by declining reserves and production. It would be forced into a long-term harvest strategy.
>
> I would view this outcome as a tragedy. Gold Fields is a world-class gold mining company with the human and technical expertise to become a world leader. It can trace its ancestry back over 100 years. During the stigmatised apartheid years, because of sanctions and exchange control, South African companies were unable to compete on the world stage. Today, in the new South Africa, there is little reason to disallow a South African company to venture out and pursue its ambition to become a global leader.
>
> In one step, the Franco Nevada transaction will transform Gold Fields into a global gold player with the strongest balance sheet in the industry and with cash means outside South Africa to acquire and/or develop new projects around the world.
>
> I strongly suspect that Gold Fields International will become a preferred global company for international investors and will, in a short period, achieve higher ratings for shareholders.

The 'warning' that some people found startling was the one that said Gold Fields would be 'forced into a long-term harvest strategy' if the deal was blocked. What could that mean? That he was predicting the slow death of Gold Fields? That, once harvested, its assets would be gone? That he might actually hasten the process? Was there an implicit threat to government?

That, anyway, is how some people read it. They thought it a most unfortunate thing to say. But it certainly illustrated the emotional depth of Thompson's commitment to the Franco-Nevada deal.

CHAPTER TWENTY-THREE

ONE ILL-CHOSEN WORD

NOTHING involving South Africa is simple. Too many interests have to be balanced. The early years of the new millennium were turbulent and confused. Unemployment was growing and so was labour restlessness; political euphoria was beginning to be challenged by lack of service delivery. Government was clinging to the lifeline of free enterprise and market economics while trying to persuade its worker allies that it was actually moving towards a labour-protected nirvana.

Nowhere was this schizophrenic approach more visible than in the mining industry, which was both the biggest single employer and the biggest single source of retrenchments. One mine after another was confronted by strikes and threats of strikes. The industry was under government pressure to hire more and pay more, an economic *non-sequitur*, especially when the gold price stayed stubbornly low and costs were soaring.

Calls to nationalise mining in terms of the Freedom Charter were beginning to be heard from within the ranks of the ANC. Later the then leader of the party's Youth League, Julius Malema, became even more outspoken. While government insisted that nationalisation was not policy, its response was curiously unconvincing. Party policy is not immutable; it can be changed. Overseas investors grew even more cautious.

A refusal to allow Gold Fields to merge with Franco-Nevada would undoubtedly serve to erode overseas investor confidence more. If South Africa was pulling down the shutters, how safe would any investor be? Again, government reassurances lacked complete conviction.

Speculation was mounting about the state's proposed new

Mining Charter. Dire forebodings were doing the rounds. Investors could not fail to pick up the uneasy vibes. The argument for saying 'no' to Gold Fields would have to be powerful indeed to over-ride such considerations. Or were there other reasons? Readers can judge for themselves.

AT FIRST, there was early semi-official encouragement. The Competitions Board approved the merger on 21 August 2000, and issued a Merger Clearance Certificate.

It found that although each company's shareholders would own 50% of the new combined entity, Gold Fields would gain board control, holding seven of the twelve seats, as well as management control. It added: 'According to the parties South African exchange control restrictions limit Gold Fields' ability to use domestically generated cash to develop new mines elsewhere in the world and the merger will liberate Gold Field's cash flows from South Africa.'

The competitions board felt no need to consider the market power of the new company since a single producer of gold could not influence prices in the international market. All producers were essentially price-takers. As for public-interest considerations, the Tribunal had been assured that no jobs would be lost; 'nor, in our opinion, does it raise any other public interest concerns listed in section 16(3)'.

To Thompson, it seemed like a good omen. Better still was a statement from a Reserve Bank spokesman saying he did not think there were sound reasons for withholding approval. Surely now the government's nod was a formality? But when someone spoke to Maria Ramos, then director-general of the Department of Finance, she insisted: 'No decision yet.'

The silence from the top impelled Thompson to give a challenging statement to *Business Report*: 'If the merger doesn't happen before December 31, the deal will cease to be attractive for Franco shareholders due to changes in accounting policy in North America. Franco would have to amortise goodwill immediately, dramatically reducing profits.' Thompson thought: if that doesn't prod the government, nothing will. It was about this time that he showed his impatience. He told a journalist:

'All that is needed for this deal to go through is that the Treasury gets off its arse.'

He didn't have to wait until December. The bombshell came in late September 2000. Nick Holland received advance warning from Manuel: government was going to stop the merger. A full statement would be released later.

Another year, another annual report, another chairman's letter and another tone – greatly subdued, angry, almost bitter:

> Looking back over the year, the key event was the denial by the South African Finance Ministry of our proposed merger with Franco-Nevada Mining Corporation Limited. This ... would have created the largest unhedged gold producer in the world with the strongest balance sheet in the industry.
>
> It was a merger, once understood by the investment community, that captured the imagination of all and the bitter disappointment that followed the turndown by government contributed to increased negative investor sentiment about South Africa. It was a blow to me and to Gold Fields.

What went wrong?

An obvious explanation is that Minister of Finance Manuel feared that Gold Fields was looking to relocate to another country, just as Anglo, Billiton and Old Mutual had done. If the trend continued it could hold serious implications for the South African tax base. But that explanation is not a complete answer. Gold Fields thought it had made it clear that it wasn't trying to duck the country. It had stated publicly that 'South African operations will remain the core of the new Gold Fields International'. It had committed itself to a R3-billion capital programme for the Witwatersrand basin over the next five years and had given strong support to a new plan to create a junior mining sector with opportunities for black empowerment.

Surely that didn't sound like a company that was packing for Perth or Toronto? Was there some other factor?

It was also undoubtedly true that the government decision had further eroded overseas investor confidence just at the moment when

ONE ILL-CHOSEN WORD

speculation was mounting about what the state's proposed new Mining Charter would do to the industry. That was another bombshell waiting to explode. So it contributed to making investors even more uneasy than ever.

The official rejection from the Ministry of Finance came on Thursday, 9 November 2000 – about four months after the application was first submitted. It said:

> Cabinet, on the advice of the Minister of Finance, Mr Trevor Manuel, has declined to approve the proposed merger between Goldfields [*sic*] and Franco Nevada Mining Limited, which would have involved Goldfields moving its primary listing from Johannesburg to Toronto.
>
> In effect, the proposed transaction was structured as a 'reverse takeover.' In terms of Canadian tax law, the new firm would have had to have its primary listing on the Toronto Stock Exchange. Although the new firm would have maintained offices in SA, it would have become a wholly owned subsidiary of a Canadian company.

Among the reasons given for the rejection was that approval would set a precedent by permitting a foreign jurisdiction to dictate terms; that it would erode the South African tax base; that it wasn't consistent with exchange control policy; and that it offered no benefits for the South African economy.

UNTIL THAT announcement Thompson had been elated. His plans were coming together. Not only had he begun to fulfil his mandate to internationalise GFL. He had found a more congenial ally as chief operating officer after the departure of Tom Dale. Things were going just as he wanted them to. The new lieutenant was none other than Ian Cockerill, the Anglo man who had once nudged his then employer into selling its Driefontein interests to GFL.

Thompson had gone to Bobby Godsell, an Anglo director, to persuade him to release Cockerill, a man with whom he had had no previous dealings. Reluctantly Godsell agreed. But that was only half the battle. Cockerill was less certain that he wanted to move. At first he said no, he was very happy at AngloGold. Thompson told him he had failed to read the script properly; he (Thompson) was not going to be around at GFL for very long and, possibly, there was an even bigger job waiting for Cockerill. No promises, mind.

Cockerill phoned his father in the United Kingdom, who had an HR background. 'What's the problem?' said his father. 'It's a challenge, isn't it?' Still he hesitated.

Finally, Thompson rounded up a couple of his board colleagues including Gordon Parker, and took the vacillating candidate to the Westcliff Hotel in Johannesburg and ordered drinks. Parker gave the candidate some friendly advice: 'Stop fucking around.' Cockerill accepted the COO appointment. Two weeks into the new job he said to himself: 'My God, what have I got myself into?' He thought the company had no modern systems and was woefully short of technical expertise. (In time he would claim that filling both gaps was one of his proudest achievements.)

For his part, Thompson remained steadfast in his commitment to internationalising, insisting that Manuel had left the door marginally ajar. He just had to find a way to give it another shove. One thing was certain: he was not about to capitulate. His crusade was not over.

Cockerill liked the idea of a deal with Franco-Nevada. Later he was to say:

> It seemed to be a marriage of convenience – a mining finance house and an operating group looking to grow internationally. FN felt the world was changing and wanted to become operators. They saw that GFL wanted to expand. We were comfortable with each other, and we all thought we could put together a company that could really compete with the Barricks and Newmonts of the world. But then we introduced the merchant bankers and the leaks began.

This is where the picture becomes murky. Thompson insists that Manuel's initial reaction was 'cautious but favourable'. Cockerill remembers otherwise.

According to him, when he and Thompson met with Manuel and his finance director-general, Maria Ramos, Manuel said he didn't like the deal because Franco-Nevada wasn't a real company – there could be problems with repatriating funds, the tax base would be depleted. 'All of these issues had been fully addressed in our submission,' says Cockerill. 'Their reasons were weak. I got the impression that government just didn't want the deal to happen.'

Whatever the case, Thompson was angered by the final decision. As far as he was concerned, any government that was ready to put a domestic industry at risk by preventing its expansion was damaging business, not promoting it.

Almost inevitably in this fevered climate, the old Gold Fields/Anglo American bogey raised its head. Someone suggested that Anglo had somehow used its influence to persuade government to block the alliance with Franco-Nevada. 'Rubbish,' says Bobby Godsell, then CEO of AngloGold, with characteristic vehemence. 'There were no conversations between Anglo and Trevor Manuel or Franco Nevada. The Treasury had set clear guidelines for externalising assets. The ones proposed did not fit. There was no advantage to South Africa Inc.'

Nevertheless, the indignation was misplaced. Anglo had never quite abandoned its desire to get its hands on Gold Fields. Cockerill had observed one such effort at first hand while still at Anglo.

Towards the turn of the century Godsell and Randall Oliphant of Barrick had been 'cooking up a plot'. Together, they would grab Gold Fields, split its assets between them and put Thompson out to grass by giving him the chairmanship of the World Gold Council (WGC). At that stage, Anglo's assets stood at R21-billion as against GFL's measly R7-billion. Like Gold Fields, it was in limbo and could only grow its gold interests by acquisition. Cockerill couldn't understand why anyone was hesitating. He thought perhaps the Anglo board didn't want any further exposure to gold.

Thompson knew the reason for the lack of action. He had enjoyed the fact that the rumour mill had got hold of the possibility of a GFL takeover because it was good for Gold Fields' share price. But that was as far as he was prepared to let it go.

He met Godsell and Oliphant for lunch at the Meridien Hotel in

London. His two lunch partners agreed that they wanted to buy GFL. 'It was a weirdly polite meeting,' recalls Thompson. 'They were actually negotiating in front of me as to how they would split up GFL between them like butchers over a live turkey. I said to them: "I know you, you're like vultures. Gold Fields is not for sale."'

One unexpected thing emerged from that little engagement – what Thompson calls 'a delicious irony'.

Godsell and Oliphant had failed to shuttle him off to the World Gold Council while they dismembered Gold Fields. But in April 2002 Thompson did indeed become chairman of the WGC, replacing Godsell. However he kept his day job too at a resurgent Gold Fields. While WGC chairman he restructured the organisation, changing its focus from gold as jewellery to gold as investment and arranged to list gold on the New York Stock Exchange. It had a profound effect on both demand and price, and earned the gratitude of the mining industry worldwide.

Soon the GFL share price would begin to outperform AngloGold significantly and it became the country's most valuable gold company and far out of reach of the two scavengers.

Bobby Godsell confirms a continuing but spasmodic interest in establishing a link with Gold Fields. He says:

> In my 12 years as AngloGold CEO I had serious discussions with Gold Fields on three or four occasions but all fell short of a formal proposal. The most recent was during Harmony's hostile takeover bid. I discussed with Ian putting the two companies together at market prices, but the talks came to nothing. Any deal would have been for a merger rather than a takeover. Anglo would not have paid a premium to take over GFL.

GOVERNMENT APART, not everyone saw the Franco debacle in the same light as Thompson. John Michael McMahon had been a non-executive director of GFL from its inception, having succeeded Gilbertson as chairman of Gencor for about a year before that. He was balding, bespectacled and blunt. He had not been convinced that the aborted GFL/

Franco-Nevada deal had been in the best interests of Gold Fields. It didn't seem to him to make much sense to merge an operating company with a royalty company.

The board discussion on the pros and cons was vigorous. McMahon was not alone in voicing serious reservations. But, in the end, there was 'sufficient consensus' in favour and McMahon readily accepted the decision.

Today he adds a postscript:

> The deal came to nothing when Thompson, in a most un-Anglo-Saxon way, elected to lay down a challenge to Manuel on the issue of exchange control. In a moment of madness, he thought to tell the world that all that was needed for the deal to go through was that the Treasury should get off its arse.

Thompson says he doesn't recall that his statement about the Treasury 'getting off its arse' was ever published. He thinks another factor influencing government was that Alec Irwin, then Minister of Trade and Industry, was going around the country bad-mouthing the deal.

When the deal was blocked by government, McMahon claimed that 'the board was not surprised and some members were relieved'. (Later Franco-Nevada had second thoughts too, and eventually proclaimed that the collapse of the merger was 'a blessing in disguise' because it encouraged the company to concentrate on royalties rather than production.)

Despite occasional differences, McMahon thought Thompson 'a good find, with entrepreneurial skills and a knowledge and understanding of South Africa'. He found him to be 'both helpful and difficult' in their working relationship. The fact that McMahon liked the contradictory combination of qualities says as much about him as it does about Thompson. These two strong-minded individuals found that striking sparks off one another was stimulating.

Says McMahon: 'So I'm a plain-speaking chap and Chris was hardly a shrinking violet, but we never had a confrontation on anything. We played the ball, not the man. That is what directors are supposed to do.'

Clearly, he enjoyed a challenge from someone with as many strong views as he himself could boast. McMahon had a formidable collection. He believed that the GFSA mindset had allowed Northam to destroy the company's reputation; that GFSA was imploding before the merger; that Gilbertson was 'an opaque character' with a unique style of doing deals without taking anyone into his confidence; that Gencor had been 'incredibly advantaged' by the merger; and that Tom Dale had a 'slash-and-burn' mentality and no feel for how to rescue good people.

Thompson offers a handful of back-handed compliments in return. He says:

> Mike was a strange director. Educated by strict Jesuit priests (as was I) he had a mental discipline second to none (unlike me). He tended to view his board role as that of a policeman. Management were inherently a bunch of heinous thieves and rogues stealing company funds and his job was to stop it. He could annoyingly detour a board meeting on minutiae to the fury of the likes of Parker and Ryan. But Mike proved to be my best director during the tough times – thoughtful, questioning and ready to take on the nasty stuff.
>
> I left with more respect and affection for Mike than I think he ever knew.

SOMEWHERE along this tortuous road, the last straw fell in the great Franco-Nevada debacle. Seymour Schulich – co-founder, chairman and co-CEO of Franco-Nevada – was becoming agitated about the inordinate delay in responding to Gold Fields' application. He knew it was government policy to encourage business growth. He decided to do something about it. He wrote a three-page letter of complaint to his old acquaintance George Soros, the billionaire investor, whom he knew to be a member of President Thabo Mbeki's recently announced international investment council. The council was created specifically to 'advise on how to attract foreign investment'.

Soros passed the letter on to Mbeki. And Mbeki, in turn, passed it to Manuel, who was not pleased to receive it. Thompson thought it a very tactless move to write such a scathing letter. Cockerill thinks one word in it might have blown the deal. Schulich referred to Manuel's 'prevarication' and suggested it was endangering the whole negotiation.

Did it influence Manuel's decision? No one will ever know. But if he thought the rejection would discourage Gold Fields from sticking its neck out again, he misjudged the company.

LIKE ANY effective businessman, Thompson had to turn his back on the project of his dreams and find other ways to grow Gold Fields. He threw himself into the job with considerable energy. But his bitter disappointment over the Franco affair never quite left him and, erstwhile colleagues say, fostered his disillusionment with South Africa and its economic direction. He made no secret of his desire to return to the United States some day, and his wife made no secret of her wish to return to Denver even sooner than that.

Nevertheless, he did not allow his mixed feelings to impair his commitment to leaving a mark at Gold Fields. With Cockerill at his side, he led the company into a golden era. In the four years of their partnership the company grew from a 2-millon-ounce producer employing 70 000-plus people to a 4-million-ounce producer with fewer than 50 000 employees. In the United States, the company's stock rose from less than $2 to more than $17. Staff morale rose accordingly.

Gold Fields became a global champion of unhedged gold production. It involved taking risks – like buying the Bank of England's gold when it came on the market at US$258 an ounce. The move helped to stabilise the price at a critical time. At first the industry was in love with hedging, and Gold Fields was the odd man out. Eventually the entire industry renounced hedging, to the massive benefit of gold producers everywhere.

Thompson had two special gifts: vision and approachability. He saw the big picture and his easy style quickly broke down barriers. He arranged dinners and lunches at his home for senior executives. He took to chatting with staff members at their desks as he did his office rounds. He was visible and friendly. As then vice-president Willie Jacobsz describes it: 'Chris brought order and restored a sense of security and morale.

He took Gold Fields people who had been sidelined by Tom Dale and brought them in from the cold.'

In short, he was an admirable boss. It is hard to imagine that one day his executive team would come to him and ask him to step down as chairman for the sake of the company.

CHAPTER TWENTY-FOUR

A BOMBSHELL LEAK

BY THE END of June 2001 chairman Thompson was trying to make the best of things: 'This has been another trying year characterised by declining gold prices and no new relief for the industry. Franco-Nevada was a big disappointment and the threat of being acquired by AngloGold was a source of concern to you all.'

Yes, that old Anglo bogey had cropped up again, and been knocked down. Thompson could see a silver lining. 'That's largely behind us now. We still have our independence and some of the best assets in the business and reason to be proud of what we have achieved so far. This will surely be a better year for Gold Fields.'

A realistic assessment or merely a fervent wish? You could almost sense the relief on the cover of the annual report for 2002. The chairman didn't actually say 'Whew!' but the report's cover did it for him. A headline in gold ink declared: 'AN OUTSTANDING YEAR FOR GOLD FIELDS.' And subliminal messages flashed across the page in grey, reinforcing the message: 'Ghana ... South Africa ... Australia ... Finland ... NYSE ... Internationalisation ... growth ... value ...'

The company was one of the world's largest unhedged gold companies. Its earnings had risen to a record R3 073-million from a net loss of R906-million the previous year, and its dividend had increased to a record 310 cents a share. It employed nearly 50 000 people and gold production had risen above 4-million ounces. It had attributable mineral resources of 187-million ounces, reserves of 79-million ounces and was exploring on five continents, ranging from the Arctic to the equator. Ex-President Nelson Mandela rang the bell to mark the company's listing on the New York Stock Exchange on 9 May 2002. It was a neat quid pro quo after Gold Fields agreed to build a new school for the former President.

'It's a watershed year for Gold Fields,' exulted Thompson. 'Our international strategy is bearing fruit and is a vindication of our sustained policy of not hedging gold. Gold Fields is now the most profitable gold mining company in the world.'

Basking in the glow, Thompson confirmed that he had resigned as chief executive on 30 June 2002 and would relocate to Denver, Colorado. He would stay on as non-executive chairman. His successor, Ian Cockerill, had vowed to continue with the strategy of ensuring acquisitions had value and current operations improved performance. Success was ensured.

Unwittingly, Thompson departed just as a cloud appeared in this sunny sky. It was not a cloud of his making but it would grow so large so quickly that it would threaten to obscure the silver lining forever. For a while, investors all over the world shuddered.

IN JUNE 2002 someone leaked to the press a copy of a proposed government Mining Charter. To this day, the author of the document is unknown, the motive for releasing it a mystery. Its central proposal was that there should be a minimum 51% black stake in every mine in the country within ten years. This had nothing to do with giving a hand-up to a previously excluded majority. It was a power grab. To hand over more than half of the industry was to disempower the original owners. It was worse than nationalisation because it offered no compensation to the losers.

It came as a bombshell to investors, wiping R52-billion off the value of mining shares on the Johannesburg Stock Exchange in two days.

Mining companies and analysts condemned the proposal. Anglo American said it was 'unacceptable'. Economist Mike Schussler said it would scare away local and overseas investors. No one knew whose interest was served by leaking the draft, but everyone had a theory. Some said Anglo American was the villain, but Bobby Godsell offered an unassailable response: 'Why would we leak a document that was going to knock 11% off our London share price and 8% off our JSE price?' Some thought the leak must have come from the Department of Minerals and Energy. To which the department responded: 'Not us.' Within days government was backpedalling frantically, insisting it was only 'a very rough first draft; everything is negotiable.'

But the damage had been done. Said chairman Thompson:

> The government was quick to distance itself from the terms of the leaked charter. Nonetheless, the leak caused quite a stir in the mining community, not just in South Africa but among the widespread groups of investors overseas who are the largest owners of South Africa's public mining companies. Their concerns are understandable, thus Gold Fields remains committed to the process of engagement with government in the firm belief that this will yield a positive result for all stakeholders.

The leak forced the mining industry to walk a tightrope. It was legitimate to express outrage at the scope of this particular draft, but politically and morally impossible to reject the idea of a charter itself. Thompson proceeded to outline for all to see where Gold Fields stood:

> It is common cause and something that we subscribe to immutably, that if South Africa is to be a success, and if Gold Fields is to survive in the long term, then the mining industry must proactively cater to ambitions of the previously disadvantaged. So too must all South Africans, black and white. Not to do so will mean that the demands of the deprived will drive political agendas in directions no one wants to see them go. This is not a matter for the privileged alone. The burden of meeting the ambitions of the unemployed and poorly paid will rest on us all.
>
> The language of the draft charter posits that the industry is the property of the 'white mine owners' and that transfer of ownership to black empowerment groups is a highly desirable event. Even if it were achievable, financially or economically, transfer of ownership in and of itself will do nothing for job creation or alleviation of poverty.
>
> South Africa's mines are not, in fact, owned by the mythical

'white owners'. Gold Fields is 53% foreign owned, for the most part by institutions which in turn invest the savings and pensions of millions of people in the street. The remaining 47% is owned primarily by South African institutions that invest the savings and pensions of South Africans, a large proportion of whom are black. There is no dominant white owner at all. And therein lies the solution to true widespread black empowerment.

Wider use of pension plans in the work force (via legislation if necessary) will rapidly expand black beneficial ownership. The encouragement of mutual funds and equity ownership for all employees would help a lot too. These are the areas that hold promise for achieving transfer without destroying the industry and, at the same time, increasing the investible pool so critical for allowing development and growth.

To encourage these directions is not novel: all Western civilisations are financed this way, and many successful models exist to copy. Pushing it will bring strains to the economy and industry, but the strains would be far more equitable.

There it was, then: a novel – not to say radical – approach to black empowerment.

Alas, it would be buried under an avalanche of comment, some informed, some mischievous, in the four edgy months until a new Charter emerged in October 2002, negotiated by all and approved by Cabinet. The new Charter acknowledged two imperatives: South Africa needed the mining industry to succeed in international markets; and the mining industry needed to address the socio-economic challenges within the country. It set a new target for black ownership – 26% within ten years, or almost half of the figure originally proposed. It ruled out nationalisation and entrenched the 'willing seller, willing buyer' principle. It added a focus on education, training and improving living conditions, and on developing black suppliers.

It brought a lot of mutual back-slapping. Said *Business Day*: 'All this opens the way for changes in the industry that go beyond enriching a mere handful of middle-class black folk to potentially providing real benefits for poorer people.'

By which time, Thompson's intriguing plan for another path to black empowerment lay dead and forgotten under the rubble of a needless, senseless and very damaging scare. In time, Gold Fields would revive aspects of it.

LONG BEFORE the notorious draft was leaked in 2002, virtually the entire industry had accepted the argument that it had a moral duty to help rectify the inequities of apartheid. Many companies had begun to look around for black partners and for other ways in which the previously disadvantaged could share in the financial benefits of mining.

Despite Gold Fields' image as a skinflint, Plumbridge had always argued that it did more good to create more jobs at lower wages than fewer jobs at higher wages. He was also the first of the mining moguls to initiate secret talks with the black National Union of Mineworkers months before South Africa's first democratic elections. Soon afterwards, the company signed a declaration recognising NUM on all its mines, declaring an end to racial discrimination and promising affirmative action.

By February 1997 Gold Fields had begun talks with its old union protagonist, Cyril Ramaphosa, in his new guise as would-be mining mogul. The talks revolved around arranging for his company – New Africa Investments Limited (NAIL) – to have an interest in Gold Fields. Both parties agreed: the arrangement should be affordable for NAIL and not amount to a free gift. Seven grinding months later a deal seemed imminent but no acceptable formula could be found and the talks were called off.

Gold Fields remained determined to get a black partner. In January 2001 Tokyo Sexwale, an ANC stalwart who was destined to become a Cabinet Minister, joined the board of GFL, sending signals that a new BEE deal might be in the offing. At least the parties would have a chance to get to know one another.

Sexwale was one of a new breed: a former Freedom Fighter who had turned himself into the very model of an entrepreneur, When South African television needed to find a tough but charismatic businessman to head a local version of *The Apprentice*, they looked no further than him.

The flirtation was slow and measured; no whirlwind affair this. It began when Sexwale was appointed a non-executive director in January 2001. About 18 months later an exploration agreement was reached with Mvela Resources, a Sexwale company, and soon after that talks began with Mvela and other potential empowerment partners. They led to an announcement in June 2003 that Mvela would acquire a beneficial interest of 15% in the South African assets of GFL for R4.1-billion.

It was the boldest BEE deal in the industry at that time. And it wasn't long before Sexwale was being tipped as the next chairman of Gold Fields.

Some time after that, a hostile takeover bid for Gold Fields complicated the relationship between GFL and Mvela because the two parties had different perspectives. 'I suppose they might have evaluated the opportunities to improve their position,' says Holland of the complications. 'That's what many investors would do.' Nevertheless, the deal was finalised – and paid for – before the year ended.

Holland explains the circumstances:

> Tokyo's company had 15% of the South African assets and an arrangement whereby it could convert this into shares in the entire company according to an agreed formula.
>
> What they could see ahead of them was that the value of the international assets was going to move up while their share of the whole pie was eroded. So we agreed to fix the formula. But then they wanted both a guaranteed floor to their entitlement and an open-ended exposure to the upside. I said: 'You can't have both.' So we settled on a guaranteed floor and a cap on the upside.
>
> From that moment on, all they were waiting for was the expiry date of the deal. They were locked into the arrangement for at least five years. It was tacitly understood that they might sell at the end of that period, but that wasn't a problem. The law required that we facilitate entry into mining for the previously disadvantaged; it didn't say that it was expected to last forever. As far as we were concerned, it lasted long enough for us to qualify for our new order mining rights.

As for Mvela, it put in R1.3-billion of its own money, leveraged the rest and walked away with R5.5-billion – a three-fold return in five years. It used its windfall to obtain a controlling interest in Northam Platinum, recapitalised it, and bought Boschendal. From their perspective, it was the best deal ever. From our point of view, we met our 15% BEE target and got our new order rights.

The experience with Mvela brought a new wisdom to Gold Fields.

The Mining Charter requires it to meet a target of 26% in the hands of the previously disadvantaged by 2014. Gold Fields thinks it is there already. In addition to the Mvela deal it has introduced an employee share ownership plan that has turned 45 000 black employees into shareholders. It introduced a broad-based BEE transaction for 10% of South Deep employers; created an education trust independently controlled by new shareholders; offered 1% to black employees at all other mines in the group.

'This is a far better way of empowering people,' says Holland. 'Far more broad-based, much closer to the grass roots. I think you'll find, between now and 2014, that you won't have the usual suspects getting richer, you'll have broader-based schemes benefiting a wider spectrum of people.'

ONE MORE THING happened in that eventful year.

Just before Christmas 2003, Holland and Ian Cockerill, then CEO, went to Moscow at the behest of Gold Fields' biggest single shareholder, a Russian company called Norilsk. How Norilsk came to occupy this influential position and to be associated with a hostile takeover bid is a story in its own right, and is told in succeeding chapters.

CHAPTER TWENTY-FIVE

FROM RUSSIA, WITH ANGER

'The surprise of 2004 was the unheralded purchase by Norilsk Nickel of Russia of the 20% Gold Fields shareholding formerly held by Anglo American.'
– Chris Thompson, chairman, GFL Annual Report 2004.

THE PENTAGON used to call it the Domino Effect – the chain reaction that occurs when a significant event triggers another, and another and so on in inexorable sequence. With hindsight, the progression of the Domino Effect on Gold Fields was as predictable as it was disturbing. In the end, the tumbling dominoes threatened to crush Gold Fields entirely.

The first domino fell in January 2001 when Johann Rupert became disillusioned with GFL's performance and decided impetuously to sell Rembrandt's investment. His choice of a buyer seemed almost mischievous – Anglo American, of all companies. But perhaps he had merely run out of other options. He sold at about R22 a share. Within months the gold price had turned around and the GFL share price had soared to more than R150. Rembrandt had thrown away the chance to make billions. Bernard van Rooyen told him he had made the biggest business mistake of his life.

'If you had been a public company,' said the irrepressible Van Rooyen, 'you would have been fired.' In time, Rupert himself acknowledged his unfortunate timing.

The second domino fell when Anglo American decided, three years later, to sell its entire holding of 98.5-million shares to a Russian company without consulting Gold Fields. Thompson called it 'a surprise'. It was much more like a shock.

True, it enabled the company to finally shake free of the Anglo albatross and sent a clear signal that Anglo American no longer aspired (if it ever did) to control its most significant competitor. That, you might think, would have been cause for celebration. In a way, it was. But down the years, and with the departure from the scene of Plumbridge and Ogilvie Thompson, relations between the two gold mining giants had lost their harsh edge.

When Tony Traher took up the top job at Anglo, Thompson went to him and said: 'If you leave us alone, we'll make lots of money for you.' And so began a more congenial era. While AngloGold CEO Bobby Godsell tried from time to time to propose a closer relationship, it never got further than amicable discussion or blunt rejection.

So there were mixed feelings when Anglo sold out without telling Gold Fields who it was selling to. Relief on the one hand; uneasiness on the other. What did the Russians really want with a 20% stake in a South African company?

THE MASSIVE deal with Norilsk Nickel was closed in a single day. The man who negotiated it was Artem Grigorian, by profession a consultant on mergers and acquisitions; by inclination, an African historian. His client, a shadowy Russian company, was the world's largest producer of nickel and palladium, and among the top producers of platinum and copper. The company began as a state venture but was privatised in 1997 when it was bleeding cash at the rate of about US$2-million a day. Soon it became highly profitable – and, according to documents, 'began paying its workers again'. It is headquartered in Moscow and has its primary operations in the permafrost wastes of Siberia, inside the Arctic Circle.

It grew to be an international company employing between 80 000 and 90 000 people and with interests in Russia, Australia, the United States, South Africa and Botswana. It had been casing the world for new opportunities. It concluded that Australia was over-mined and its labour expensive; South America was politically problematic; North America offered little to foreigners; India and China were too difficult for outsiders. Southern Africa was the place. So Grigorian kept a lookout for opportunities from an office in Cape Town.

Keeping his ear to the ground, he got to hear that Anglo American's stake in Gold Fields was up for grabs. On a Friday in March 2004, Norilsk made a bid for it. Its offer of US$1.4-billion was accepted by close of play on the same day and announced on the Monday. The first Gold Fields knew of it was when a Canadian contact phoned Cockerill late on Sunday night to tell him that it had happened.

Jimmy Dowsley, then senior vice-president in charge of corporate development, took a group of people to look at the Norilsk assets. 'They were pretty good,' he says, 'but the people and the accounting – they were opaque. I was very nervous about the individuals. I was amazed when Chris came back from Moscow and said: "Jimmy, you'll like these guys."'

THOMPSON AND COCKERILL headed off to Moscow to meet their new shareholders and to enter the labyrinthine world of Russian business where politics and economics were often intertwined. Russians had their own way of doing business, sometimes alien to the West. There would be differences of culture, of style, of approach. Besides, at least one of Norilsk's leading lights had been too close to the former KGB, to put it no higher. How would such a relationship work?

The new shareholders were two of the richest men in Russia. Vladimir Potanin was richer – worth something like $25-billion – and more politically influential, but Mikhael Prokhorov, with a mere $17-billion, was more visible – in every sense. At well over two metres, 6ft 9ins in fact, he justified the nickname of 'Giraffe' which he had earned as a youngster. He was a man who enjoyed parties and blondes. In time he would be arrested at a French Alpine resort on a charge of procuring prostitutes for his guests, but the charges were dropped after four days and eventually he got an apology from the French government.

They met Potanin first, and liked him immediately. He spoke English fluently. Thompson told him: 'Look, many people have tried to take over Gold Fields. All have failed – and you will too. All that happened was that value was destroyed. Let's avoid that and work together to create a major international company.' Potanin's eyes seemed to light up at the prospect.

Prokhorov was different. Thompson found him arrogant and a playboy who didn't like Westerners. Cockerill thought he wasn't so much arrogant as defensive. They didn't take to him too much. Finally, they met Leonid Rozhetskin, a Russian-born, US-trained attorney who was very smart and didn't look at all like the Machiavelli he turned out to be.

Together, the new shareholders did their best to persuade their visitors that GFL had nothing to worry about. 'It's not a bad deal for you,' Potanin insisted. 'We don't want to change anything. We're just a minority shareholder.' All they wanted were two seats on the GFL board. No problem: Grigorian and a Norilsk employee called Sergei Stefanovich were appointed as directors.

And there the situation might have settled – comfortable and apparently unthreatening – had the Gold Fields' imperatives not come to the fore again: explore, grow, internationalise. But they did come to the fore, and that was what caused the third domino to fall. It led, eventually and inevitably, to an upstart mining company concluding that Gold Fields was ripe for a hostile takeover.

Oh yes, and it also led to a betrayal by Norilsk which, in its turn, felt betrayed by Gold Fields.

The problems that followed came partly from the law of unintended consequences and partly from a communication lapse. Nevertheless, when all was said and done, it was the malice aforethought that stuck in most minds.

DESPITE THE SETBACK of Franco-Nevada, chairman Thompson had not abandoned his dream of internationalisation. If anything, he was more determined than ever. He was convinced that Gold Fields' future lay in spreading its net internationally and he never stopped looking for opportunities. Indeed, he was becoming irritated that Ian Cockerill, his successor as CEO, didn't seem to have the same level of commitment.

And then one day he thought he had found the perfect opportunity again.

IAMGold is an odd name for a company, but there was nothing odd about the company itself. With headquarters in Toronto, it mines in Canada, Africa and elsewhere. In time it would become a junior partner with Gold Fields in the Tarkwa and Damang mines in Ghana. (In 2011 it sold its interest to GFL for $667-million and, with a war-chest of $1-billion, went looking for other investments.)

The spark between the two companies came when Thompson discovered that IAMGold shared GFL's desire to acquire new assets, and was enthusiastic about joining forces. The plan was simple: Gold Fields would sell its assets outside South Africa to the Canadian company and use the proceeds to acquire 70% of that company, leaving the South African company in control. This new giant – Gold Fields International – would be bolstered by other acquisitions Thompson was working on, giving it a potential market capitalisation of US$25-billion. It would be registered in Canada, based in Denver and led by South Africans. Thompson would be the chief executive.

The deal would solve the perennial problem that Gold Fields had identified: grow abroad or face a slow death at home.

Unhappily, not everyone shared Thompson's enthusiasm. Some shareholders and observers thought the deal was a ruse by Thompson to take Gold Fields to Denver. They felt strongly about it. Denials and explanations by Thompson and Cockerill fell on stony ground. The unfounded perception created fierce resistance; made Cockerill uneasy about pushing too hard for the deal.

Says Thompson:

> Early in 2004 I showed the deal in principle to Ian. I was due to stand down as chair in late 2004. Along with the board, I was getting more and more concerned about the growing anti-mining sentiment in the ANC, the stronger rand and the declining gold industry in South Africa. The growth imperative was over-shadowing us again and Ian had shown little or no urge to do any acquisition in his first 18 months as CEO.
>
> I had made it clear to both Ian and Nick Holland that, if the deal came off, they would have to move to Denver and take over the reins because I had no plans to run a company any more. Ian and

I had been a very successful partnership, doubling gold production during our time together. He was a very good operator, and good with his subordinates. Now, suddenly, he was dragging his feet on the IAMGold scheme. I had backed him as my successor and I began to wonder if I had put the right guy in the job.

In the end I said if he didn't put it to the board, I regarded it as my final duty to explain what could be done with the deal. The board loved it and asked me to stay on to oversee its completion.

Cockerill hotly denies dragging his feet. 'I supported growing abroad. But the political objections were a reality. They could not be ignored. Neither could the wishes of major shareholders.'

So far, so good. In August 2004, Chairman Thompson once again proclaimed to the world at large that a deal had been struck. It needed only to be approved by shareholders at the annual meeting in December. The law didn't actually require shareholder approval, and advisers urged him not to bother. But Thompson and the board felt a moral obligation to give them a say; after all, the deal would change the face of Gold Fields.

What Thompson didn't realise, at first, was the strength of the resistance that was building up. Attitudes were hardening, particularly among some shareholders. Feelings were running high. He was in for some rude awakenings. The first came from his deputy chairman, Alan Wright. It was relatively mild.

'You know, Chris, if the IAMGold deal goes through you won't be the top man any more,' Wright remembers telling him. 'You might be the top man in Denver but you will have to report to the chairman and CEO of Gold Fields in Johannesburg.'

Thompson said: 'No, I'll still be the boss.'

And Wright replied: 'You can't be. Denver can only be a subsidiary and the main people in Johannesburg are going to be the main operating people.'

Thompson seemed surprised. As he understood things, there would be an independent board, and he would be CEO and Gordon Parker chairman. Was there some misunderstanding somewhere?

THE NEXT RUDE awakening was precipitated by a communication lapse. In early 2004, long before the critical December meeting of shareholders, Thompson and Cockerill met the Russians' representative, Rozhetskin, in a private dining room at London's Barclay Hotel. Says Cockerill: 'We discussed the issues relating to the IAMGold deal and I wrote the details down on the back of a menu. Rozhetskin was enthusiastic. I left the meeting feeling that we had communicated with our senior shareholder.'

But Norilsk itself was convinced that it had not been briefed and, as a major shareholder, was deeply offended.

As to why Norilsk was kept in the dark, there is a third, darker explanation that appeals to conspiracy theorists. Some Gold Fields people believe it; some don't. It relates to Rozhetskin, the man. The conspiracy theorists say he didn't tell Norilsk about the deal because it suited him to create a rift between Gold Fields and the Russian company. He wanted Norilsk to become angry because, if it were angry enough, it might be persuaded to support a hostile takeover bid against Gold Fields. By this tortuous route, Rozhetskin thought he could reach his own goal: a takeover by Norilsk of a much more powerful gold mining combination of Gold Fields and the takeover company. It would earn him a US$25-million commission.

Rozhetskin was charming, brilliant, two-faced and quite capable of devious plotting. He lived two lives. He was the father of a son by his wife, an extraordinarily beautiful Russian model called Natalya Belova. He craved wealth and status. But he also craved gay young men and could indulge himself because he had made several fortunes. And several serious enemies too, especially when a business deal went sour while he was living in a Moscow penthouse with floors of pink and purple marble and a pink poodle.

For years he kept his homosexual instincts in the closet, probably because Russian society was very straitlaced.

In March 2008 he took an unexpected break at his Latvian seaside home. On the night of his arrival, two rent boys were seen entering his house. They left about 1.30 am to return to the gay club from which they had been hired. Some time during that night or early next morning, Rozhetskin vanished. Police found blood on his apartment's marble floors and, later, when they recovered his missing car, blood on the back seats too. Friends were convinced he had been murdered by contract killers.

He has never been seen again and his body has never been found. But under Latvian law he cannot be officially declared dead until ten years have elapsed. So he remains merely 'missing'.

Cockerill says he tried several times to contact Rozhetskin to confirm that he had informed his principals, but got no response – until an hour before the deal was announced. That was when his phone rang.

'You can't do this. You've got to stop,' said Rozhetskin.

'Stop what?'

'The deal with IAMGold.'

'Why?'

'My principals are not in favour of it.'

'Leonid,' said Cockerill, 'we told you what we were doing. It was your responsibility to brief them. We can't turn back now.'

'There may be unfortunate consequences,' said Rozhetskin, and rang off. He turned out to be absolutely right.

In August 2004, GFL announced the IAMGold deal to the world. It was sooner than the South African company would have liked, but its hand had been forced. In terms of Canadian law IAMGold had to tell its own shareholders the news as soon as the deal was agreed. GFL realised it would look very silly indeed if it kept silent. But to confirm such a deal four months before a scheduled meeting to get shareholder approval – and while government was still considering it – was to invite trouble.

In its August announcement, GFL was careful to stress that the deal still needed to be ratified by shareholders. That didn't placate Norilsk, still angry about being kept in the dark. It chose to put the worst possible construction on things. Thompson, it concluded, wanted to feather his own nest by moving the bulk of Gold Fields to Denver – or, as director Grigorian put it, to 'over-smart their shareholders'. Besides, Norilsk wanted a holding in a company with 50% South African assets and 50% international assets and the merger would skew that situation.

On top of that, the Russians felt that GFL's assets had been undervalued and IAMGold's over-valued; that Norilsk's interest in GFL would be diluted; that the whole deal was too expensive. Then and there, Norilsk decided to vote against the merger. Or, rather, was persuaded to by a Gold Fields ill-wisher named Bernard Swanepoel, CEO of an up-and-coming gold mining company called Harmony. Domino Number Four tumbled when Norilsk changed its allegiance.

Harmony's attempt to take over Gold Fields with the connivance of Norilsk would dominate the headlines day after day for well over half a year – cheeky, bitter, cunning. It had echoes of the Minorco debacle of the 1980s with twists of its own. It would keep South Africa and investors round the world on tenterhooks, half fascinated, half bemused.

CHAPTER TWENTY-SIX

Predator on the Prowl

IT IS POSSIBLE to pinpoint precisely when the fifth domino fell. It was in the evening of an early summer Saturday – 16 October 2004. Cockerill was celebrating his mother-in-law's 70th birthday with a barbecue in the garden when the phone rang.

The caller said: 'Hullo Ian, it's Bernard Swanepoel. I'm phoning as a courtesy to tell you that Harmony will launch a takeover bid for Gold Fields on Monday morning. I need to know, within 48 hours, where you stand.' The tone was cool and businesslike, not hostile.

'Oh, really? What are the terms?'

'We're offering 1.275 Harmony shares for every Gold Fields share.'

Cockerill kept his cool too. 'Okay, fine. I will convey your proposal to the board. But I must tell you I think it highly unlikely that the directors will accept it.'

Swanepoel pressed on: 'You should also be aware that I have got an irrevocable from the Russians for their 20%.'

'Fine,' said Cockerill, though his mind was racing. An 'irrevocable' meant a firm undertaking from Norilsk that it would throw in its lot with Harmony. He knew one thing for certain: for him, the birthday braai was over. He handed the barbecue tongs to his son and excused himself from the family gathering. 'When you've worked in the gold mining industry, you're used to all sorts of curved balls coming at you. You almost kick into a slow-down mode because, if you don't, you can make some very hasty decisions that you might regret.'

The first thing to do was get hold of chairman Thompson, who was racing his car somewhere in the United States. They agreed: an urgent board meeting was necessary. He called the company secretary to put it together – for the next day, Sunday. There would be a conference call hook-up for those who couldn't be there in person.

The directors had a fiduciary duty to consider any offer. At the hastily called board meeting there was ready agreement that Harmony's offer was totally unacceptable. Derisory, really. Swanepoel had made it clear that he would proceed with his bid whatever the board said. Cockerill decided to take as much time as he needed to put in place the strongest defence possible.

To the public – and at least one member of the board – the initial silence smacked of indecision. How can you stay almost silent for nearly a fortnight after receiving a hostile takeover bid? And when GFL did at last respond – on 30 October – it was cursory and dismissive, describing the bid as 'a coercive attempt to gain control of Gold Fields via an early settlement offer rather than a single offer conducted in the normal way'.

It was not a response calculated to stir the blood. Nor did it reveal that GFL's blood was boiling. But it was. It was preparing to fight for its life.

SWANEPOEL'S COURTESY CALL was not a complete surprise. Thompson and Cockerill had met with Swanepoel a few weeks before when rumours were flying about Harmony's intentions. Something was up – but what? Secrets are not easily kept in the tight-knit world of Johannesburg mining. The market – and mining circles – had been buzzing with rumours for days. Some were wildly inaccurate. Newspapers, revelling in their ignorance, tried to outdo each other in their speculation. An unidentified predator was on the prowl. Gold Fields was alert but not alarmed. It was used to rumours about itself.

As Cockerill himself liked to say: 'If you are the father of pretty daughters, you expect predators to come calling. Gold Fields was a very pretty daughter indeed.'

Adding fuel to the rumours was a false perception that GFL had been made particularly vulnerable by unsettled times in the entire industry. The market liked nothing better than to predict crisis ahead. The Mining Charter and BEE requirements were proving insurmountable obstacles, they reasoned. False. An innovative deal with Tokyo Sexwale's

Mvelaphanda Resources would see it acquire 15% of GFL within five years. And pay R4-billion in cash for it.

Chairman Thompson had described fiscal 2004 as 'difficult but eventful'. Was he saying that the company had been harmed? Wrong. He was merely presenting an honest picture, mostly of common industry ailments. As he reported to shareholders:

> Some of the difficulties in the form of the transformation mandates imposed by government were predictable, but the principal problem, the strengthening of the improbable rand, was not. The rand averaged R6.90 to the US dollar compared with R9.07 for fiscal 2003, a rise of over 24%. As a result the indomitable South African gold mining industry is struggling to achieve profitability despite a gold price that hovers around $400 an ounce. But for the success of our non-South African operations, the financial results for the year would have been quite poor. The South African operations are now under extreme pressure.

Costs had risen in rand and dollar terms, driven largely by an expensive union settlement in July 2003. If things continued on this path, there would be shaft closures and lay-offs.

Was he saying that GFL was shaky at the roots? Not at all – GFL was doing better than merely coping. But it was one of those uneasy times when the more far-fetched a claim was, the more likely it was that it would be believed. Envious rivals found it all too easy to interpret Gold Fields' focus on international growth as a sign of weakness rather than a simple recognition that South African gold was a diminishing asset. The mere existence of a deal with IAMGold, they argued, proved that GFL felt the need to find a prop for itself. False. The deal was equally advantageous to both parties and met GFL's oft-repeated imperative to grow abroad.

But no doubt something was brewing – and the media had long since realised that speculating in print often forced real information into the open. It worked again this time. Such gossip would not usually have occasioned much more than a ripple in the mining-camp psyche of Johannesburg. But Swanepoel found himself under pressure from the media and from others and decided to make his bid public sooner than planned.

Hence the call to Cockerill; hence the press release announcing the takeover bid on Monday 18 October. Being Swanepoel, he came out swinging. First public reaction was a mixture of incredulity and grudging admiration. Harmony was a successful upstart; Gold Fields an established giant. He couldn't be serious, could he? – a shark attacking a whale? It was thoroughly cheeky, typically Swanepoel – and whatever the outcome, it should make for a riveting spectacle and a rare old battle.

And so the contestants went to war.

ZACHARIAS BERNARD SWANEPOEL is not your stereotypical mining mogul – nor does he look like a man who once aspired to creating and controlling the biggest gold mining company in the world. He bounds into a recent interview in blue jeans and unfashionably casual shirt; no jacket, no tie. But looks are deceptive.

He seems surprised to learn that Gold Fields' executives had been seriously stressed by his hostile bid all those years before. His reaction is a shade disingenuous; after all, as the whiz-kid of the industry, he had much to lose too. His reputation, for instance.

'Oh really?' he says when told of GFL's reaction, and proceeds to present his business philosophy, only he doesn't call it that. 'I've had my share of successes and failures. I enjoyed the successes and I learnt from the failures. In the case of Gold Fields, I tried, I failed, I moved on. It was always going to be a long shot.' He pauses, finds it irresistible to add his own sardonic footnote: 'Do you think Gold Fields learnt from its failures too?'

Back in 2004, Swanepoel didn't much like the idea that Harmony was thought of by some as an upstart. The company warranted greater respect than that. He was riding the crest of a wave, the blue-eyed boy of the industry. His peers regarded him as very bright and very self-assured; an assessment he no doubt shared, although his preferred style was more self-deprecating. It was an endearing trait.

With a BSc in mining engineering and a BCom (Hons) he launched himself into mining as a hands-on learner with Gengold, subsequently becoming a highly successful mine manager and spending a year on secondment as a mining analyst. He had three of the essential ingredients for progress in this tough world: vision, charisma and cockiness.

In 1995, at the age of only 34, he became Harmony's CEO. Over the next 12 years, he grew production from 650 000 ounces to 3-million ounces, turning the company into the fifth-largest gold producer in the world. Inevitably, the media called him the man with a Midas touch. They called him less flattering names too, but usually with grudging respect. In his heyday, in a newspaper interview, he presented himself as just an ordinary bloke. His hobbies, he said, were reading, jogging and family; his favourite book was the Bible; and his long-term ambition was 'to be exactly where I am now, only wiser'.

In fact, his ambition was larger than that. In 2004 he decided that fifth place in the gold hierarchy was not good enough for Harmony. It needed to make a great leap; something more than the step-by-step growth of before. He thought he saw a golden opportunity. Could he sabotage the GFL deal with IAMGold – and replace it with a coup of his own? He thought he could. In fact, he knew exactly how it could be done.

He decided that he would try to swallow Gold Fields. Cynical observers saw it as cheeky but enjoyed the audacity. Swanepoel saw a bigger picture. Combined, the shark and the whale would become the world's number one gold producer almost overnight. But he had to act quickly –before GFL shareholders met on Tuesday 7 December, to vote on the merger. If it were approved, it would very likely place Gold Fields beyond attack. So he had exactly 50 days – seven weeks and one day – to persuade the shareholders of Gold Fields to vote down the IAMGold deal and open the door to a Harmony bid.

GFL's Achilles heel was Norilsk, angry as it was about being kept in the dark over the IAMGold proposal. Could he suborn this 20% shareholder? He determined to try.

About the time when Gold Fields was announcing the IAMGold deal, Swanepoel made his move. He asked his advisers at HSBC (Hong Kong and Shanghai Banking Corporation) to make an appointment for him with Norilsk. He wanted to tell the Russians that he thought Gold Fields was selling itself short to the Canadian company. The suggestion fell on fertile soil. Its board agreed that Gold Fields had undervalued its own assets. Did he have an alternative plan?

Yes, indeed he did – a double-whammy of a plan, to be implemented in two stages.

In the first stage, Norilsk would use its 20% holding to vote against the IAMGold option. Hopefully that would persuade other shareholders to follow suit. In the second stage, Norilsk would throw its shareholding into the pool to support the Harmony takeover bid. The poetic justice appealed to the Russian company. Gold Fields had kept it in the dark; very well, two could play that game.

On Saturday 16 October Swanepoel learnt that the Norilsk board had approved his strategy. It signed an agreement to support Harmony and made it irrevocable for six months. In a single move he had sewn up the holder of 20% of his prey's capital.

He had always believed that time and momentum were critical in any business venture. That same day, he picked up the phone to Cockerill.

Harmony's bid became South Africa's most sensational takeover attempt. It made international headlines. It had all the elements of high drama: a Johnny-come-lately mining house trying to take over an established giant, to create the most powerful gold mining company in the world. It would command headlines from the world's media. It would go on for seven exhausting months until an almost farcical court ruling put an end to the misery. By that time, both companies were bleeding and investors were saying: a plague on both your houses.

At the beginning, there was a hero and a villain too, both essential to a good drama. Gold Fields was the Goliath, perceived to be smug and complacent. Swanepoel was the boyishly engaging David. The public liked the imagery. The underdog was the media favourite, and the underdog knew how to milk the publicity for all its worth. The battle unleashed a weird and wonderful menagerie: never mind sharks and whales and underdogs, there were red herrings and rabbits emerging from hats. Scapegoats too, and snakes in the grass and spitting cats. It was a show worthy of a Roman circus.

ON THE MONDAY of Harmony's public announcement, Swanepoel set up an international conference call to tell the world of his plans. It was the first shot in the battle for the hearts and minds of investors and analysts, and Harmony's man oozed confidence:

> Good afternoon ladies and gentlemen, or good morning to the people in North America. Thank you very much for joining us. I am told there are over 200 people dialled in. I am going to do a very quick overview ... and try and give maximum time for questions and answers.
> The offer that we put to Gold Fields shareholders today, as you are all aware, is 1.275 Harmony shares for every Gold Fields share. This offer values Gold Fields at just over eight billion US dollars, and represents a premium of 29% to Gold Fields' 30 business day volume weighted average price, up to and including the 14th. We just picked the 14th because obviously after that incorrect rumours were beginning to impact on share prices. The value proposition for Harmony shareholders sits in our proven track record of reducing costs. We back ourselves to achieve the 15% cost reduction on the three big South African mines in order to break even in terms of the premium we have offered.
> For Gold Fields shareholders that holds true. What also holds true for Gold Fields shareholders is that this transaction is demonstrably better than the IAMGold transaction. One of the main considerations therefore is that the IAMGold transaction gets voted down as we get to that point in time on the seventh of December.

He explained that Harmony had made a rare two-tier bid. The first stage provided for early acceptances of the Harmony offer within 30 days. Acceptors would get their money sooner and avoid entanglement in a lengthy takeover battle – 'if it comes to that.' After that there would be a compulsory follow-on offer on the same terms. Of course, all regulatory processes would have to be complied with. That was when Norilsk would throw its 20% into Harmony's takeover pool.

QUESTION: What do the South African authorities have to approve?
BS: We certainly couldn't foresee any problems with the Reserve Bank because we are not asking for any

special dispensation. The Competition Commission may take time, but it is a pretty well understood process. Our legal advisers say that there shouldn't be significant competition issues raised that can't be addressed. But the time period that the Competition Commission allows itself is 60 days, plus a right to extend that by another 30 days; that is the bottleneck.

QUESTION: Bernard, you've got a large amount of South African assets under one roof there. What makes you feel sort of easy that the Competition Bureau is going to approve this?

BS: We have had many filings by many gold companies in the past. Our Competition Commission has historically always come to the conclusion that the level of concentration in no ways whatsoever impacts on the price setting of gold.

QUESTION: Why would Gold Fields shareholders pander to Harmony when in fact you are making large losses and their cost of production is a lot lower than yours?

BS: When Gold Fields shareholders do the analysis I think what will become very clear is that Harmony's ability to reduce costs will be very advantageous. The Gold Fields assets in South Africa have slipped into quite a marginal position and it actually found itself in cash negative territory until the capital expenditure was curtailed. You can curtail capital expenditure for a few quarters, but you shorten the life of those mines quite significantly. We are very comfortable that our proven ability to reduce cost structures will significantly enhance the cash flow of the Gold Fields assets.

QUESTION: Have you spoken to any Gold Fields shareholders?

BS: We got overtaken by time and the fact that the market started to speculate, albeit incorrectly. It forced us to bring forward our announcement to this morning. We didn't speak to any Gold Fields shareholder other than Norilsk. Obviously for the reasons of them being the biggest and us wanting to secure their irrevocable undertaking to vote against the IAMGold transaction and to accept the Harmony offer.

QUESTION: My understanding is that the follow-up offer only gets triggered if you get to 34.9%. Could there be a situation where you end up with, say, 20-25% of Gold Fields, Norilsk with 20%, the balance in the market? How does that play out?

BS: You guys obviously get paid to generate a thousand possible scenarios. And we can speak about all 999 of those. Our offer is to get to 50.1%, and that is the condition that is still in place. There are a few critical benchmark points. The first one is 30 days from now. We will get some acceptances. They will be shareholders who will exit as soon as they can mop in the profit.

Then you will be into the period up to and including the Gold Fields AGM. If the IAMGold transaction gets approved there, then obviously our offer goes away. So that is the second sort of benchmark point. And then we run up to the end when all of the other conditions have been met, and we go over the 50%, and that 50% of course is inclusive of Norilsk. I am trying to give you the process. I think people are going to have to make their own interpretations of possible outcomes.

QUESTION: If I were Gold Fields I might consider using delaying tactics and so make a timing mismatch between the upcoming [IAMGold] vote and your ability to close the early settlement offer.

BS: I am sure that by now Gold Fields would have had many opinions suggesting delaying tactics and frustrating actions. Frustrating actions, of course, are something that the courts and the regulators do not look kindly on. Quite honestly we think they will be barking at their own shadows. That may not stop them, but I would be extremely surprised if they waste shareholders' money on frustrating actions.

SWANEPOEL was in for an 'extreme surprise'. Before the seven months were out, Gold Fields had spent R316-million on legal fees and Harmony had spent about R184-million. Swanepoel recalls that there were something like 23 legal actions on the go at one stage. The figure may be exaggerated – but not by much.

Almost every statement by one party or the other was challenged in one forum or another, and counter-challenged thereafter. Shareholder disillusion reflected in the share price of both companies. Cockerill calculates that both companies lost value amounting to nearly R2-billion in the protracted battle. Yet neither side could escape the roundabout with honour before the fight was settled, and that didn't happen until May 2005. By that time, the public had become tired of the spectacle and the final judgment, when it came, was a massive anti-climax.

Or a farce, as some journalists called it.

CHAPTER TWENTY-SEVEN

DEADLINES, DAMN DEADLINES

By its nature, there is something insulting about a hostile takeover bid. The challenger is sending a very clear and public message to existing management: Get out of the way; we can do it better.

It is inherently personal. And it accounts, in part, for the ferocity, not to say animosity, that characterised the takeover battle.

What made Harmony's CEO Swanepoel believe that Gold Fields – so much bigger and more powerful – was vulnerable? Says Swanepoel today:

> It was quite obvious to me. My perception was that the management team had run out of ideas. They were getting a lot of bad PR for the way they treated Norilsk; it seemed like they were trying to manage their shareholder as opposed to managing their business. The catalyst, from an outsider's perspective, was the IAMGold deal, a very convoluted transaction to split up the company. There was significant shareholder dissatisfaction – like I say, they were not the most favoured management team around in the gold mining industry. They put themselves in play.

In the same interview, he acknowledged the personal nature of the bid – obliquely and perhaps unwittingly – when he added:

> The one thing it would have been very hard for Gold Fields to ever accept is that we brought a simpler, smarter way of operating a mine. Our share price didn't go from R9 to R180 only on hype and bullshit. But the whole thing was cast from day one as an aggressive

attack on their egos or their credibility, which it had to be. The result was we never sat down and said: How do one and one make more than two?

The comment invites a fundamental question: Did there need to be a crisis over the Harmony bid at all? If Swanepoel was offering all those good things – bigger profits, better management, more efficient systems, happier shareholders – why resist it? Why not just accept the goodies gratefully?

Why not indeed?

It is likely that Gold Fields' immediate reaction to the bid may have been coloured by bruised pride as much as anything. But Cockerill, too, was aware of the dangers of a personal war. He asked his executives to make a much harder choice.

'This is not about you,' he told them. 'It's about what's best for shareholders. Ultimately we want to ask shareholders a single question: Who would you rather have manage these assets – Harmony or Gold Fields?'

The assessment dictated the strategy. Cockerill appointed a defence team that included Nick Holland, John Munro, Jimmy Dowsley, Willie Jacobsz and Terence Goodlace.

The team would work on nothing else but debunking what had come to be known as 'Harmony's Way'. Each member had a specified role. 'We wanted to show that Harmony's Way was nothing but a hall of mirrors, a hollow shell,' said Cockerill.

But the day-to-day business had to go on too. Mike Prinsloo led the operational team. And then there were international operations. Says Cockerill: 'We said to them: "Guys, just go out there and break rock and produce gold. Performance is the best defence."'

ONE IMPORTANT element in the defence was still missing. It was all very well to say that the executive agreed that the bid was undesirable. How did ordinary staff feel about it? Were they as loyal to the company as the people at the top? Perhaps they would actually prefer a new owner? Cockerill decided to find out for himself.

Consulting ordinary workers would, he hoped, boost morale. More importantly, it would enable him to apply the first rule of warfare: know your enemy. He needed to know who would be with him in the battle to come.

He started at head office, saying:

> Look, we don't believe that the Harmony offer is good for us. We will be trying our level best to resist it. I can't promise you it's going to be over quickly. The best thing you can all do is to make sure you do your job well. Don't worry about the bid because it's the job of the defence team to do that. If we all worry about the bid we take our eye off running the business day to day. We can't afford for that to happen.

He was pleasantly surprised at the warmth of the response.

But that was the easy part. How would the people on the mines feel? Almost by tradition, miners tended to deride their head offices. Would the people of Gold Fields instinctively react that way?

He got his answer when he went to Driefontein. About 10 000 people were waiting to hear what he had to say. Cockerill gave them a simple message: 'We know what happens when Harmony takes over mines. The only way they can afford this particular transaction is to take out jobs. I don't want you people to lose your jobs.' The crowd gave a rousing cheer. A similar response came when he went to Kloof.

But it was only when he went to Beatrix in the Free State that the human dimension really hit home. A large group of wives were waiting for him at the gates. They carried placards saying 'NO TO HARMONY'. He realised they were encouraging their men not to bow down. It gave him an adrenalin rush to know that the heart of the company, the DNA of the organisation, was with him.

He told his defence team: 'Guys, you know what? Even if we go down in flames it doesn't matter. We are not going to allow this to happen.'

THE DEFENCE TEAM began to delve furiously into 'Harmony's Way' – the strategy that had underpinned that company's acclaimed early successes. Was it all that it was cracked up to be? Gradually it became apparent, at least to Cockerill and his team, that the strategy was flawed and had, at its heart, a built-in guarantee of failure.

Former President Thabo Mbeki put his finger on the central conundrum. 'Tell me,' he once asked Cockerill at a meeting, 'how is it that a company that is not making money can make a bid for a company that is making money?'

Mbeki's question was apt. Harmony had not paid a dividend for several years; Gold Fields was making money and paying dividends.

Cockerill told Mbeki: 'It's simple. The company that's not making money needs to feed off the bones of Gold Fields. But Gold Fields is not going to be dismembered to feed Harmony. Yes, it may create the world's largest gold company but it would be the world's largest gold company that didn't make money.'

Doing the analysis that many analysts had failed to do, the defence team uncovered what it thought was the trick to it all. The official Response Document – when it finally appeared on 3 November – was devastating. Coolly and clinically it tore Harmony's claims and pretensions into pitiful shreds in 42 pages of analysis, graphs and facts.

Its introductory letter from chairman Thompson set the tone: 'It is rare indeed that a hostile takeover bid has combined such a serious threat with such little merit ... Harmony's hostile and unsolicited offer is structured to buy Gold Fields on the cheap.'

Harmony had boasted of its ability to cut costs. It was easy enough to reduce corporate overheads quickly after acquiring new assets from companies like Anglo and Gold Fields. But that was a once-off benefit. Research revealed that, within four or five quarters, costs rose to the old levels again. That didn't matter so much when the gold price was rising on the back of a falling rand and it was profitable to mine more of Harmony's lower-grade ores. But when the rand began to strengthen and the gold price settled ... why, a strategic variation was called for.

It compelled Harmony to continue to issue new equity to acquire higher-grade assets to give the illusion of growth. Even then, it failed. In the first quarter of the 2005 financial year Harmony posted a net operating loss of R112-million; Gold Fields made an operating profit of R120-million. And so the Response Document went on. And on. The demolition job was withering.

Says Cockerill: 'The Harmony model was always going to work while it could acquire fresh assets at knockdown prices to do this little front-end engineering. But when you run out of things to acquire, the model runs out of steam.'

Of course Swanepoel didn't accept then that Harmony's Way was flawed. He still doesn't. He counters: 'If you start off, as we did, with the worst ore body in the country it's not hard to upgrade. All 15 assets in Harmony, except the original mine, came in through acquisitions. Even if you're buying AngloGold's biggest pile of crap, it is still better than your own. So that, unashamedly, was our corporate strategy.'

The argument for rejection gained momentum. Gold Fields had Saks Fifth Avenue assets against Harmony's Walmart selection which, very likely, had been overstated anyway. Promises of increased productivity were too glib. The only beneficiaries of a takeover would be the shareholders of the lesser company.

Gold Fields came to the conclusion that if it acquiesced in a takeover, it would in effect be signing its own death warrant as a company. Worse, it would be entering into a relationship with a partner whose long-term strategy it considered doomed. That would be a betrayal of shareholders and investors.

By happy chance, the conclusion served the best interests of the executive team too, For individual executives, it didn't need much insight to recognise that the writing was on the wall. Swanepoel's jibes about the quality of leadership at Gold Fields, his insistence that executives should resign over the failed IAMGold vote, his regular public denigration – all confirmed that their jobs were on the line.

It was time to fight.

At the start, Harmony seemed to have victory in its grasp. It won three legal challenges in a row. Swanepoel's chutzpah, GFL's curiously muted initial response, courtroom defeats, sympathetic media reporting … all combined to suggest that the senior mining company was on the ropes.

EARLY ON, Gold Fields learnt one important fact about Swanepoel: he was a formidable opponent and he enjoyed a public scrap, the tougher the better. His regular and provocative statements were designed to chip away at confidence in Gold Fields. The media spotlight was harsh and constant. Swanepoel spared no one.

At first the campaign of personal denigration seemed to catch Gold Fields off-guard. A gentlemanly organisation, it wasn't used to a streetfight of that kind. Apart from announcing that it was preparing a counter-document, it said little publicly. Internally, it was asking itself a question: Do we go head to head with Swanepoel? Match him blow for blow? Get down in the gutter with him? The decision was to play it straight; ignore insult, innuendo and slur; stick to facts; keep the tone dignified.

Or, at least, that was the intention. Sometimes Gold Fields couldn't resist getting in its own little digs. It appeared to have the result of provoking Swanepoel even more.

The most provocative campaign against Harmony was devised by the communications team lead by Jacobsz. It featured a cartoon character who bobbed up everywhere – in newspaper advertisements, even on the big scoreboard at the Wanderers cricket ground – asking: 'Bernard, where's the Competent Person's Report?' A Competent Person's Report (CPR) is akin to an auditor's report. It comes from an independent and qualified outside source and authenticates a mining company's own estimates of reserves and resources, critical elements in assessing the worth of a company.

Irritated by the implication that he had overstated Harmony's prospects, Swanepoel undertook to produce a CPR – and then failed to do so. Gold Fields made the most of it. Swanepoel retaliated by christening Jacobsz 'Comical Willie', after Saddam Hussein's bumbling sidekick Comical Ali.

It amused the public – even if it didn't amuse the combatants.

JUST AS MOOD music sets the scene in movies, so the series of explicit deadlines in the battle between Harmony and Gold Fields ratcheted up the tension, increased the strain on the warring parties.

First was the deadline for early-bird acceptances, the so-called first stage. Those who wanted to take immediate advantage of the Harmony offer had until noon on 17 November to accept, exactly 30 days from the time the offer was made. Would Harmony get the 35% or so of acceptances it was hoping for? Would this provide a pointer to the eventual outcome?

As it happened, Harmony got only 11.8%. Did this mean triumph for Gold Fields, then? It wasn't as simple as that. Harmony had Norilsk's 20% in the bag, and other big shareholders were reputed to be unhappy about the foreign merger. It was still anybody's game.

Besides, the next critical deadline was a mere 20 days away – Tuesday 7 December, the day when GFL shareholders were due to vote on the IAMGold proposal. On the face of it, this vote had nothing whatever to do with Harmony. But Swanepoel had cunningly inserted his company into the equation by insisting from the beginning that a vote in favour of IAMGold would mean an end to Harmony's bid.

So would this day of reckoning reveal who was winning the takeover war? Not necessarily.

It is true that some shareholders were confused, and had come to believe that the two issues were inextricably linked. They thought they were facing an either/or choice: IAMGold or Harmony. Cockerill tried to restore some sanity. 'A vote *against* IAMGold is not a vote *for* Harmony. These are two different matters,' he cautioned. 'If Gold Fields loses the Canadian company it's not the end of the world. We are considering alternatives, and they don't include Harmony.'

Harmony promptly expressed dismay at Cockerill's 'surprise' announcement that it had alternatives. If Gold Fields was looking at other options while Harmony's bid was still on the table then, it said, that was surely a matter for the stock exchange regulators.

There was one more deadline to contend with – the most important of them all. Stock Exchange rules require that a takeover bid must remain on the table for at least 60 days, giving shareholders ample opportunity to accept the offer if they wish. But if the takeover party fails to gain control by that deadline, the bid automatically falls away and the takeover is deemed to have failed. This raised a key question: when, precisely, did Harmony's offer lapse? Sixty days after the first stage? Or 60 days after the second?

GFL's legal adviser, Michael Katz, was confident he knew the answer. Harmony, just as confidently, disagreed with him. It took until May 2005 before a court ruling finally resolved the dispute. By that time, the war had lasted seven months. It ended not with a bang but a whimper.

IN THE MIDST of this thicket of deadlines, one legal skirmish followed the other in one venue or the other, leading to appeals in yet other venues and each time creating an entirely new set of deadlines. Dates for rulings were set and, very often, delayed as the clock ticked. For the participants, it made for frantic times. Lawyers were bobbing up everywhere; so were legal costs. Accusations and counter-accusations were traded with abandon. It was legal ping-pong on a grand scale. Thompson felt strongly that the event had become a 'fee fest' for both companies' lawyers and advisers.

To an increasingly bemused public, it seemed like an interminable legal wrangle with no goal in mind and no end in sight.

The ping-pong began on 18 November when the competition tribunal rejected an urgent appeal from GFL to stop the deal at its first stage. Its chairman cautioned that the Competition Act shouldn't be used to chill hostile takeovers, an important part of the competitive process. From then on, it was non-stop warfare.

Bankers and other advisers were drawn into the fight. Nearly all had worked for both parties at some time or another and were vulnerable to accusations of conflict of interest. One of them, working for Gold Fields, had advised its client early on to surrender gracefully because Harmony had clearly won. Another, JP Morgan, found itself in the uncomfortable position of having recommended a merger with Harmony a few months earlier. Now it was helping the company to fight it off. No wonder Gold Fields began to wonder where primary loyalties lay.

Imprinted on deputy chairman Wright's memory are interminable meetings 'sitting in that boardroom in Parktown and having a sea of faces around us – all the thousands of experts and advisers who weren't giving us any bloody advice or helping us at all. It was a very difficult time. I counted how many meetings I went to that year. It was close to 100, and I was a non-executive director.'

Thompson thinks he knows how the resistance to the IAMGold deal (and himself) had started. Capital Group of London had a significant interest in Norilsk. Neither group liked the deal. Both ensured that their views became more widely known, especially to GFL advisers. Thompson got 'several strange phone calls' suggesting that it might be appropriate for him, as father of the IAMGold proposal, to step down. 'The caller didn't try to explain why I should and I told him that I wouldn't.'

As things heated up, Thompson and Cockerill found themselves dashing round the world, putting out fires. Behind the scenes, odd things began to happen. Cockerill got an unsolicited call while he was in London. It was from Swanepoel, who said: 'Let's get together, see if we can have a chat on this.' What was this – a peace offering?

They met in Hyde Park and went for a long walk. It was a typical grey November day:

COCKERILL: Bernard, I'm quite happy to sell you some of the more marginal assets in Gold Fields, but not the whole company.
SWANEPOEL: No, no ... I want to buy the hotel, not rent a room.
COCKERILL: To be perfectly honest, putting the two companies together makes no investment sense whatsoever. Our companies appeal to two very different kinds of investor. Yours are raging bulls who think the gold price is going to the moon. Ours want high-quality dividend yielding and international growth.
SWANEPOEL: No, no, I disagree entirely.
COCKERILL: Look, if you are saying let's take some of the better parts of Harmony and put them together with the better part of Gold Fields and create two entities? Is that what you're saying?
SWANEPOEL: No, I want the whole thing. I want to manage the whole thing.

COCKERILL: I don't care who manages it. All I care about is whether it's right for shareholders. And in all honesty I believe the offer you are making makes no sense.

And after that somewhat pointless exchange, the two warriors departed to continue battle. An even odder incident was yet to come.

INEVITABLY, keeping up with so much hectic activity led to lapses and setbacks on both sides. Some of the court experiences were embarrassing for one party or another.

One of the more awkward episodes occurred in mid-November 2004. The scene had shifted to the United States, just as it had done in the days of the almost-forgotten Minorco bid. Gold Fields had asked US District Judge Richard Berman to declare information provided by Harmony to be so inadequate or misleading as to make it impossible for Gold Fields' American shareholders to make an informed decision. It was a long shot. Berman turned the application down and noted: 'Gold Fields has proceeded – thus far unsuccessfully – in the following fora: SA Securities Regulation Panel [SRP]; the High Court of South Africa, the Competition Tribunal of SA; and the Johannesburg Stock Exchange.'

Swanepoel gloated: 'Gold Fields has been spectacularly unsuccessful in trying to frustrate Harmony's offers through every possible legal and regulatory means.' To which GFL's Jacobsz responded: 'We may have lost, but we've got appeals on everything.'

Thompson became so concerned at what he saw as the reckless abandon of the lawyers that he sent a memo to Holland, who was acting as a go-between with the legal team: 'Please, no more legal actions unless you are absolutely sure we can win. Court defeats are making our shareholders think that the company is inept.' He had good reason to want to avoid embarrassment, both for the company and himself. He had just come through an embarrassing experience in Judge Berman's court.

The following extract from the record says it all:

COURT: Just so I understand, so this 147-page prospectus

	and this 32-page brochure [from Harmony] that you refer to in your declaration, did you read those documents?
THOMPSON:	I've reviewed them very lightly. I haven't reviewed them in detail.
COURT:	You haven't reviewed them in detail. So do you think you're in a position to say what they say?
THOMPSON:	I couldn't give you chapter and verse on them, no.
COURT:	You couldn't really say if they're accurate or inaccurate?
THOMPSON:	No.
COURT:	Because you haven't read them?
THOMPSON:	No, that's correct.

The next day Gold Fields abandoned all its claims against Harmony in Berman's court, bar one directed to the alleged improper disclosure by Harmony of material information relating to gold reserves. Berman noted drily: 'This decision may be related to comments made by Thompson.'

However, that exchange was a side-issue. The central issue was always whether Harmony had correctly estimated its ore reserve figure. Or whether an independent expert had come up with a lower figure. There is no agreement between the contestants on that issue.

The District Court action led to embarrassment for Cockerill too. He fell into the trap that he himself had warned against: he forgot to put himself into slow-down mode and responded too impulsively to an e-mail from his Norilsk colleague Rozhetskin. There was no reason for Cockerill to believe his e-mail response would ever enter the public domain; it was, after all, a private exchange. But it did, thanks to smart footwork by a Harmony lawyer. It happened like this:

During the course of the District Court action, both parties had demanded that the other 'discover' – ie produce – innumerable documents, a standard practice. Later the Harmony representative had asked the court with elaborate innocence: 'Your Honour, just as a housekeeping matter, can I ask counsel if they continue to insist on the strict confidentiality designation that they have provided?'

To which a Gold Fields lawyer responded: 'No objection.' He should have realised it was not an innocent question.

Among the documents thus placed in the public domain was Cockerill's e-mail. It dealt with a request from Norilsk not to make an issue of its attitude to the IAMGold merger because it was under scrutiny from the Russian authorities over its deal with Gold Fields. It was a ridiculous request: the grapevine was making no secret of the Russian company's attitude. Everybody knew where Norilsk stood. Cockerill tried to convey his discomfort at meeting the request.

His e-mail to Rozhetskin said:

> As you are aware I have been trying unsuccessfully to talk with you for over a week now and it is absolutely vital that we talk before next week as I am going on a roadshow in Europe and I suspect I will be asked the obvious question: 'What do Norilsk think of the IAMGold deal?' Now I can continue to lie, as I have done to date, and say I have had no contact with you other than the five-minute conversation on the day of the announcement.
>
> This has been my party line to protect Norilsk in what is clearly a very difficult situation you're currently in. Basically, I didn't want to say anything that caused you any unnecessary embarrassment with the Russian authorities.

Harmony's lawyers seized on three little words: 'continue to lie'; took them out of context; embroidered them into a Cockerill conspiracy to lie to shareholders. It was that kind of war.

CHAPTER TWENTY-EIGHT

A Victory at Last

IT WAS NOT until November 2004 that Gold Fields won its first court battle. It was a symbolic victory rather more than a legal triumph. It arose when Harmony announced that it intended to use whatever Gold Fields shares it had acquired in the 'early bird' stage of the takeover bid to vote against the IAMGold deal.

'Oh no, you're not,' said the Gold Fields legal team.

The arguments against Harmony exercising these votes were complicated and technical. But the central issue was clear: could the initiator of a takeover bid use the votes it had acquired to foil a legitimate deal being planned by the target company? The South African Competition Tribunal decided it couldn't. Harmony promptly appealed – only to be knocked back yet again. On 27 November, just ten days before the critical AGM vote was due, the High Court confirmed the ruling.

Harmony was outraged, saying that it amounted to disenfranchising a shareholder. It appealed yet again, this time to the Supreme Court as a matter of urgency. The higher court suggested that Harmony didn't need an urgent remedy. Let the vote take place and if it transpired that the block vote would have been decisive ... well then, that was the time to seek relief from the courts.

Harmony decided that it would go ahead and vote its acquired shares anyway.

'You can't,' said Gold Fields spokesman Jacobsz. 'The high court has ruled against it.'

'We'll vote our block anyway,' said Harmony.

'And we won't count it,' said Jacobsz.

Soon after, Gold Fields won another little victory. The High Court ruled that Gold Fields could vote the American Depository Shares for which no instruction had been received by the Bank of New York. Harmony protested loudly and threatened to challenge the ruling. To no avail.

On the eve of the big vote, both sides were superficially confident. Harmony said: 'If all the shareholders are allowed to vote, we think we will vote the IAMGold proposal down.' And Gold Fields went on the record to say: 'We are bullish. We continue to get very supportive feedback.'

But beneath the surface, doubt gnawed. Both sides were forced to contemplate the unthinkable.

Gold Fields began to accept that it might, just might, lose the IAMGold vote. Harmony, which had stubbornly refused to improve its offer, suddenly issued a press statement that implied that it might be persuaded to do so. It promised that first-stage accepters would get a top-up if it was obliged to better its second-stage offer. (Before long it was forced to back down and improve its first-stage offer to hedge funds – 1.35 Harmony shares for one Gold Fields instead of the original 1.275. Even so, it made little or no inroad. And most of the shares it did acquire came from US retail investors who thought the takeover was a done deal anyway.)

Business Day concluded: 'It will be a close-run thing, but the smart money is on Gold Fields scraping through.' On that note, the two parties prepared to face each other down at the crucial AGM on 7 December. It was hardly surprising that what was normally a routine event turned into a drama-filled day.

MEANWHILE, neither party was earning any Brownie points on the public relations front. International media had begun to show their distaste for the tone of the debate, while revelling in reporting it faithfully.

The (London) *Financial Times* remarked on the metaphors being used: 'One commentator compared the battle to mud-wrestling; another thought it like a protracted game of paintball with toxic paint; and a third said it seemed more like a post-cabaret mascara fight between two, by now, exhausted drag queens.'

An analyst said: 'This is like a small corner café trying to take over a large chain store. The fight is getting ugly.'

On 26 November the *Wall Street Journal* began a report thus:

> These should be glittering times for shareholders of Gold Fields Ltd, the big South African gold producer. In recent week the price of gold has been marching steadily higher, setting a 16-year high this week. So what have investors in Gold Fields' US-traded shares got to show since Harmony made its offer? Nada.

Dow Jones called it 'arguably the most bitter takeover battle in the Europe-Middle East-Africa region this year', and reported on 2 December: 'Tuesday's extraordinary meeting of South Africa's Gold Fields Limited shareholders is shaping up to be a cliffhanger.'

The (London) *Times*, in its on-line edition of 6 December said:

> A surprise of the battle has been the depth of bitterness, the well of hostility, evident between the two compatriots. Direct negotiations have been eschewed in favour of public slanging matches played through the press, and private ones via lawyers. It is reaching pretty ugly stages on both sides.

Swanepoel seemed to agree: 'I accept that we are all responsible for the extent to which this battle has deteriorated into a mud-slinging, name-calling battle, where the team with the best spin-doctors has its way in the media.' Print media, he said, had got a R6-million bonanza in advertising in just ten days – more than half from Harmony, the rest from Gold Fields. Not to be left out, a NUM spokesman called it 'money down the drain'.

The Silver Fox, aka Bernard van Rooyen, was a former Gold Fields director who had changed companies and allegiances too. He was now deputy chairman of Mvelaphanda, a Tokyo Sexwale company. And Sexwale was seeking to benefit from the Gold Fields/Harmony battle. Van Rooyen couldn't resist putting in an oar. 'I haven't seen anything like it in 20 years. It's turned into a corporate circus with both parties getting personal, and lawyer battles taking place left, right and centre.'

So nearly everyone agreed that the fight had become too rough and nasty. But no one seemed to know quite how to stop it.

IN AN ATMOSPHERE thick with tension, curious events occurred on voting day; so curious that the announcement of the result was delayed by three hours, leaving outsiders bewildered. Had things gone awry? Was something wrong?

Well, yes – things had gone awry, and in almost inexplicable ways.

A biggish investor with close links to Rozhetskin voted no. So did a fund manager who had a significant holding in Norilsk. That was more or less predictable. But what happened next wasn't. Jacobsz recalls that one important investor, the America South Africa Investment Fund, filled out its proxy form in favour of the deal – and then somehow forgot to send it in.

The strangest happening of the day involved Sanlam Investment Management (SIM) – an institutional investor with a total stake of 3.5% in Gold Fields and 2.41% in Harmony, a combination bound to create a conflict of interest. The previous day spokesman Stephen Roelofse had told Reuters: 'We've decided to support the deal.' The same day, chief investment officer George Howard was somewhat less specific. 'SIM hasn't made a decision yet. We will consult our clients.' But later he confirmed that the agreed vote was yes. Finally, CEO Johan van der Merwe said SIM had voted for the IAMGold deal, but 'it was a very marginal call and we didn't try to influence our clients. Most of our clients elected to vote their own shares.'

How then to account for the fact that, on the very day of the vote, a Sanlam representative arrived at Gold Fields' headquarters with an unusual request?

One-time GFL Vice President John Munro takes up the story:

> I was involved in making sure we got the proxy processes right. I was sitting there after all the votes were in and this guy from Sanlam comes to us and says, 'I've spoilt my paper, I need to change it.' So I asked Chris [Thompson, company chairman] what we should do and he said: 'We've got to get the votes right.' So we told this

guy, here's a phone, here's a new form, go and get it right. Then he got new numbers from head office and changed Sanlam's vote and swung the decision.

We phoned the guy afterwards and asked him why he changed the vote. He said: 'It's been taken out of my hands.'

When at last the votes were counted, checked and rechecked, the IAMGold proposal was defeated by the narrowest of margins: 51.44% to 48.23%. Harmony had cleared the first hurdle; the way was open for it to pursue its hostile bid even more vigorously. After all, more than half the shareholders had shown that they were against management's plan for the future. Surely this would impel them towards the only apparent alternative on offer?

Swanepoel recognised a raw nerve when he saw one. He promptly announced that GFL management should regard the outcome as a vote of no confidence and called for management changes. Dennis Tucker, a banker for Investec, was more specific: 'The shareholders have spoken. Surely it is time for Gold Fields management to leave for sunnier pastures.'

Thompson was unrepentant. He wasn't going anywhere, he said; at least not until the Harmony bid had been defeated. In Gold Fields' next annual report, he lamented:

> Growth for this company must come from new discoveries and/or acquisitions outside the country. Some critics have attempted to paint this external growth focus as unpatriotic. However, management is charged and rewarded to create value for shareholders and grow the company ...
>
> IAMGold was the perfect target, for not only is it our joint venture partner and owner of 18.9% of Tarkwa and Damang, it has other attractive interests in Africa, and was also in need of a transaction of the nature proposed.
>
> While by far the majority of Gold Fields shareholders by number supported the transaction, three significant shareholders, including 20% shareholder Norilsk, voted against it. As a result the transaction was marginally rejected. Not included were some institutional

votes in favour that went missing and could not be accounted for. The outcome was a setback for the company.

Swanepoel wanted a final word. In a press statement he said:

> We are surprised by Gold Fields' behaviour since we are aware that over 40% of its shareholders oppose the proposed IAMGold transaction, including its three largest. We find it impossible to believe Gold Fields' management does not consider that this represents substantial opposition. Management is committing one of the most blatant breaches of corporate governance best practise in recent years. It is seriously damaging South Africa in the eyes of the world. All GFL shareholders should be rejecting this outrageous behaviour.

CHAPTER TWENTY-NINE

Palace Revolution

IT SEEMS paradoxical, but the threat of a takeover unleashed internal tensions in Gold Fields' head office even as it united its executives as never before. How could two sets of contradictory feelings co-exist? The answer was that it could only happen if one overwhelmed the other for a time.

The tension began at the top, between the chairman and the chief executive. It had been developing slowly. Thompson thought that Cockerill was dragging his heels on the IAMGold proposal. He couldn't understand why. The public announcement that it would happen had lifted the stock price of both companies – a rare phenomenon indicating that shareholders on both sides approved. The plan had been warmly received by commentators, analysts and the media. He had received calls from 'all over the world' praising the deal. Too bad if Norilsk was unhappy. He was looking after the best interests of GFL.

Cockerill, on the other hand, paid heed to the political rumbles that suggested Gold Fields was fleeing the country; thought it necessary to try to placate Norilsk; was uneasy about possible political repercussions and the damaging gossip about Thompson hijacking the company to Denver. They were singing from different hymn sheets.

The differences culminated in confrontation.

In the light of the Harmony attack, Cockerill had invited Thompson to return from Denver to South Africa. He told his chairman: 'You know Chris, this nine-hour time difference is very difficult. We need to be able to talk. You should be back here.' And the chairman had replied: 'Fine. Whenever you want me there, I'll be there.'

Thompson picks up the story:

> I jumped on a plane a few days after the first board meeting after the Harmony bid and started directing traffic in Johannesburg. Very quickly I arranged with JP Morgan that they would in principle underwrite a rights issue that we could use to buy out Norilsk. Rozhetskin loved it – he would get paid, of course. But Prokhorov dilly-dallied and then turned us down.

But 'directing traffic' wasn't at all the role that Cockerill had in mind for the chairman.

He had envisaged Thompson as a kind of elder statesman, making his experience and tactical skills available on request but leaving the day-to-day activity to the executive team. And that's what the executive team wanted too. Hell, they had been doing just fine until Thompson returned. For the chairman to grab the reins back would amount to a vote of no-confidence in management. That definitely wasn't what they wanted.

One particular event rang alarm bells, according to Jacobsz. The executive team discovered that Thompson had invited Patrice Motsepe, chairman of Harmony, to the Gold Fields' offices for a private meeting; the team had no idea why. It thought the action a step too far by the chairman.

Says Thompson:

> Ian was at once hostile to my interference. He had absolutely no experience of mergers and acquisitions whereas I had lived through several dog-fights of that nature.
>
> I confess that I was irritated by Ian's cockiness, thinking he could manage all this and his presumption that I would consult for him. Shit, I was his chairman and still his boss. I knew I would be better at managing the defence than him and that if I asked the board for a mandate to run the defence they would have given it to me. But then I would have to move back to Johannesburg for quite some time and that didn't suit me at all.

Eventually he decided to let Cockerill 'sweat the dogfights'. He would revert to being a non-executive chairman, using his authority to 'prevent the CEO from making mistakes or inappropriate commitments'.

It was an uneasy solution to a messy situation. It created a relationship that was several degrees less than cordial.

IT WAS IN this climate that things came to a head. Cockerill called it 'a painful duty'. Thompson described it as 'a palace revolution'. Call it what you will, it amounted to the fall of the sixth domino for Gold Fields.

Soon after Thompson landed back in South Africa, shortly before the IAMGold meeting on 7 December, Cockerill felt impelled to convey an unwelcome message to his boss. 'Look Chris,' he said, 'Don't shoot the messenger, but from what I'm hearing, my sense is that you have become an obstacle in this whole transaction.' His championing of the IAMGold merger had alienated shareholders, he said; antagonised the Russians; and aroused unfavourable comment in investment circles. Some politicians were interpreting it as a flight from South Africa. He was doing the company more harm than good and it might be helpful if he stood down.

Cockerill said he had the backing of the full Gold Fields executive in talking to Thompson. Furthermore, he felt duty-bound to take the same message to the board.

Thompson could hardly believe his ears. He quickly convinced himself of two things: that the Capital Group and merchant bankers JP Morgan had got at Cockerill – and Nick Holland too – and persuaded them that the way to save the company was to get the chairman out of the way; and the second thing was that Cockerill couldn't possibly have the support of the full executive. Says Cockerill today:

> Telling Chris was probably the most uncomfortable thing I have ever had to do. But it would have been intellectually and professionally dishonest not to raise the issue. At the end of the day it's about the company, not the individual. We're looking after other people's money and we can't protect our own self-image at the expense of the company.

THE UNOFFICIAL executive meeting that preceded the confrontation was one of the most harrowing that any can remember. Thompson had been, *was*, a hugely popular and admired CEO and chairman. He had led the revival of the company – and the revival of staff morale – with consummate skill. Tom Dale apart, he probably didn't have an enemy anywhere in Gold Fields. He had brought human warmth and brilliant skills back into the business. Ironically, his main accuser, Cockerill, was also his most fulsome praise-singer when the time finally came for him to leave.

In a book specially created to mark the occasion of his farewell to Gold Fields, Cockerill wrote the foreword. It described Thompson's legacy thus:

> Having just come through the merger, and the successive waves of restructuring and retrenchment that reduced the headcount from 80 000 odd to just over 40 000, the people of Gold Fields were shell-shocked. There was no sense of belonging, no sense of purpose. There was no vision for the future.
>
> By the time that he stepped down as CEO four years later, he had turned Gold Fields from a moribund South African gold producer into a truly global company; he infused us with a spirit of entrepreneurship that we did not know before; he cared about people, about those amongst us with HIV/AIDS; he saw the need for black empowerment long before it became fashionable. From a nervous start he had come into his own as a visionary leader … Chris gave Gold Fields soul.

No one took any pleasure in asking him to step aside. But as Cockerill went round the room, obliging each executive in turn to commit to an opinion, all present agreed, some reluctantly: Thompson had become a liability.

Says Cockerill today:

> That was my management style. I mean, what is the point of having a hand-picked executive team with complementary skills and then ignoring their views? I don't pretend to know everything. If you don't consult your colleagues first, you might miss something that

you don't know. Besides, it's a good way to find out where everyone stands. If you're going into the trenches, you need to know in which direction your colleagues are shooting.

I felt that the board needed to know what was being said about the chairman. It was my duty to speak up. It was up to the directors to decide what to do about it. Chris and I had spent many hours talking to his critics, trying to convince them they were wrong; that the Denver move was not featherbedding but in the real interests of Gold Fields. But some were not persuaded.

There's no doubt our ultimatum spoilt a very solid relationship and I still have the highest regard for Chris. I understand that he was deeply hurt. But at least he couldn't say that I was conspiring behind his back because it was done openly.

One question remains unanswered: did Cockerill have the support of the full executive? He says so; Thompson insists only Holland, Dowsley, Jacobsz and John Munro were involved. Either way, they were the key people in the company so it didn't much matter if others abstained.

TO THIS DAY there is confusion in the minds of executives as to how, precisely, the news should have been imparted to Thompson: bluntly, or with a sugared pill? Executive vice-president Dowsley describes his own reaction. He says:

> It was a very divisive time for the company. We assembled two teams – those who were going to Denver and those who were staying behind. It was like Chris was pulling the talent out of Gold Fields. We weren't sure who was going to be in control. There were the seeds of a problem there. He asked me to go with him but I said South Africa was my home, I didn't want to leave.
>
> Well now he'd set up a structure and he'd pissed off our major shareholder. They were spitting mad. It became critical that we appease our shareholders. They were telling us: 'Chris is the problem. We don't like this deal. IAMGold is not top of the pops.'
>
> So I think Ian had gone to Chris and said Exco wants you out;

rather than saying: 'Chris, recognise you're not liked by the new shareholders, get out of our hair and let us run this. In other words, keep your head down.' But Ian was right. Either way, we *were* saying 'kill the king'. So whether or not he put it exactly as we would want, the spirit couldn't be interpreted any differently. Exco was saying: 'You're the problem.' You couldn't have Chris getting up at a shareholders meeting and telling shareholders: 'I have been advised that I should not chair this meeting, therefore I will not.' The relationship was broken. He had no choice but to go.

Every now and then he phones and we still chat. I've always had a lot of admiration for Chris despite the way it ended.

THOMPSON DID the only thing he could do in the circumstances. First, he phoned a few executives to ask them whether they were party to the Exco decision. He got mixed responses according to whether the executive belonged to the blunt or diplomatic faction. But the central message could not be evaded. They had agreed that the chairman should be made aware that he was a stumbling block.

With tears in his eyes Chris Thompson informed the board of the ultimatum he had received, and asked if that was the view of the directors too. The response was – outrage. Board members were appalled at what they saw as the disloyalty and presumption of the executives. Thompson got the impression that the board might instruct him to fire his two most senior executives, Cockerill and Holland. Non-executive director Michael McMahon said: 'If this ever happens again, it will be the chief executive and the chief financial officer that will be looking for a job, not the chairman.'

There were nods all round. 'Besides,' added McMahon, 'it would be suicide to remove the chairman in the middle of a takeover bid.'

In the midst of the turmoil over IAMGold, Harmony had indeed sensed the disarray in Gold Fields, seduced its largest shareholder and made a hostile bid for the company. It would herald the most turbulent time in modern memory for the new Gold Fields. The repercussions made world headlines. It bought sleepless nights and anxious, disturbing days. In the end, it came close to destroying the company.

The sudden resignation of a chairman could only have made things worse.

IN ANY GROUP of ambitious men and women, there will be rivalries and jealousies. Gold Fields was no exception. But by and large these were set aside in the face of a threat not only to their jobs but what they saw as the soul of their company too. Even the chairman and CEO hid their personal feelings well enough to be able to work together.

Nevertheless the hot-house atmosphere created ideal conditions to test the temper of people under pressure and to stir hidden resentments. More often than not, the stress moulded the team rather than divided it. But its members would have been less than human if they hadn't succumbed from to time to time. So strong feelings seethed beneath the surface and the strain told on everyone.

There was tension between the board and the executive too. Some executives thought the board remained too aloof from the realities. Others insisted that a hands-on board trying to second-guess management would have been worse.

Some directors thought that the company had been slow off the mark. Other directors thought they were being unduly criticised by management. The CEO was beginning to get tetchy over what he saw as a lack of support, particularly from director McMahon.

COCKERILL CALLED the takeover battle 'the most stressful time in my working life'. As a boy he had asked his father, a bomber pilot, what the Second World War had been like. His father had refused to discuss it. But when they talked about the Harmony battle his father finally replied: 'Now you know what the war was like. Only your lives weren't in danger.' To the Gold Fields executives, the hyperbole didn't seem out of place.

Nick Binedell, founding director of the Gordon Institute of Business Science, debriefing the team later, described the experience as the corporate equivalent of going to Vietnam and back. Said John Munro, then head of international operations: 'Basically, we worked two years in a year. We were determined to save the company.'

Gradually the defence team coalesced. Its members spent up to 17 hours a day in the office, weekends included. Families were neglected. It was a see-saw time of high adrenalin followed by utter weariness followed by adrenalin bursts. Holland learnt that his wife was dying of cancer; he had to compartmentalise his life so that he could still concentrate on his job.

'I don't know how he did it,' says Cockerill. 'I don't think I would have been able to.' Holland doesn't know either – but he did.

Jacobsz was in charge of communications. Dowsley thinks his contribution was invaluable. 'Look, everybody had a role to play. But Willie more than anybody else got under Bernard's skin and had him make public utterances that made people say: "Hang on – this guy isn't all that he's cracked up to be."'

Jacobsz hid his stress behind a mask of composure. He believed he was being followed and spied upon, and suspected that his phone was tapped. He remembers his children watching TV one day when Swanepoel was being interviewed on CNN. His son came to him and said: 'Dad, did you hear what he said about you?' He was clearly upset, just as he was when comments were made by his friends at school.

When, finally, the tension was released, Jacobsz was felled by a stress-induced complaint – 'quite a diabolical thing; it affects your immune system. People can die from it.' It left him with a continuing health problem.

Dowsley says:

> It brought stressful times for some of the senior management in terms of conflicts between them. The battle got to the gutters very quickly. It's the nature of those things. Individuals get involved. It did become pretty personal. We tended to harp a lot about their short-sightedness, their management and the way they cut out muscle rather than fat. That's a personal affront against the whole ethos that Swanepoel was developing. So it was always going to get pretty personal.

Cockerill gathered his family together and said: 'This is not something that is going to disappear overnight. You're going to see a lot of stuff written in the media. A lot of it will be rubbish, not very pleasant. But understand this is the way of the world.'

His daughter Nikki was at university, studying economics. The lecturer decided that it would be useful to have a live case study on Harmony vs Gold Fields, the biggest story of the time. Frank comments were exchanged by lecturer and students. Then, one day, the penny dropped. The lecturer stopped himself and said: 'Nikki Cockerill? You're not by any chance related to this bloke Ian Cockerill are you?' She said: 'Yes, I am.' He asked: 'In what way?' And she replied: 'He's my Dad.' The class seemed stunned. No one else had made the connection. Later she confided to her father: 'I thought the debates were lively, actually quite good.'

His son Michael, three years younger, found a more insouciant response when teachers at his school asked him how his father was coping. 'It's fine, it's not an issue,' he would say. 'By the way, you should buy Gold Fields stock.'

Cockerill discovered – or thought he had discovered – that Harmony had hired investigators to follow him and Holland to see what dirt they could pick up. They found nothing – but it was a disconcerting experience. As it was when Harmony took to quoting him out of context to make it look as though he supported the takeover. 'It was very cleverly done,' he says, 'but I wasn't going to play that game. It was all spin and no substance. Our team chose to stick to fact.'

On top of all that, takeover battles are messy and anguished affairs. Emotions often get the better of logic, even among allies. Put grown men in a pressure-cooker situation and they will sometimes confuse their friends with their enemies. Heated arguments on direction or strategy will break out. Gold Fields was a hot-house. It took its toll on nerves.

ONE THING wasn't in doubt: the persuasive power of the Official Response Document. In the view of those outside the Gold Fields fortress, the document – when it came out – was decisive and devastating. If confirmation were needed, it came in an extraordinary way, from none other than Leonid Rozhetskin, Norilsk's agent. He approached Cockerill with a surprising request.

'Ian,' he said, 'could you spin out this takeover battle for a bit longer? Say, until April or May?'

'I don't know if I can,' said Cockerill. 'Why do you ask?'

Rozhetskin replied: 'I'm not prepared to renege on our irrevocable undertaking. But I don't like what I'm seeing. I wouldn't mind if the irrevocable expired.'

He felt that Swanepoel had duped Norilsk into believing it could take all the SA assets and dump them into its own gold company. Now the company wanted to be free to reconsider its options.

Thompson took this as proof of the duplicitous nature of the Russians and wanted to continue treating them as hostile. Cockerill argued for trying to mend fences with their single largest shareholder. They seemed at odds with one another yet again, and Cockerill thought: there goes another nail in the coffin of our association.

With hindsight, Thompson's assessment of the palace coup has mellowed. 'I do believe,' he says, 'that it was well-intentioned and not evilly rooted. For the most part, we made a good team, Ian and I.'

CHAPTER THIRTY

Brutal Ping-Pong

THE GAME of legal ping-pong turned into something more like mud-wrestling. Both parties were determined to score points when they could. Opportunities to do so came regularly.

A revelation that Russia's central bank was investigating whether Norilsk's $1.4-billion stake in Gold Fields was properly authorised cast doubt on Harmony's main public supporter. This was followed by the revelation that Gold Fields was prepared to buy Norilsk's stake back and had made a secret offer to do so.

Before the critical vote, Gold Fields renegotiated the deal with IAMGold to save itself $200-million. The official explanation was that currency controls had been loosened, making it unnecessary to pay as high a premium. But it was hard not to relate the saving to the need to win over shareholders, who presumably would appreciate the windfall.

Immediately after the IAMGold setback, Swanepoel irritated his opponent by assuming the success of the takeover bid. He looked forward now, he said, to friendly talks to agree a merger with Gold Fields. Not a chance, said GFL.

Swanepoel announced that if he won the day he would take the new company out of the World Gold Council, saving $7-million a year. Gold Fields responded incredulously: 'What, and lose all the benefits of a very successful marketing arm?'

Harmony promised that it would restrict job losses to about 1 500. Terence Goodlace, Gold Fields vice president for strategic planning, told the Competition Tribunal that the figure was wrong. it would have to sacrifice more than 7 000 jobs if it were to reach its publicly announced cost savings target of R1,6-billion.

Mudslinging reached a new high (or low). Harmony accused its opponent of hiring a spy to gather information on it. The compliment was returned when Cockerill and Holland began to believe that they were being followed. Swanepoel says: 'It's simply not true.' Nothing came of it all, but it was disconcerting.

Swanepoel put a full transcript of evidence from the US court action on a website and wrote to GFL shareholders: 'You may be interested in seeing what your directors are saying under oath.' It sounded suitably sinister, but meant nothing.

The air was thick with allegations of duplicity, cries of defamation and implications of bribery. The share market was less than enamoured. The value of Harmony's initial bid was reckoned to be $8,1-billion. But the declining share price of both companies had reduced it to $6.35-billion.

FATE SEEMS to take a malicious pleasure in aggravating tense situations. On Wednesday 15 December 2004 Cockerill and Holland found themselves in the same business class lounge at OR Tambo as Swanepoel – all bound for Moscow. Both parties had been invited to 'consult' with Norilsk. They reported that their accidental airport meeting was 'friendly', which was a lot more than could be said for their business relationships.

A Harmony spokesman, Ferdi Dippenaar, confirmed the meeting with Norilsk but added: 'I'm not sure what the agenda will be. I think that all parties realise the need to talk.' Holland describes the talks thus:

> Norilsk told us that if we were going to work together we'd have to stop the fighting. Ian just sat there and listened, so I actually took the lead. I said we would meet with the advisors and we would sit and chat. But I was just buying time. I remember Bernard sitting there eating these boiled sweets and Ian sitting there with a sullen look on his face. We're in freezing Moscow three days before Christmas and we're asking ourselves: 'What are we doing here when we should be with our families?'

Both companies were invited to the Norilsk Christmas party, but only

Cockerill and Holland accepted. 'I've never seen anything like it,' said Holland. 'It took place at an old army barracks. It was the most amazing Christmas party I've ever been to. They had the top ten pop groups in Russia performing live; guests from all over the operations, including Siberia. There was champagne and caviar and everything.'

The visit to Russia solved nothing.

At one stage Tokyo Sexwale, chairman of Mvelaphanda Resources and Gold Fields' BEE partner, bobbed up in Moscow. He sensed that the stand-off could be exploited to the advantage of his company. Perhaps he could get a better BEE deal out of Gold Fields by offering support? But nothing came of that either.

Ironically, the only real beneficiary of the takeover battle was Norilsk itself. It walked away from Gold Fields 15 months later, still nursing a grievance but now nursing a handsome profit too. It made $700-million on the sale of its GFL shares, which were dispersed piecemeal. At least Gold Fields no longer had to contend with a single large and hostile shareholder.

ONE THING is certain: not even a Solomon could reconcile the accounts – and memories – of the two companies involved in the takeover battle. There is no point in trying.

Gold Fields believes its response document demolished its opponent. The attack on the valuation of Harmony's assets and its inherently flawed business strategy opened the eyes of the investment community. Suddenly, the romanticised biblical analogy didn't ring so true any more. Gold Fields was no longer automatically the Goliath to Swanepoel's David. Public sentiment began to swing.

Swanepoel says: 'Our response to their response was my personal favourite piece of corporate communication. Unfortunately it must have been mislaid in the Gold Fields file.' Harmony never 'mis-stated or restated' its reserves. It never increased its offer to hedge funds. It won the battle in the American court. And so on.

But this is Gold Fields' story, and this is how it goes. When Swanepoel went on leave that December, he thought he was leaving behind a reeling target and a victory assured. He came back to find a revitalised opponent and a changing tide. Time, the great enemy of many business deals, was beginning to turn the tables.

Much later Cockerill got confirmation that the mostly 'dignified' defence strategy had worked. He had been to see his doctor for a routine medical check. She said she had followed the takeover battle avidly:

> The one thing that struck me from the beginning was that the Gold Fields guys said this is the story, this is why it's not value-accretive, do not accept the offer because you're actually buying a crock of shit. You didn't change your story right from day one. Harmony, on the other hand, were all over the show, they kept on changing their story. One minute it was this, one minute it was that, they really looked like a three-ring circus.

The date when the battle formally ended is easily pinpointed. It was Friday, 20 May 2005, when a final court ruling officially brought things to a halt. But the date when both parties *realised* that the battle had been won and lost is not so easy to establish.

Gold Fields thought it was some time in late December 2004 when Harmony (in its view) seemed to lose its fighting heart and was just going through the motions. Swanepoel insists that he was still in with a chance right up until the final court case.

What is certainly correct is that hostilities continued for five months after the Christmas holiday period. It continued because one party wouldn't accept that it had lost; and the other couldn't afford to stop fighting until that party did accept defeat. It was a fight that cost both companies large sums of cash and significant chunks of reputation.

For spectators, it became about as mechanical and meaningless as watching two toy boxers in a ring – doomed to slug it out for ever, or at least until their batteries ran out.

THE BOXING analogy is apt for another reason. The takeover fight was eventually won on a TKO. Technical knock-outs rely on the judgment of a disinterested third party, and are necessarily subjective. The winners hail it as a glorious victory; the losers usually disagree; and the spectators feel cheated of a good fight.

A court battle can create a similar outcome.

Swanepoel was a very confident competitor. He had taken the trouble to get the Securities Regulation Panel to approve his unusual two-stage bid. His legal team was supportive and he knew that the competition authorities did not like to discourage hostile bids because they were a healthy feature of a competitive business environment.

Besides, the two-stage bid gave an evident and immediate advantage not only to Harmony but to new shareholders too. If they accepted the first-stage offer and swopped their Gold Fields shares, they would be free to convert their new shares to cash at will – and at a profit. Clearly, Harmony shares would gain value from the mere prospect of being associated with the birth of a new mining giant, not to mention the boost that an actual merger would bring.

As Swanepoel had said when announcing the bid, he expected a significant number of shareholders to be attracted by the opportunity to make a quick buck. He thought he would have no difficulty in obtaining just under 35% acceptances quickly. That would give Harmony a very handy beachhead for launching the second stage of its bid.

Better still, it would buy time to win over some of Gold Fields' bigger players. With 35% acceptances and Norilsk's 20% already in the bag, he would hold more than half of his prey's shares. Surely that would encourage others to throw in their lot with the new company.

Swanepoel saw another advantage too. Under stock exchange rules, the takeover bid would lapse if Harmony didn't acquire a majority holding within 60 days. It was a tight schedule. But the creation of a second stage would automatically extend the deadline by introducing a new and later starting date. So, as Swanepoel believed, time would not be a problem.

Or would it?

MICHAEL KATZ, chairman of Edward Nathan Sonnenberg, is one of South Africa's most prominent lawyers. He has practised for more than 40 years and is an expert on takeovers and mergers, among other qualifications. His credentials are formidable: chairman of the Minister of Finance's tax advisory committee, member of the King Committee on corporate governance, trustee of the Nelson Mandela Children's Fund and a dozen other positions. His motto is: 'Be passionate and committed in everything you do.'

He is also legal advisor to Gold Fields Limited. He became involved in the Harmony battle from the beginning. Like Cockerill, he was celebrating a birthday – his own – with family on Saturday evening, 16 October, when he was interrupted by a phone call at 9.30 pm. It was Holland. He said: 'Michael, we've received an unsolicited bid from Harmony. We need to meet tomorrow.'

That was the start. They met on the Sunday and discussed possible strategy. That evening, Katz left for New Zealand – but he took his commitment to Gold Fields with him. The phone wires from Johannesburg kept humming. 'Things started hotting up,' says Katz. 'But there was a 12-hour time difference, they were meeting at noon and it was midnight for me. I said to myself: "This is not on, I'd better come home."' So he did.

'Michael is the sort of individual who likes to sit and think about something, not rush into a decision,' says Holland. 'Eventually he offered some very wise advice. I don't know what we would have done without him.' Katz returns the compliment: 'I don't want to take anything away from other members of the Gold Fields defence team, but without Nick the outcome would have been very different. He grasped instantly what my strategy was about, and he supported it doggedly.'

It didn't take Katz long to reach his own conclusion on the takeover bid. Swanepoel and the Securities Regulation Panel were wrong. There was no such creature as a two-stage takeover bid. You were either trying to take over a company from the start, or you weren't. He never wavered in that opinion. A merchant banker saw that Katz was determined to fight aggressively, and said to him: 'Michael, the game is up. It's just a question of how much the price will be. We've got to go and debate that in Moscow because of Norilsk.'

Katz replied: 'That may be your view. Until I am instructed otherwise, I will keep fighting.'

His argument was simple. Harmony could insist all it liked that there was a first and a second stage, each discrete and self-contained. That was a nonsense. The so-called stages had to be seen for what they really were: two parts of a single, indivisible offer for 100% of the company. Once the first stage came into effect, the second stage followed inevitably. They were inextricably linked.

It wasn't just an arcane legal quibble. It mattered. Securities law sets a 60-day deadline after which a takeover bid lapses; establishing when the clock started ticking was crucial. Katz insisted that it began ticking from day one of the first stage, which meant that the bid had lapsed long since – on 18 December 2004, to be precise. On the other hand, if Harmony's interpretation was right and the second stage was separate, the deadline stretched well into the future.

Now all Katz had to do was persuade a court he was right.

He was conscious of the fact that law libraries are full of instances where opposing lawyers believe they have an unbeatable case. One of them is always wrong. It didn't faze him. He even concedes readily that courts are composed of people who make all-too-human decisions. Different courts, different judges could arrive at different conclusions. But his confidence in his own argument remains undiminished.

He delights in quoting a former United States Chief Justice on the nature of America's ultimate court: 'We are not ultimate because we are infallible. We're infallible because we're ultimate.' To his mind it sums up the situation perfectly. No case is without risk.

It was in this frame of mind that Katz approached the High Court on the morning of Friday 20 May 2005. Norilsk's irrevocable undertaking had expired only hours before. Harmony believed that Gold Fields shareholders had until noon that day to accept its offer; that it was – by a slim few hours – inside the deadline that would bring the bid to an end. The situation was on a knife-edge as the parties waited for the judge to deliver her judgment. The battle was about to be resolved, one way or another.

The judgment vindicated Katz completely, and finally lifted a load from the shoulders of Gold Fields. It declared that Harmony's takeover bid had lapsed on 18 December 2004, just as Katz had argued. In terms of the rules, Harmony was precluded from making another bid for at least a year. The judgment had elements of farce. In effect it ruled that everything that had happened in the last five months had been wasted effort – the court actions, the battles, the insults, the ever-increasing costs. Everything.

The parties had been fighting over a takeover bid that didn't exist, an ultimate definition of futility. For Katz, the case crystallised two rules for such cases that he would impart to any law student: 'The first is simplicity – keep it simple. The second is that the longer a hostile bid takes to happen, the less chance it has of happening.'

Gold Fields celebrated. Only later did it stop to consider a sobering question: could it be said that anyone had been victorious, given the loss of value that both companies had experienced? Gold Fields' share price had suffered; Harmony's had been decimated. Neither would recover quickly. Each would have to work very hard to restore its public image.

It was a high price for Gold Fields to pay to get the Harmony monkey off its back.

IT WILL BE of no comfort to Harmony to learn that two of its most ferocious adversaries believe that Swanepoel came within a whisker of winning the war.

Senior vice-president Dowsley says:

> There was a time in December just prior to Swanepoel going on leave where he had Gold Fields in the palm of his hand. All he had to do was up his price. I know his advisors tried to get him to sew it up before he went away. But his attitude was: 'I've got them over a barrel. It's done and dusted. We'll wrap it all up when I come back.' He had that kind of arrogance. But when he came back, it was too late.

Legal adviser Katz supports the view: 'If their offer had been in simple form – a vanilla offer – they would have had control by Christmas. It would have been game, set and match.'

'Wrong,' says Swanepoel. 'Even my own advisers were telling me to increase the offer to win over undecided shareholders, But it was my stubborn belief that that would destroy value for my shareholders that stopped me; not my arrogant belief that we had won.'

Chapter Thirty-one

Changing the Guard

THE BITTERNESS generated by the takeover bid lingered. It was evident in the tone of the annual report for 2005, which came out four months after the final court case. In ways subtle and overt, it conveyed the message that Harmony had damaged not only itself (which was fair enough – it deserved it); it had damaged Gold Fields too.

Chairman Thompson reported:

> The hostile takeover attempt should never have happened. Motivated for the wrong reasons, namely to revive and perhaps even rescue a failing Harmony, cloaked in hypocritical patriotism, and buttressed with gold reserves that did not conform to industry standards, the bid was unappealing to Gold Fields shareholders from the start.
>
> The whole affair had only negative consequences. The fact that the company was able to report an increase in production, reduce total cash costs and achieve flat operating profits is quite remarkable ... It has been a disturbing and challenging year. This industry, which survived gold below US$275 an ounce, is strikingly unprosperous at US$425 an ounce.

CEO COCKERILL underlined the message: 'The repercussions for business in general, and the mining industry in particular, remain to be seen.'

But there was something more to it than financial disadvantage; something less tangible. For a while, the battle seemed to have knocked the stuffing out of the company or, at least, some of its executives. It coincided with a series of hiccups and calamities – almost as if the mining gods were seeking vengeance on every front.

From his vantage point as the executive in charge of investor relations, Jacobsz watched in dismay as Gold Fields' share price fell – and fell again. Public confidence had been eroded. He remembers it as a time of treading water, of going nowhere. He thought the company was becalmed and listless. So was the industry.

Cockerill challenges that perception. 'That's strange,' he says. 'We acquired Bolivar Gold in Venezuela, sold it about 18 months later, approved the Cerro Corona project that now embodies the spirit of the new GFL, expanded Tarkwa and acquired South Deep mine. Hardly a period of inactivity, I would suggest.'

Indeed, the 2006 annual report tended to confirm this assessment. Said chairman Wright: 'Gold Fields is once again a sharply focused business with a crystal clear vision, direction and intent. We are a truly global player with an operational footprint on three continents.'

It happens – perceptions are perceptions. Contradictory views can exist, and be defended. It all depends on the viewpoint. Insists Jacobsz:

> Perceptions of both Harmony and Gold Fields were very negative. Then the Russians got out and sold their shares into the market. It almost led to a … well, not exactly a collapse but a sharp decline. Between mid-2005 and the end of 2006 the company was not going anywhere. It was fairly much in a funk.
>
> In 2007 we went on a roadshow and told investors: 'We're turning the ship around. Just watch the December quarterly results.' But in October more than 3 000 miners were trapped a mile underground at Harmony's Elandsrand mine. All were rescued – but for government it was the last straw. The mine was closed for six weeks and President Mbeki ordered an inquiry into mine accidents generally. The implication was that the industry was cavalier with black lives.

Murphy's Law ensured a flurry of new mine fatalities and temporary mine closures:

> Our quarterly results were horrendous, so we started saying: 'Watch the first quarter of 2008 – that's when the turnaround will become

evident.' But what became evident instead was the great Eskom power crash, which forced mines to close and knocked production for a loop.

True to his word, Chris Thompson resigned as chairman after the Harmony bid was defeated. He was replaced by former CEO and deputy chairman Alan Wright. The tone of the 2006 annual report under its new chairman was notably more cheerful but the Harmony spectre had not quite disappeared: 'The Group has produced a most pleasing set of results. Although gold production was down, in line with the international industry trend, this was more than offset by the higher gold price that increased year-on-year by 28% to US$524 an ounce.'

So everything was back to normal then?

Not quite. That darned share price just kept dropping. Investor confidence had not been restored. And Gold Fields had yet another blow to deliver to its shareholders. Or, at least, it seemed like a blow at the time.

WHEN THOMPSON retired to Denver, Colorado, in November 2005, it was to start a new life. He carried with him a lasting memento in the form of a printed and bound hard-cover book entitled 'Christopher MT Thompson' with the subtitle: 'You will go to Africa and run the greatest gold mine there.' It consisted of tributes and reflections from colleagues and friends. It is remarkable for what it didn't say. In the face of his many contributions, the IAMGold episode was wiped from official memory. Perhaps that was the most sincere compliment of all.

Thompson continued to serve on several boards while making more time for his real passion, which was for racing fast cars. However, the link with his old company was not entirely severed. Whatever harsh memories remained for him – and he gave no indication that there were any – he was lovingly supervising a cosmetic change to a Porsche housed in a workshop about an hour's drive from his home. He had suggested that our interview be conducted while driving there for an inspection in loco.

This sleek mechanical monster was getting a new livery – a coat of finest gold plate. It seemed to shimmer in the soft workshop light – a thing of fragile beauty. It wasn't worth thinking about how easily the gold leaf could be damaged by a nudge, let alone a crash.

Before it was ready for its next season of motor racing it would be adorned with a company logo proclaiming that it was sponsored by Gold Fields. Thompson would be part of the team which would race it at a series of meetings around the United States. Thompson and Jacobsz gazed upon the golden glory with a proprietorial air: the one because he was going to drive it; the other because he had endorsed the idea of sponsorship.

The Porsche would certainly attract attention on the circuit. To the last, Thompson was promoting his old company.

IAN COCKERILL says he would hate to be remembered for the Harmony affair only. Right from the time he started at Gold Fields he recognised that Tom Dale's retrenchments had deprived the company of much-needed expertise.

'It was all very well saying, "We don't need technical resources; we can always get it from outside." But there needed to be someone internal with enough skill to judge external information,' says Cockerill. 'Otherwise you're going to be paying outsiders to tell you the time with your own watch. The cull of technical excellence at the centre had been overdone.'

He set out to bring expertise back – 'it's one of the things I'm particularly proud of.' There are others: helping to create Gold Fields as a brand; devising a formula that enabled junior companies to get access to Gold Fields finance for exploration at 48 hours' notice; continuing the internationalising process that Thompson had started; buying South Deep; ensuring succession planning. Oh yes, and best of all: developing people: 'In the last four or five years Gold Fields has become a place that other companies look to when they need staff. Eight of the executive team that worked directly for me have become chief executives in their own right. If you ask me what I'm most proud of, it's that.'

His management philosophy was simple: 'You have a vision, you sell that vision to the team and you put the right people in to ensure that the vision is achieved. Then you let them get on with it and you don't interfere.'

It was an enlightened form of delegation – and owed a great deal to the philosophy of his old boss Thompson – but it had a hidden danger.

Unless accompanied by visible involvement, it can be interpreted, or misinterpreted, as ducking out.

Musing on his contribution, Cockerill says: 'A lot of people have said to me that the Harmony bid must have been the defining moment of my time at Gold Fields. That's not the way I see it. There are other things, like growing internationally.'

He looks back with satisfaction on the fact that the company is now what he calls half-half – half in South Africa; half abroad. Despite Thompson's belief that he was dragging his heels, he thinks there was no real difference between them on this objective, save on the question of timing and pace. 'You've got to recognise the political dimension. Government is sensitive about companies which appear to be moving overseas. You have to take that into account,' he says.

He has intriguing ideas on the role of executives; it is not a philosophy that would have had much traction in the Gold Fields of 25 years before: 'Ideally, you should have people on your team who are probably smarter than you. But then of course you must have the self-confidence to be challenged and not see it as a threat.' He cannot understand bosses who hire skilled people and then fail to involve them in decision-making:

> I mean, what's the point of handpicking an executive team with breadth of intellect and opinions and then not using them? When you come to situations like Harmony, situations that are off the wall for you, if you don't consult your colleagues first you may miss something you don't know. Besides, you can also use it to gauge where they stand: are they for the cause, against it, ambivalent?

His management philosophy was put to the test by his PR team from Brunswick during the Harmony bid. He was advised: 'Gold Fields needs a rainmaker. You must be the figurehead in this battle. Make all the public statements yourself.' He had an instinctive feeling that this would be wrong. He said: 'Harmony's bid is personal; it's all about Bernard Swanepoel. I want the public to see that our whole executive is at one in fighting this battle. That it's not just me opposing Harmony.'

It worked. Journalist Brendan Ryan came to him after a press conference to launch Gold Fields' counter-attack on Harmony and said: 'That was incredibly powerful. Did you realise that all your team were dressed in dark suits, blue shirts and red ties? Was that deliberate?'

Cockerill replied: 'No, I never even noticed.' But he found the unintended message of team unity reassuring. That's how he liked to operate.

SOMEWHERE ALONG the way, something went sour. McMahon says that relations between the CEO and the board deteriorated from the time of the attempt to remove Thompson:

> Ian was fed up with a board of non-execs who had stamped on the palace coup. He became brusque and hyper-sensitive. I concede that I, probably more than any other director, spoke my mind. I may indeed have made Ian unhappy but I wasn't just being a grumpy old sod.
>
> By definition, management would prefer a board staffed by congenial, compliant and 100% supportive old codgers and run like a gentlemen's club. That's how it used to be, by and large. Then along came King and others. Shareholders and exchanges today insist that directors are accountable and must demand accountability. The unavoidable consequence is a greater potential for confrontation and stress. It's not pleasant for either party but it's now a duty call. Why does that seem to attract criticism?

Viewed from outside, Gold Fields' defence against Harmony operated like a well-oiled machine. A specially-created board committee under the chairmanship of Alan Wright debated strategy with the CEO and his consultants. The CEO devised a master plan and his executives executed it. Result: victory.

But in reality – and inevitably – it didn't always work that way, perceptions to the contrary. For instance, some Gold Fields executives felt the board was too disengaged: 'They sort of came and went to meetings and that was it. They had no idea what management went through.'

Wright disagrees vigorously:

> The defence was orchestrated behind the scenes by the board and the

board defence sub-committee, but we never tried to usurp the functions of the executive. I certainly know all about it because I chaired the sub-committee with the fantastic support of a few non-executive directors.

Disengaged? The annual report shows that the board met 27 times and the sub-committee nine times. In normal years the board might meet ten times. We averaged a meeting every fortnight and, remember, we were non-executives. Both the board and the executives played very important roles. I believe that the real brains behind the defence were Nick Holland and Michael Katz, often in discussions with John Hopwood (an expert on mergers and acquisitions) and the defence sub-committee.

As for the contribution made by the consultant bankers, Wright shares the cynicism of many in Gold Fields:

Most of the strategies they concocted were shot down in flames by the sub-committee, usually with the support of Holland. No wonder that some thought we were disengaged. The truth is that most of the suggested strategies had little chance of success – except in lining the pockets of the consultants.

Director Rupert Pennant-Rea – former editor of *The Economist* and now a London businessman – said: 'Admittedly, we were a little slow off the mark at first but when we got going we did everything that we possibly could. And we triumphed.'

BUT THE TENSION wasn't only between board and management. Some senior executives began to wonder if Cockerill was becoming too preoccupied with other things. Perhaps they had misread his commitment to delegating; there was always the danger that delegation could be seen as copping out.

Cockerill believed – believes to this day – that he handled the campaign like a general handling a well-planned military operation. He deliberately remained slightly divorced from the direct action. He explains: 'You could very easily get bogged down in the details. I stood back and tried to act as an independent arbiter. You sit down, discuss broad outlines with the team, let them get on and produce something. When they come back you can look at it and say: That's good, or tweak this, tweak that.'

But others didn't see it quite that way. Jacobsz thought that the operation cried out for greater hands-on direction – 'you can't just formulate a plan and expect others to carry it out without supervision'. Dowsley felt it was more 'a process of learning on our feet' rather than implementing specific steps. And Holland came away with the impression that Thompson's attempted intervention and Cockerill's style led to 'headless chicken syndrome' – executives running around aimlessly without proper direction.

Cockerill believes that his young team emerged from the Harmony battle 'battered, bruised but without doubt a lot stronger'. Jacobsz has his doubts: 'For about a year afterwards, the company was not going anywhere. Everyone was exhausted and dispirited.'

Thompson was even more blunt: 'The truth is that, after Harmony, senior management came to view the company as a dead horse trapped in SA with nowhere to go. That's why so many left. It was an easy decision to move from GFL to better prospects.'

AS COCKERILL saw it, McMahon was his nemesis. He says:

> Mike was a very, very difficult non-executive director. There were times when he played the role brilliantly, and was top class. But then every so often he went wobbly. His knee-jerk reaction then was always to accuse management of being rogues and scoundrels; of running away with the cash book.
>
> I told Chris I believed he should sort it out because this was exactly what he had done when Chris was CEO. I said Mike could accuse Nick and me of being naïve, stupid, making dumb decisions, anything he liked – but he should never ever question our integrity.

McMahon agrees that he has an aggressive manner. 'It's the way I work,' he says. 'I believe in raising issues vigorously. I don't mind if people disagree with me, but I like to ask the questions anyway. If the majority disagrees with me, I go along. I accept it. I don't harbour grievances.'

The undercurrent of tension lingered and came to a head on a Friday in November 2007, during a board visit to the company's recently acquired Cerro Corona mine in Peru. Gold Fields' share price was still failing to recover – an imperfect barometer of a company's fortunes but enough to rattle those responsible for directing those fortunes.

Directors had been expecting to find a mine in good shape and on the brink of production. Instead they found a property nowhere near ready and costs running US$78-million higher than estimated only three months before. They felt they had been misled about the investment, and didn't try to hide their feelings. Cockerill felt they were unreasonable in not making allowance for the serious socio-political problems that had cropped up unexpectedly.

The terse board minute did nothing to disguise the strain:

> The Board received from Mr [John] Munro a detailed presentation ... Mr Munro noted that since his last report in August 2007 there had been a severe deterioration in capital cost and completion schedule ... The headline cost of the project was now forecast to be some US$421-million against US$343-million in August 2007 while the completion schedule was now expected to be delayed by some three months. The Board expressed its concern.

The next board meeting took place in Franschhoek in February 2008. It was to be Cockerill's last.

Says McMahon:

> I don't think Ian enjoyed life for his last 18 months at Gold Fields. For a few board meetings, the directors had been calling his bluff. The general message was: why do you need to be out of the country for 180 days a year? You're Mr Gold at conferences, out promoting the company – but it's not making any difference and we're not making progress with the operations. At two meetings he got aggressive

because of the lack of blind board support. It got to the stage where members would say openly that he was talking nonsense.

Cockerill responds:

Out of the country for 180 days? If only I were, I wouldn't need to pay SA taxes. I spent time offshore because I was visiting our international operations in Ghana, Peru, Venezuela, Australia. Not to mention seeing foreign GFL investors, attending World Gold Council meetings and other global conferences. Sadly, another Mike exaggeration I'm afraid.

Holland says:

I remember Ian telling me that he didn't know how long he would have the support of the board. I heard that, at the Franschhoek meeting, Ian told the board he was tired of all the criticism of management and it had to stop. Some very direct stuff was spoken. That's the last board meeting Ian attended. He submitted his resignation six or seven weeks later.

Cockerill doesn't deny the clashes but insists that it was only the lure of another exciting offer that prompted him to resign.

His resignation was announced on the JSE's news service on 1 April together with the name of his successor, Nick Holland, who would take over at the beginning of May. The unexpected announcement invited speculation, as did Cockerill's explanation that 'an intriguing opportunity came along sooner than expected'. *Business Day* reported the news under the headline: 'Cockerill mysteriously quits Gold Fields job.'

In reality, there was no mystery but there were unanswered questions. What was the 'intriguing opportunity'? What job was more inviting than being the CEO of a major international mining company? More significantly: why such short notice? Normally, a chief executive might give months of warning of his intentions to ensure a smooth succession. In this case he was departing within 30 days. What was the story behind that?

Even Cockerill seemed taken aback by the speed of the process. He protested that his new employers were not ready to make an announcement, but the board said it wanted to avoid speculation and ensure continuity.

As it happened, his new employer was revealed within days. It turned out to be his old employer – Anglo American. He was going to head up a new division under the new broom of Cynthia Carroll. Eighteen months later Anglo restructured its hierarchy and Cockerill found he no longer had a job. When this book was published he was executive chairman of Petmin, a multi-commodity mining and processing company and a leading producer of quality anthracite and silica. In 2011 it paid its maiden dividend.

On the very day when Cockerill's resignation from Gold Fields was announced, 1 April, another top-level departure from Gold Fields was revealed. Munro, executive vice-president and head of international operations, was leaving to join GFL's recent opponent, Harmony. He would head up its newish uranium subsidiary. Munro had at one time been considered a favourite for the CEO's job at Gold Fields. He had been passed over.

What was going on at GFL? The share price fell more than 6%.

That same day Gold Fields presented its shareholders with what some thought was another uninspiring bit of news. Cockerill would be succeeded by Nick Holland, a virtual unknown. Most of those who did know him thought of him as a low-profile bean-counter. As GFL's chief financial officer, he had earned a reputation for being tough, inflexible and less than sensitive. Was that really the kind of leader needed to restore investor confidence?

In time, Holland would come to surprise his critics.

CHAPTER THIRTY-TWO

Looking Ahead

TWO TOP executives suddenly gone, an image dented, share price becalmed. Gold Fields needed to demonstrate that it was not bereft. It needed to name a new chief executive promptly. It wasted no time. Chairman Wright came to Holland and said: 'We have two people on the short list for the CEO's job – you and Terence Goodlace. We need to know whether you'd be interested.'

Holland replied: 'I'd be more than interested. I'd be honoured.'

Cockerill calls Goodlace a 'hidden gem'. He had been badly shell-shocked by the brutal retrenchments that marked the early days of GFL, fearing that he might be next for the chop. As the company settled, his confidence returned and he became 'a quiet, behind-the-scenes professional, highly respected'. When he was asked to assume responsibility for the South African mines, he blossomed. And he was part of the group that drafted the Harmony defence document. He was a formidable contender for the CEO's job. But the board opted for Holland and rewarded Goodlace with the title of Chief Operating Officer.

In a chummy kind of way, chairman Wright advised Holland that the job required him to develop a broader vision for the company and better HR skills. Would he like a coach to help him break the accountant's mould?

'No thanks,' said Holland, 'I'll do it myself.' It was a far cry from the diffident employee of yore, who wondered whether Gencor would find a job for him. Then he laid down his own marker too:

> I said to the board straight away, look, I can't do this job if we're going to have a continuation of the current relationship between

management and the board. I need everyone's support, otherwise I'm going to fail. I'll come around and talk to you individually, find out what your concerns are, what we've got to change. It was very evident to me that the board gap had widened and widened. So it was a pretty unhappy time generally.

It is relatively rare that a new CEO has the temerity to lecture the board that appoints him on the way they should handle him. It caused a stir. But the board rallied quickly.

Holland was told that the directors had every confidence in him, despite the little lecture on his perceived weaknesses. Meanwhile, he took Wright's advice to heart. In remodelling himself he improved his handling of subordinates and widened his vision. After three years his closer colleagues began to remark on how much he had grown in the job. Holland readily agrees that he has changed. 'Look,' he says, 'when my first wife died of cancer I went through a bad spell. I was depressed and demotivated. Then there was the aftermath of the Harmony affair too. It was not a good time, but that's all behind me now.'

His second wife Roslyn agrees that he has changed – but not completely. She takes credit for developing his dress sense, but doesn't believe he was ever short of human warmth. 'He was always more caring, more concerned about others, than most people recognised or that he cared to let on,' she says. 'I always knew that side of him.'

Chris Thompson remembers him as a chief financial officer who was 'quite narrow and very much the accountant'; tough on his people, but absolutely reliable when it came to getting his numbers right every quarter. He wondered if an accountant could ever change his spots. He thinks he has found the answer. 'I have been surprised, pleasantly surprised. I believe he will be at least as good as his predecessors; perhaps better.'

Current chair Dr Mamphela Ramphele has no doubt that Holland has changed:

> I can attest to a major change just in the one year I have worked with him. The problem with mining is that it is a male-dominated culture; it skips the essentials which are about how people feel. Even before I came he brought in a vice president for HR; Gold Fields

had never really had someone of that seniority to handle human relations.

Now take Nick himself, for instance. He worked like a dog, people used to say he was in the office until 8pm, 9pm. I said to him: 'Nick, you have to give people permission to go home by going home yourself. If you nurture yourself then you'll be a nurturing CEO.' It's more or less a rule now that there is to be no one in the office after 5pm on Fridays. He is still a tough taskmaster but there is a more relaxed atmosphere. I was at an executive meeting the other day and I said to them: 'I can feel the team. I can feel the morale.' They are really focused on delivering the fantastic projects they have on the go – South Deep, the Far Southeast.

ONE TERRIBLE event was to shape Holland's period in office and his personal philosophy. It happened on the day he formally took over as chief executive officer – 1 May 2008.

The family had spent the Workers' Day holiday, a Thursday, at their home on the Pearl Valley Golf Estate near Paarl in the Western Cape winelands. Holland was enjoying breakfast in Paarl before returning to Johannesburg to take up the reins when he got the phone call alerting him to the news. There had been a shattering accident at Gold Fields' South Deep mine. A steel rope had snapped as a cage carrying passengers was descending a secondary shaft. The cage had hurtled down the shaft for almost 60 metres. Eight men and one woman had died instantly. All mining had been halted. Government was on the warpath. Minister of Minerals and Energy Buyelwa Sonjica was expected at the mine on the Friday to meet with unions and management. Holland had better get back as soon as possible. He caught the next plane.

He arrived at the mine to be met by a tirade from Minister Sonjica. The mining industry, she said, had scant regard for lives, especially black lives. It forced workers to experience needless dangers. It was cavalier about death tolls, cared only about profits.

By unhappy chance, President Thabo Mbeki had ordered an official probe into mine safety practices only a few months before, after 3 200 miners had been trapped underground at a Harmony mine. All were eventually rescued unharmed, but that didn't extinguish the spotlight that had now been focused on the industry.

Instead of the usual defensive response – human error was to blame, not callous owners – Holland was jolted into considering whether the Minister had a point. Was there a germ of truth in her charges? Was Gold Fields – and the whole darned industry – too accepting of the inevitability of accidents and deaths on the mines, notwithstanding the frequent public commitments to safety?

On Wednesday, 7 May, Holland attended a memorial service and day of mourning at South Deep. 'I've never seen so many of our workers just sitting there and saying nothing,' says Holland. 'I saw the wives and girl friends and loved ones and they seemed to be looking at me accusingly, and I said to myself: We have got to do something.'

There and then he made his decision and gave the mourners his word: 'If we cannot mine safely we will not mine.' But what, actually, *could* he do? The question haunted him. Everyone in the industry could place a hand on the heart and insist that the safety of miners was their absolute priority. What more could anyone do?

Later, at another funeral, Holland listened to a Xhosa lament and asked someone to translate the words. The mourners were singing: 'I don't want to die; I want to go home.' He was shocked by the implication. 'It seemed to me they didn't really believe that mining could be done safely; they thought that miners were living on borrowed time and sooner or later it would be their turn to die.'

Another realisation followed: 'Perhaps they didn't believe it because their bosses didn't really believe it either.'

Somehow he had to make employees believe, really believe, that mining could be safe; that it was not akin to an inevitable death sentence to be avoided only by returning home. Which meant that the conviction had to come from the top. Starting with himself. He had to prove that safety was more important than production by shutting down unsafe areas voluntarily – before government demanded it. Managers had to stop emphasising the need for production and learn to say: 'Your workplace is not safe, you had better stop and fix it before you do anything else.'

In short, he had to prove that the promise he had made – *If we cannot mine safely we will not mine* – wasn't just an empty slogan but a real commitment. So he backed it up with a slogan that captured the company's priorities: Stop, fix and continue.

HAVING MADE up his mind on the solution, the rest was simple – simple but expensive. He ordered an independent audit of infrastructure at Gold Fields' mines. The result gave him a shock. The steelwork at one shaft turned out to be so badly corroded it was a wonder it had not collapsed. To fix it meant closing the shaft for seven months. He alerted his board: 'This is going to be a big hit at the market. We're going to lose about 10% of our market value.' To its credit, the board accepted the decision and the underlying principle without hesitation. Safety had trumped production.

But Holland got one thing wrong. Gold Fields lost 20% in value, not 10%.

The audit revealed disturbing signs of infrastructural decay on several other mines. No one had let it happen deliberately, but the law of unintended consequences had ensured that the pressure for production had unwittingly overshadowed the greater need for safety.

At first, Holland's slogan caused derision in much of the industry, even among his own staff. But gradually awareness grew that putting safety first was actually a sound business proposition. Fewer accidents meant greater productivity in the longer run. The real gold in the company was in its people.

There was one other unexpected consequence.

Holland became the first CEO to go underground on a regular basis. Miners often resent what they see as the bosses spying on them. But as the safety-first principle became established, workers began to come up to him, shake his hand and thank him for making their jobs safer; for not just talking about safety but doing something about it too.

> If I look at the additional ground support we've introduced underground, it's chalk and cheese from what it was four years ago. We've narrowed the spacing, put in netting to catch falling rock, introduced roof bolting. New techniques are helping us get the men away

from the danger zones. I think we are beginning to win the hearts and minds of our employees. They are losing the belief that fatalities are an unavoidable part of the industry.

In the week of the South Deep calamity, Gold Fields had 14 fatalities in all. The year before, the death toll for all Gold Fields' mines was 38. Three years later it had dropped by half – to 18. Says Holland:

> I think the workers are beginning to believe. The Kloof, Driefontein complex made 2-million fatality-free shifts just before Christmas [2011]; 35 000 people worked for four months without a single death. It's unheard of. South Deep completed a whole year without a fatality in January 2012; Beatrix went for nine or ten months without a death last year. So the guys believe they can do it. That's the change.

CURIOUSLY, the issue of safety is controversial in the industry – not because anyone is opposed to the idea. Only a handful of politicians believe mining companies are cavalier about human lives. Mining executives, past and present, reject with contempt any suggestion that they put production before safety. Fatality-free shifts are recognised and rewarded by the Chamber of Mines. Posters everywhere proclaim the importance of working safely and offer slogans to drive home the message. The focus is unmistakeable. So why the controversy?

It arises because there are two broad schools of thought, just as there are over road accidents. The one is the accidents-are-inevitable school, which believes that the industry must do as much as it can to prevent them, but recognise the limitations. The other is the accidents-can-be-avoided school, full stop. Both schools accept that acts of God are beyond their power. But the simple truth is that by far the most accidents underground are caused by human error, lax procedures or faulty equipment. These are, or should be, preventable.

Mining regulations and government inspectors set a base-line. Government has the power to close down shafts, even whole mines. But that is where the individual decision-making starts. At the risk of oversimplification, mining companies have to decide what precautions they are obliged to take; what degree of risk they will tolerate; where on this sliding scale they wish to place themselves. The choices range from 'safe enough' to 'zero tolerance'. Clearly, the richer companies are better able to follow the second course, but all have to make a choice.

Dr Ramphele, with her links to both companies, believes that Gold Fields and Anglo American have demonstrated their willingness to sacrifice profits for safety. She says:

> The issue of safety is emotive. A lot of mining companies have been asking themselves: is it ethically defensible to send people into an environment which we know can have a seismic event that could result in a massive loss of life? Nick, I think, is genuinely uncomfortable with what has happened in the past. Cynthia Carroll [Anglo American CEO] shut down Rustenberg, and not just for one day.
>
> If you go to Anglo American you will hear them talk about zero harm. If you go to Anglo-gold Ashanti you will get the same kind of language. So Gold Fields' language – 'if we can't mine safely …' – is part of the new awakening. It used to be against the pattern to think safety. They said: mining and death are fellow-travellers. So I think we are seeing greater commitment by several corporates to safety issues.
>
> And then, of course, there is Section 54, which gives the government power to shut you down. So there is a business imperative to this thing too. And I think that, notwithstanding all this, or maybe because of it, we are seeing a significant drop in fatalities and greater care all round.

ANOTHER CONTROVERSIAL though less emotive action by Holland has been to change the way that the cost of producing an ounce of gold is reported. The practice in the industry is to report only total cash costs and to exclude capital expenditure on the grounds that it is 'growth capital'. Most mining companies still use this approach. But Gold Fields has introduced the concept of Notional Cash Expenditure which brings all capital expenditure, including sustaining and growth capital, into the equation because it gives a more realistic idea of the actual cost of wresting the precious metal from the ground.

The old way, Holland believes, is profoundly misleading and could result in 'significant risk' to the industry as costs continue to rise. As he told shareholders in the 2010 annual report:

> In an industry that continues to favour cash costs instead of all-in costs it is not surprising that external stakeholders will demand a greater share of the apparently higher operating profit margins. It is becoming more urgent for the gold mining industry to move towards a more inclusive and transparent reporting of costs. We believe that Notional Cash Expenditure [NCE] provides a more reliable measure than the commonly used cash costs.

His justification for including all operating costs and all capital costs as well as near-mine exploration is simple and compelling.

Most capital expenditure today, he argues, is aimed not at increasing the supply of gold (as once was the case) but simply at replenishing the industry's declining output. 'If this is not the case, then surely we should have seen primary gold supply increasing over the last ten years instead of remaining stagnant, particularly in the face of significantly higher gold prices,' he says.

In essence, he is warning of the danger of producing rose-tinted results that give an inflated idea of the profitability of gold mining. Everyone wants a share of this apparently bigger pie: governments, unions, shareholders. Such demands deplete the cash flows that mining needs. They could threaten the stability of the entire industry, especially in times of rising costs.

IT IS TOO EARLY for final judgments on Holland's performance as CEO. He had been in the job for less than four years when this book was written; time will tell. But early signs are propitious.

It is possible (if slightly risky) to gauge the state of a company by its annual report. The 2011 report of Gold Fields Limited had a confident ring to it. It was operating eight mines on four continents and had four major projects in the pipeline. Annualised gold production was 3.5-million ounces – and on track for its target figure of 5-million ounces in production or development by 2015. In 2011, for the first time, just over half of its total production (51%) came from outside South Africa, a significant milestone in its pursuit of global recognition. The gold price ended the year higher in both dollar and rand terms.

Yes, the share price failed yet again to adequately reflect its optimism – but shareholders had reason to be pleased. Gold Fields paid a total dividend of R3.30, giving a yield of 2.6% – the highest among the leading gold companies of the world.

IT IS, of course, easy enough for a company to make airy-fairy promises and predictions; more difficult to set specific goals that enable outsiders to judge success and failure. On the face of it, the formal annual-report caveat relating to 'forward-looking statements that involve known and unknown risks' provides an escape route. But Gold Fields has defined unambiguously what it plans to achieve. It says it is making a determined effort to enable investors, governments, local communities and employees to judge the company and its ability to 'flourish in the new growth environment of tomorrow'. It says it is committed to transparency.

For instance, it has announced its intention to increase gold production from 3.6-million ounces to 5-million in production or in development by 2015. It aims to earn a place in the upper ranks of the Dow Jones sustainability index within three years. Recognising that exploration growth is cheaper than buying ounces through mergers and acquisitions it is committed to seeking new international opportunities. Within two years it will take construction decisions on four advanced projects – in Mali, Peru, the Philippines and the Arctic Circle in Finland. It has promised that the pursuit of profit – essential as it is – will not be at the expense of its ethical values. Most of all, it has reiterated its promise that it will not mine if it cannot mine safely.

Measurable goals, all of them. And it is prepared to be judged by the extent to which it achieves them.

Chapter Thirty-three

A Woman's Touch

ALAN WRIGHT stepped down as Gold Fields' chairman in 2010 after more than 40 years in the mining industry. He had enjoyed almost every moment of it – but was equally pleased to see the end of it. Now, at last, he had the time to travel.

His successor, Dr Mamphela Ramphele, is the author of a number of books illuminating the socio-political state of the country. She is also one of the most astute businesswomen. At first glance, her ambition as new chair of Gold Fields is preposterous. She wants to bring a woman's touch to the masculine world of mining. Of course she doesn't put it quite like that. Her aim is more nuanced but – as she told CEO Holland and her board – she proposes to encourage change in the male-dominated culture of the industry; to be more responsive to people, especially people from poor communities which have traditionally endured, but not necessarily enjoyed, a mining environment.

'I don't have mining skills, I don't need to have,' she says, disarmingly and not quite accurately. Smart as paint, she couldn't have spent six years as an Anglo American director without picking up a sound understanding of the industry. But, again, her message is more subtle. 'I'm a little long in the tooth, so I've got some idea of how institutions work. You know, one of the problems about a male-dominated culture is that it skips the essentials. And the essentials are about how people feel.'

Dr Ramphele is – and wants to be – recognised as a standard-bearer for a new era in mining.

Her record suggests an academic turn of mind. She has a medical degree from the University of Natal – the only university in South Africa to admit black students without reference to government in apartheid times; a doctorate in social anthropology from the University of Cape Town; and 20 honorary degrees, including a doctorate in law from Cambridge and a doctorate in science from Tufts University, an American university centred on Boston and more than 150 years old. She was the first South African to be appointed a managing director of the World Bank and has served on the boards of the Anglo American Corporation, Transnet and a number of other companies.

But ask her outright where her interests lie, and she will reply:

> I have always been an active citizen. I am an activist. I dedicated my life to fighting for freedom. And since 1994 every job I have done has had something to do with making people aware of their rights and responsibilities as citizens, of the fact that they're not oppressed subjects any more.
>
> I mean, I'm 64. I should be relaxing. And here I am involved with Gold Fields for all these reasons ...

What reasons? Ideas and ideals bubble out of her. Dr Ramphele has thought deeply about her connection to mining. Somehow she manages to combine firm views on almost everything from politics to people with a non-dogmatic manner, a rare skill. She believes there hasn't been sufficient recognition of what she calls the 'woundedness' of the repressed population under apartheid.

She posed an intriguing question to delegates at the 2012 Mining Indaba: 'Why is there this disconnect between the industry's sustainability efforts and the rising clamour for action against it?' and proceeded to offer, bluntly, four possible reasons for it.

First was the woundedness of communities who bore the brunt of past unjust policies. The mining industry had to acknowledge this:

> The unacknowledged social pain suffered by many such communities who endured broken families, poverty level wages, lack of training and education opportunities need to be dealt with. Societies have much to gain by engaging in conversations that can begin the journey of healing.

Second, the industry was very bad at promoting itself. It needed to marshal independent data to provide a convincing overview of the positive economic impact that it could have: 'The outcome would surprise many and would perhaps mitigate some of the criticism.'

Third, stakeholders needed to be more realistic about their expectations:

> As communities, trade unions, NGOs and governments issue ever-greater imposts on the industry and regulations become ever more stringent, these stakeholders often forget that mining is a capital-intensive, high-risk industry that needs to reward the providers of capital with a significant return. The mining industry can only continue on its path of sustainable growth if it is allowed to operate profitably. I'm afraid that in many jurisdictions, including South Africa, we are getting close to the point where this is no longer guaranteed.

Fourth, and most importantly, the industry needed to do a lot more to entrench sustainability and so minimise the risks of further regulatory interventions, It needed to demonstrate its unique ability to create innovative approaches to leverage economic value for communities:

> I would like to see a situation where a mining company comes into a community and starts to sow these sustainability seeds from the initial exploration to the eventual and inevitable mine closure. Unfortunately what we have seen far too frequently is a hole left in the ground.

Community partnerships were imperative to increase economic benefits. But there was an onus on government too. It ought to integrate the training and skills-development abilities of mining companies into its own educational systems: 'Such co-operation has been talked about a lot in South Africa but very little has come of it.'

SUSTAINABILITY IS the new code word in mining circles in South Africa. It is a word hardly heard a generation ago. Today it is bandied about by almost everyone: by those who believe in it; by those who pay lip-service to it; by those (like Aurora) who ignore it. It has acquired a far deeper meaning than merely 'the ability to keep something alive'.

It encompasses a vision of an industry that offers benefits to communities while it is operating and a legacy of good when it dies. It has been slowly evolving.

Fifty years ago you could recognise Johannesburg by its mine dumps (or slimes dams, to use the less picturesque term). They were composed of slurry – the detritus of the process by which a strong acid was used to extract gold from ore. The lifeless dumps baked in the Highveld sun until they caked, forming man-made, flat-topped yellow hills around the city. They gave Johannesburg its unique skyline and were widely seen as an attractive and distinctive feature.

True, when the wind blew, the southern suburbs and central business district were often left with a coating of fine yellow dust, but that was regarded by most as the unavoidable price of being the city of gold. It partially explains why the mining gentry moved to the northern suburbs on the other side of the Ridge of White Waters.

In time the yellow dust became intolerable and mining companies were obliged to do something about it. Research helped them find a way to grow bush and scrub in the acid soil. Progress reached a peak when someone tarred the flat-top surface of a mine dump and erected a drive-in cinema there.

That was the beginning of the concept of sustainability; the acceptance of the notion that mines had responsibilities too; that they couldn't just dump their unwanted residue anywhere.

The concept today has gone far past that. In a nutshell, sustainability has come to mean using part of the profits of mining to compensate those who have paid a price without sharing the benefit of the riches beneath their feet. It is all-embracing. It includes offering employment and training, developing skills, creating opportunities for small business, improving the environment, healing the scarred earth and contributing to the welfare of local communities.

Says Dr Ramphele:

> Of course mining isn't exactly the flavour of the month politically.

South Africa has got this legacy of conflict over who benefits from its natural resources. There is a legitimate resentment and a sense that the injustices of the past haven't been redressed. The people who are making the loudest anti-mining noises are not against mining *per se*. They are calling for a fairer distribution of the benefits of mining. And in that they are correct.

The question is how to foster a fairer distribution?

In my view the mining industry, in conducting its business, paid very little attention until recently to the impact it was having on poor communities, on how it sourced mine labour, or polluted water.

In her first statement as chair of Gold Fields, in the company's 2010 annual report, Dr Ramphele returned to a theme that has almost become a signature tune: her confidence that, properly directed, mining could be a powerful force for change and prosperity in South Africa. Gold's upside potential, she concluded, 'is greater than the downside risk'. And the company was firmly on track to achieve its target of 5-million attributable ounces of gold, either in production or in development, by 2015.

Some of that money was being ploughed back, to the benefit of poorer communities. Over the past year alone the company had committed R26-million in support of mining faculties at South African universities, in addition to numerous ongoing partnerships with tertiary institutions in all its host countries.

Wrote Dr Ramphele:

> Gold Fields creates significant economic value not just for our employees but also for our local communities and host governments through royalties, taxes and social upliftment programmes. This is based on the understanding that mineral rights are, justifiably, viewed as part of the national patrimony. This is founded on the belief that we wish to create a positive and lasting post-mining legacy.
>
> Economic value creation applies above all to our investors who must be rewarded for their investment – a goal we prioritise as we position ourselves as the investment of choice in 2011 and beyond.

It was a firm but gentle reproach to those who believe that nationalising the mines will bring greater good to all.

IN AN INTERVIEW for this book it becomes apparent that her natural optimism does not allow her to dwell too much on the obvious mistakes of the past, but rather concentrate on what can be done about them. Here are some of her thoughts:

On BEE:
The first wave of BEE was really a kind of an abusive relationship story. It was payback. Now, because our BEE is slanted more towards staff and poor communities, in my book it is a more balanced process. It should really focus on making staff the beneficiaries of hard labour and making the communities round our mines benefit from our presence there. After all, they are inhaling our dust and enduring our intrusion. Oh yes, and the labour-sending areas, they should benefit too. That's how it's structured now and I am much more comfortable with that.

Yes, but will it satisfy government?
I think government itself is becoming embarrassed by this revolving door with the same people being involved a thousand times with little impact.

The baggage of the past?
One of the big problems which the mining industry and the country must own and acknowledge is that we have invested too little in South Africans. They provided the bulk of the unskilled labour and because of that very little was invested in them. Of course, part of it had to do with the labour laws at the time – which were pushed by the likes of Cecil John Rhodes, incidentally. So it wasn't, as is now being rewritten, those bloody Afrikaners who did this. No, no, no. Mining barons needed this pool of labour. The mining industry cannot just walk away from that.

It's in this context that I believe that today's mining industry needs to be reminded of its responsibilities. They have to be better corporate citizens. That's part of the reason why I'm in this. Even TB and HIV/AIDS came in through the mining industry and was perpetuated by the migrant labour system. It's not just finger-pointing; it's a question of taking ownership. And then we can find joint solutions – the government, the private sector and the citizens.

Has there been any progress?
I'm pleased to see that many mines now have a '24 hours in the life of a mineworker' approach. It's no longer a question of not caring where they came from, where they sleep and so on. A wrong move has been this living-out allowance which has spawned shacks around our mining areas which are spreading HIV. In a sense it is contributing to mining accidents. If you live in a noisy shack environment with poor eating habits and too much drinking, you're not a safe pair of hands. So the issue of family housing is not just a human concern, it's a very sensible business approach.

On the shortage of skills:
We are running out of skills. The qualified mining engineers and other skilled workers are getting into their 50s. It's going to happen. It's a global problem but it's particularly acute in South Africa. Secondly, we have an artisan problem. That is because, against the advice of many of us, the government went for the SETA system. The old apprentice system was killed for the simple reason that it was discriminatory in the past. Why don't they just open it up again? It works. Don't break it. Just open it up to all.

Why was the apprentice system abandoned?
If you have dealt with teenage children, you'll know that they can cut off their noses to spite their faces.

But we're dealing with grown-ups?
As a democracy, we are teenagers. And the psycho-social impact on black South Africans of being treated as inferior has left very deep wounds. White South Africans suffer from wounds of a superiority

> complex. The combination of these two complexes makes it difficult for us to work together as South Africans using our pool of talents to address our challenges to seize the opportunities available.
>
> **How can they be healed?**
> One, acknowledge the fact. Two, sit down and talk about how we can deal with it. I was shocked to find that deep in our mines we still use Fanagalo. Using that master-and-servant language just rubs salt in the wounds. We need to change the way we talk to one another. Mine captains must learn the dominant language in each area of operation. If we can meet one another halfway, we can change the dynamic. These are the symbolic acts we need to have. At mine level, we need to promote teams that put human dignity at the centre.

If Dr Ramphele has a single goal it is to improve the lives of ordinary people. It's why she fought apartheid and racial discrimination, and why she wants ordinary people now to wrest their democratic constitution from the hands of politicians and take ownership themselves. She is passionate about these things.

She believes she is striking a chord in the minds of industry leaders.

IT WOULD BE a bold and foolish author who predicted a smooth road ahead for a company in an unpredictable and volatile industry. Nothing in Gold Fields' history – nor in current conditions – suggests that this is likely. Too much can go wrong. Politicians can interfere; companies lose their way; gold and metals fall from favour; production falters and fails; economies flounder.

But it is fair to say that, as things stand, there is an air of quiet confidence about GFL that is reflected in its annual report and in staff morale; a sense that the company knows where it is going.

But there have been disturbing factors too. The fall-off in gold production in South Africa has been steeper than expected.

Says Holland:

> We didn't see that coming. No one did. Our approach now is to accept

that we are not going to get the South African assets back to where they were. The challenge is to make them profitable at a lower level. Our whole bedrock is shifting. The original bedrock of the company was in Kloof and Driefontein, but within the next five to ten years that mantle will shift to South Deep. The challenge is to make the older South African assets profitable at a lower yet sustainable level.

We're starting to think about the bedrock of the future – it's going to be things like South Deep and Far South East Asia in the Phillipines. Those last two will probably produce as much as Beatrix and the Kloof/Driefontein complex together.

And South Deep, once expected to be the last great gold mine in South Africa and the only significantly mechanised underground mine in the country – will it meet expectations?

It's proven to be harder than expected to get to the prize, but once we get there it'll be a great mine. We have taken gold analysts and investors there and the potential blew them away. However, if we are going to go into some kind of expansion mode in South Africa we have to mine differently. Fewer people at the face; more robotics.

Will Gold Fields meet its target of 5-million ounces overall?

Yes, either in production or in development. It will be a great day for us.

And the million-dollar question: the share price remains static. When will shareholder confidence grow stronger?

The market likes our strategic plan, our projects. I don't think anyone is critical of that. But we don't have a track record of delivering projects. We've only built one mine in the last 15 years. South Deep is not exactly finished. They want proof that we can deliver on our strategy. So that's what we're going to do – deliver! When we do, the confidence will come surging back.

Time will tell.

Index

Abbott, Brian 196, 201
Abrahamse, LG 3
Adan, Mike 177, 178, 198, 201
Agnew (W Australia) 211, 213–216
Agnew, Rudolph 3, 7, 9, 11–14, 30, 33–36, 41, 43–45, 47–51, 55, 57, 59, 61, 64–68, 71
Alvey, Graham 177
ANC (African National Congress) 53–56, 58–61, 88, 142, 143, 153, 154, 175, 219, 225, 226, 228, 243, 250
Andersen, Roy 182
Anglo American Corporation ix, x, xiii, 3, 4, 7, 8, 9, 10, 15, 17, 20, 21, 23, 24, 24, 26, 28, 34, 36, 41, 43, 45, 46, 64, 65, 66, 67, 68, 80, 81, 82, 86, 91, 100, 111, 112, 122, 127, 169, 176, 182, 189, 202, 204, 207, 208, 221, 222, 233, 240, 246–248, 311, 318, 321, 322
AngloGold Ashanti 127, 232–234, 237, 239, 247, 269
Asteroid 23, 62, 93, 176, 182
Avgold 201

Beckett, Michael 42–44, 51
Barnard, Dr Niel 54, 57
Berman, Richard 274, 275
Botha, Louis 78
Botha, PW 54, 57–59, 103, 106
Boustred, Graham 91
Boyd, Leslie 91
Brown, Daryn 131, 135
Brown, Peter 22
Buhrmann, Emil 87, 183, 203
Busschau, Dr William 21, 22, 37, 69, 83

Carroll, Cynthia 208, 311, 318
Central Mining 82
Cerro Corona 216, 218, 302, 309
Chamber of Mines ix, 3, 24, 40, 78, 79, 97, 99, 100, 102, 128, 138, 155, 168, 213, 317
Clarke, Neil 34
Cockerill, Ian 4, 127, 206, 222, 225, 226, 232, 233, 237, 240, 245, 248–253, 255, 256, 258, 260, 264, 266–269, 271, 273–276, 283–288, 290–292, 294–296, 298, 301, 302, 304–312
Competition Board 24, 25, 44, 62, 68, 69
Consolidated Gold Fields of London (Consgold, CGF) 1–27, 29, 30, 32–35, 40–51, 53, 55, 61, 62, 63, 70, 73, 74, 78, 82, 83, 84, 85, 86, 91, 111, 123

Dale, Tom 193–197, 201, 205, 206, 210, 221, 231, 236, 238, 286, 304
Daling, Marinus 59
Damang 125, 211, 250, 281
Davison, Barry 112
Dawn Raid, The 4, 5, 6, 9, 23,
De Beer, Bridged 163
De Beer, Tony 159–163, 165–168
De Beers 6, 7, 8, 11, 23, 45, 63, 64, 69, 73, 76, 162, 176
De Klerk, FW 19, 20, 152
De Villiers, HP 3
Deelkraal 84, 145
Department of Trade and Industry (DTI) 44, 86, 235
Dippenaar, Ferdi 294
Doornfontein 21, 73, 145

331

Dowsley, Jimmy 110, 111, 208, 248, 266, 287, 290, 300
Driefontein 5, 21, 70, 80, 146, 153, 159, 182, 189, 202, 203, 205, 221, 222, 232, 267, 268, 317, 329
Drummond, John Hays 75, 76

Edwardes, Sir Michael 43, 44, 50, 70
Eksteen, Mike 112–114, 131, 133, 136, 141
Erroll of Hale, Lord 5, 6, 8, 23
Esterhuyse, Prof Willie 54, 58, 60
Evander 202

Fairview Mines 202
Federale Mynbou 82
Fenton, Colin 112, 113, 149
Fitzpatrick, Percy 73
Flack, Peter 183
Fleischer, Col Spencer 78
Franco-Nevada 224–237, 239, 249
Friends Proposal 10, 12, 14, 24, 62

Garoeb, Moses 164
Geingob, Haike 165, 168
Gencor 91, 176, 182–186, 193–197, 201, 206, 208, 235, 236, 312
General Mining (Genmin) ix, 5, 8, 91, 182, 200, 207
Gengold 113, 181, 185–187, 191, 193–196, 198, 258
Gilbertson, Brian 88, 91, 92, 182–189, 193–199, 201–204, 210, 220, 221, 235, 236
Gnodde, Andries Michael Drury ('Dru') 17, 19–22, 27, 34–36, 94, 114
Godsell, Bobby 169, 222, 223, 231–234, 240, 247
Goldco 189
Goodlace, Terence 266, 293, 312
Gordon, Donald 85, 92–94, 114
Gordon Institute 93, 289
Graeme, Dick 211
Great Miners' Strike (1987) 102
Grigorian, Artem 247–249, 253
Gush, Peter 3, 21, 68–70, 151

Hanson, Lord 50, 51, 61, 62, 70

Hanson PLC 2, 50, 51, 70
Harmony 202, 234, 254–256, 258–272, 274–281, 283, 284, 288, 289, 291, 293–306, 308, 311–314
Harmony's Way 266, 267, 269
Harris, Lord 77, 78
Harvey, Robert (author, *The Fall of Apartheid*) 53
Harvie-Watt, George 42, 82
Heath, Edward 54
Heslop, Philip 22
Hertzog, JBM 79
Hewitt, Gordon 171
Hichens, Antony 26, 33–35, 43
Holland, Nick xii, 182, 183–187, 193–196, 200, 201, 205, 106, 215, 216, 218, 222, 230, 244, 245, 250, 266, 274, 285, 287, 288, 290, 291, 294, 295, 298, 307, 308, 310–319, 321, 328
Hope, Robin 120
Hopwood, John 177, 179, 188, 307

IAMGold 250–253, 257, 259–261, 263, 265, 269, 271, 273, 276–278, 280–283, 285, 287, 288, 293, 303
Irwin, Alec 235

Jacob, David Lloyd 6
Jacobsz, Willie 237, 266, 270, 274, 277, 280, 284, 287, 290, 302, 304, 308
Jameson Raid xiii, 74, 76
Jameson, Starr 74, 75
Jamieson, Bill (author, *Goldstrike – The Oppenheimer Empire in Crisis*) 7, 14
Janisch, Peter 39, 137, 148
Johannesburg Consolidated Investment Company (JCI) 108, 111, 122, 156
Jones, Alan 113
Jones, Guy Carleton 80

Kahle, Helgo 126, 127
Katz, Michael 225, 272, 297–300
Kebble, Brett 156
Keys, Derek 91
Kloof Gold Mine 70, 109, 112, 130–136, 145, 146, 154, 156, 159, 176, 182, 189, 202, 267, 317, 329
Knight's Deep 77

INDEX

Kombat 159, 161,162
Krahmann, Dr Rudolf 80
Kruger, Paul 74, 75

Leeudoorn 197, 202
Levy, Richard 22
Lewis, Glynn 126
Libanon 21, 145, 202,
Liberty Life 70, 85, 92–94, 114, 115, 182
Liebenberg, Johan 97–99
Louw, Ian 6
Lowe, Dr Peter 132
Lowe Bell Africa 171, 172

Main, Tom 155
Malherbe, Dilly 184
Manuel, Trevor 224, 226, 230–233, 235, 237
Mbeki, Thabo 59, 60, 61, 225, 237, 269, 303, 314
MacNab, Roy (author, *Gold Their Touchstone*) xiii, 5, 6, 73, 79, 80, 84
McMahon, Michael 113, 115, 185, 235, 236, 288, 289, 306, 308, 309
Mandela, Nelson 54, 58, 60, 143, 152, 154, 155, 164, 239, 298
McAlpine, Roy 93, 94
Mells Park 11, 13, 42, 59, 61
Mineworkers' Union of Namibia, (MUN) 159–162, 167, 168
Minorco (Mineral and Resources Corp) 5, 10, 11, 12, 15, 16, 18, 23–26, 34, 41, 42–51, 62, 63, 65–69, 71, 254, 274
Moore, Brian 109, 120, 121, 124, 125
Motsepe, Patrice 284
Mukasey, Judge Michael 45, 50
Munro, Alan 113, 136, 139, 141, 148, 153, 177
Munro, John 266, 280, 287, 289, 309, 311
Mvelaphanda Resources 87, 118, 244, 245, 257, 279, 295
Myburgh, Judge John 141

National Union of Mineworkers (NUM) 97–99, 102, 129, 153, 154, 167, 243, 273
New Africa Investments Ltd (NAIL) 176, 188, 243
Newmont Mining Corporation 44, 45, 48, 50, 63, 124, 203, 220, 223
Norilsk Nickel 245–249, 252–255, 259–261, 263, 265, 271, 273, 275, 276, 280, 281, 283, 284, 291–295, 297–299
Northam Platinum Mine 87, 94, 107, 109–119, 130, 141, 144, 156, 188, 236, 245

Ogilvie Thompson, Julian 11–14, 20, 34, 43, 44, 64–67, 71, 91, 183, 189, 247
Oliphant, Randall 233, 234
O'okiep 158
Oppenheimer, Sir Ernest 11, 21, 22, 82, 208
Oppenheimer, Harry 4, 6, 7, 8, 11, 13, 21, 23, 32, 33, 34, 62, 71, 73, 82, 111, 208, 222
Oppenheimer, Nicholas 189, 208
Otjihase 159, 161, 162

Parker, Gordon 113, 203, 220, 221, 232, 236, 251
Pennant-Rea, Rupert 307
Plumbridge, Robin Allan 1, 4, 5, 14, 19–37, 39–41, 44, 51, 70, 84, 86–89, 91, 94, 96, 99, 100, 101, 104, 105, 108, 111, 114–116, 118, 122–124, 126, 137–139, 141, 143–146, 148, 151–153, 155, 157, 169–171, 173, 177, 179, 180, 183, 184, 220, 243, 247
Potanin, Vladimir 248, 249
Prestea 120, 121, 122
Pretorius, Willem 59
Prokhorov, Mikhael 248, 249, 284

Ramaphosa, Cyril 97, 99, 102, 176, 188, 243,
Ramphele, Dr Mamphela 313, 318, 321, 322, 324, 325, 328
Rand Club 73
Rawlings, Jeremiah John 120–122
Reagan, Ronald 44
Reinecke, Dr Leopold 80
Relly, Gavin 68, 69, 91
Rembrandt Group (Remgro) 39, 43, 62, 64–68, 70, 85–87, 89–91, 93, 114, 137, 176, 184, 188, 203, 246
Rhodes, Cecil John xiii, 3, 11, 37, 72–77,

333

83, 176, 192, 207–209, 326
Rio Tinto Zinc 13
Robinson Deep 79
Robinson, Richard 124, 177, 189, 190, 193, 194, 197–200, 206, 220
Romain, Ken (author, *Larger Than Life*) 92
Rozhetskin, Leonid 249, 252, 275, 276, 280, 284, 291, 292
Rudd, Charles Durrell 72–75, 83, 151, 192, 207
Rupert, Anthony Edward ('Anton') 5, 85–87, 94
Rupert, Johann Peter 43, 65, 67, 68, 70, 85–91, 93, 94, 110, 114, 115, 117, 118, 137, 138, 146, 170, 176, 179, 183, 186, 190, 207, 209, 246
Rustenburg Platinum 108, 111, 112
Ryan, Patrick J 203, 236

St Helena 202
St Ives 211, 215, 216
Sanlam 5, 280, 281
Schulich, Seymour 236, 237
Sexwale, Tokyo 87, 116, 118, 243, 244, 279, 295
Slack, Hank 12
Sonjica, Buyelwa 314
South Deep 120, 156, 245, 302, 304, 314, 315, 317, 329,
Southern Life 34
Stegmann JA 3
Steyn PG 3
Sub Nigel 79
Swanepoel, Bernard 254–260, 264, 266, 268–271, 273, 274, 279, 281, 282, 290, 292–298, 300, 305

Tagg, Mike 220
Tambo, Oliver 56, 219, 295
Tarkwa 88, 121–127, 144, 199, 210, 211, 250, 281, 302,
Teberebie 210
Terreblanche, Sampie 59
Thatcher, Margaret 54, 59

Thompson, Chris 125, 196, 197, 203–206, 210, 211, 215, 221–227, 229, 231–241, 243, 246, 247–253, 255–257, 268, 272–275, 280, 281, 283–288, 292, 301, 303–306, 308, 313
Toros, Maurice 120
Toivo ya Toivo, Andimba 164, 165, 167
Traher, Tony 247
Travis, Peter 53
Tsumeb Corporation (TCL) Mine 158–161, 162, 166, 167, 177
Tutu, Desmond 143

Union Corporation ix, 5, 81

Van der Merwe, Johan 280
Van Rooyen, Bernard (aka the Silver Fox) 13, 16, 17, 23, 24, 26, 28, 29, 33, 35, 36, 70, 91, 110, 113, 118–126, 203, 246, 279
Van Zyl Slabbert, Dr Frederik 56
Venterspost 21, 81, 145
Viljoen, Richard 191, 192
Vulindlela 174, 176–180, 188, 198, 220

Waddell, Gordon 111, 112
Watson, Ian 110, 112
Wedding of the Romans 10, 11, 24
West Witwatersrand Areas Ltd (West Wits) 21, 22, 67, 69, 80–82, 84
Western Deep Levels 82
Wiehahn Commission 97
Witwatersrand ix, 2, 19, 21, 39, 73–75, 80, 82–84, 177, 209, 230
Wolfe-Coote, Clive 177, 193, 198, 199, 201, 206
Wood, JHA (Humphrey) 3, 35
Wright, Alan 87–89, 115, 116, 118, 136, 138, 148–152, 156–158, 169–175, 178–180, 183, 184, 186–194, 199, 201, 251, 302, 303, 306, 307, 312

Young, Michael 53–61

Zuma, Jacob 59, 61